THE DALTON BROTHERS

AND THEIR

ASTOUNDING CAREER OF CRIME

THE DALTON BROTHERS

AND THEIR

ASTOUNDING CAREER OF CRIME

BY
An Eye Witness

ALSO INCLUDES THE CLASSIC BIOGRAPHY

Black Jack Ketchum:
The Last of the Hold-Up Kings

BY ED BARTHOLOMEW

Skyhorse Publishing

First Skyhorse Publishing edition 2013
Special contents copyright © 2011, 2013 by Palladium Press

Skyhorse Publishing books may be purchased in bulk at special discounts for sales promotion, corporate gifts, fund-raising, or educational purposes. Special editions can also be created to specifications. For details, contact the Special Sales Department, Skyhorse Publishing, 307 West 36th Street, 11th Floor, New York, NY 10018 or info@skyhorsepublishing.com.

Skyhorse® and Skyhorse Publishing® are registered trademarks of Skyhorse Publishing, Inc.®, a Delaware corporation.

Visit our website at www.skyhorsepublishing.com.

10 9 8 7 6 5 4 3 2

Library of Congress Cataloging-in-Publication Data is available on file.

ISBN: 978-1-62087-586-5

Printed in the United States of America

EDITOR'S NOTE

As we noted in a companion volume in your Frontier Classics Library, *The Authentic History of Sam Bass and His Gang*, the most obvious targets for the bad guys in the Old West were the places where the money was: stagecoaches, banks, and trains. The four Dalton brothers and Black Jack Ketchum gained their principal notoriety from robbing trains. It was a violent activity, and during the last quarter of the nineteenth century, all save one of these characters were to die as violently as they had lived: two of the Dalton brothers in 1892, another in 1894, and Black Jack Ketchum in 1901. The stories of their colorful lives were told in two separate books, brought together for the first time in the edition before you.

The Dalton brothers — Gratton ("Grat") (1861–1892), Bill (1863–1894), Bob (1870–1892), and Emmett (1871–1937) — were sons of Adeline Younger Dalton (aunt of outlaws Cole and Jim Younger). They were born in Missouri, part of a large family that ultimately included fifteen children. In 1882, the Dalton family immigrated to the Indian Territory (now Oklahoma), and four years later moved to Coffeyville, Kansas.

Although these four young men were to become the main members of one of the most brutal band of outlaws on the western frontier, their older brother Frank (1859–1887) was a highly respected deputy U.S. marshal. He was killed in pursuit of whiskey runners in the Indian Territory near the Arkansas border.

Perhaps in hopes of avenging their brother's death, Grat, Bob, and Emmett became lawmen (Bill, who would later join the gang, moved to California and became a farmer). But enforcing the law was clearly not suited to the brothers. At age nineteen, Bob, now a deputy U.S. marshal, killed a man, and declared he had done so in an official capacity, although this was disputed. Soon thereafter, Bob and Emmett were accused of introducing alcohol into the Indian Territory. Later that same year, a charge was made against Grat for stealing horses.

Bob and Emmett fled first to New Mexico and then to California, where Bill and Grat joined them. The brothers and their gang robbed trains in California and throughout the Indian Territory.

In 1892, the gang began to rob banks. Bob Dalton boasted that he would "beat anything Jesse James ever did — rob two banks at once, in broad daylight." On the morning of October 5, 1892, Bob, Grat, and Emmett, along with two other members of the gang, rode into their hometown of Coffeyville, dismounted, and divided into two groups to rob the C.M. Condon & Company Bank and the First National Bank. As one group of robbers entered the Condon Bank and pointed their guns at the tellers, a passerby looking through the bank's window recognized the Daltons (despite their fake beards). When the gang left the two banks, townspeople fired at them. Three residents and Town Marshal Charles Connelly were killed, as were Bob, Grat, and two Dalton gang confederates. Emmett received twenty-three gunshot wounds and was soon captured. After fourteen years in the Kansas penitentiary, he was pardoned. He died in California in 1937.

Several gang members and Bill Dalton continued to commit robberies throughout the Indian Territory for several years. Yet all were ultimately killed by lawmen, Bill by Loss Hart on June 8, 1894.

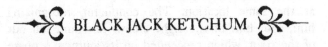

BLACK JACK KETCHUM

Thomas Edward "Black Jack" Ketchum (1863–1901) was born in Texas, and during his early years worked as a cowboy and cattle driver. In 1890, at the age of twenty-seven, he moved with his brother Sam to the Pecos River Valley in New Mexico, formed a gang of outlaws, and began robbing trains. The group's first robbery, of the Atchison, Topeka & Santa Fe Railroad, took place in 1892 near Deming, New Mexico; the gang netted twenty thousand dollars.

On June 10, 1896, the two Ketchum brothers robbed a shop and post office in Liberty, New Mexico. They killed two members of a pursuing posse and then escaped into Wyoming, where they linked up with other outlaws at Hole-in-the-Wall Pass in Johnson County.

Operating from their hideaway at the Hole-in-the-Wall, Black Jack and Sam Ketchum, along with several gang members, started robbing trains in an area near Folsom, New Mexico, known as Twin Mountain. On September 3, 1897, they robbed a train of about twenty thousand dollars in gold and forty thousand dollars in silver. On July 11, 1899, the gang (minus Black Jack) took fifty thousand dollars from a train in the same area. An ensuing gunfight with a posse near Cimarron, New Mexico, resulted in the death of three posse members and the wounding of several outlaws, including Sam Ketchum. Although Sam escaped, he was soon tracked down and arrested. He died of his injuries in the New Mexico Territorial Penitentiary.

On August 16, 1899, just weeks after his brother's train robbery, Black Jack tried to rob the same train at the same location. The conductor, recognizing him, shot him in the right elbow. Ketchum fell out of the train, which proceeded on its journey. A posse found him the following day, and after he had his arm amputated and underwent recovery, he was convicted of the capital crime of "felonious assault upon a railway train." The law was found to be unconstitutional, but this determination was made too late to be of benefit to Black Jack. He was hanged on April 26, 1901, an event with a grisly aftermath. Through a combination of circumstances — the inexperience of the hangmen, the excessive length of the rope, and Black Jack's considerable weight gain during his incarceration — he was decapitated, at that time the only recorded instance of decapitation in a judicial hanging in America.

This Skyhorse Publishing Library edition consists of exact facsimile reprints of *The Dalton Brothers and Their Astounding Career of Crime* (first edition, 1892) and *Black Jack Ketchum: Last of the Hold-Up Kings* (first edition, 1955).

Les Adams
Chairman, Editorial Board

BIRMINGHAM, ALABAMA
SEPTEMBER 20, 2011

THE DALTON BROTHERS

AND THEIR

ASTOUNDING CAREER OF CRIME

BY
AN EYE WITNESS

With numerous illustrations reproduced from photographs
taken on the spot

———————

CHICAGO
LAIRD & LEE, Publishers

CONTENTS.

PART THE FIRST.

CRIMINAL BOYS.

CHAPTER VI. PAGE

PART THE SECOND.

CRIMINAL MEN.

CHAPTER I.

CHAPTER II.

CHAPTER III.

CHAPTER IV.

CHAPTER V.

CHAPTER VI.

PART THE THIRD.

DEAD CRIMINALS.

CHAPTER I.

CHAPTER II.

CHAPTER III.

CHAPTER IV.

CHAPTER V.

CHAPTER VI.

THE DALTON BROTHERS
And Their Astounding Career of Crime

PART THE FIRST

CRIMINAL BOYS

CHAPTER I.

A STRANGE NIGHT'S WORK—UNDERTAKER LANG'S GHASTLY
VISITORS—THE DALTONS' COVERED WAGON AND ITS
SILENT OCCUPANT—SHOT IN THE BACK AND
DISHONORED BY HIS MURDERERS.

A dark, dreary night in December, 1888.

On the open plains of Southern Kansas, the wind blows a hurricane of snow. The roads disappear under the white covering, and the city of Coffeyville, in Montgomery county, Kansas, just three miles from the Indian Territory limits, sleeps the sleep of the just.

It is a prosperous, strictly law-abiding community, populated with bright, active, sociable people who are proud of their promising town and of the good days ahead for it and for them. The spires of numerous churches rise, here and there, as material evidence of the people's culture and religious feelings, while, in the business part of the city, several blocks of substantially-constructed brick buildings are clustered in sign of business activity. Indeed, Coffeyville is a worthy representative of that indomitable American spirit which has made the West a joy for the eyes and the hearts of men.

But to-night, the inhabitants have all withdrawn to their cosy homes, and doubtless enjoy the sweets of well-earned repose. It's almost one o'clock already, and hardly a light is visible inside the closed houses.

Suddenly the dull rumbling of a covered wagon is heard at a distance. It is rolling from the western direction, and the driver on the front seat is talking with some one seated behind him.

"Are you sure you know where he lives?" he asks, in evident ill-humor.

"Just half a block ahead, on Ninth street, I tell you; a two-story house with a brick basement, on the next corner to the right," is the precise answer given in a tone of command.

The driver grumbles something unintelligible, then shuts his lips tight, as if to keep the icy air out. At the place designated he stops his horse in front of a comfortable looking dwelling. Strange to say, there is a light burning on the upper floor; a sick one is perhaps keeping the mother awake. Anyhow, this sign of life brings out a satisfactory grunt on the driver's part:

"They won't keep us waiting long in that ——— of a weather," he swears. Then he begins calling out in a stentorian voice:

"Lang! Oh! Lang!"

At the second or third appeal, a window on the second floor is slightly lifted and a bearded man's face leans over, while a muffled voice answers:

"What are you after, you fellows, waking up a man in the dead of night?"

"It's a job for you we are after, Mr. Lang?" is the cool retort.

"Who are you, anyhow?"

"The Dalton Brothers from the territory, with a little parcel in this wagon to be delivered you C. O. D. Do you catch on?"

" 's that you, Bob Dalton?" the householder queries.

"Bob it is; and Emmet's behind me with a silent customer he wants to introduce to you, Mr. Lang. Are you coming down? It's mighty cold here I tell you. Will drive you to the store."

"Is it a cash on the nail business?" queries the Coffeyville citizen, in a cautious way.

'Oh! it's all right. It's court money and it can't fail you, this month or next. A job on the square, I tell you. By G——, won't you hurry up? We'll be soon as stiff as our friend back there, if you don't hustle ——"

"I am coming, I am coming ——" is the welcome answer, and the window closes with a bang.

Five minutes later, the two occupants of the wagon are increased by one, not counting the strange freight they have been lugging around so mysteriously.

The horse's head is turned toward the business portion of the village—*city*, they like to call it, over there—and the party soon reaches the large store of

LANG & LAPE,

Furniture Dealers and Undertakers,

on Walnut street, three or four doors south of Eighth street.

They all alight, throw a blanket over the perspiring horse, and, while Mr. Lang fumbles with his key in the lock of the store-door, the two Daltons, tall, stalwart young men, lads rather, hardly out of their teens, walk to the back of the wagon and begin to unload its gruesome freight.

As the reader has doubtless surmised already. it is a corpse which has been the silent companion of the brothers during their midnight ride. It is a powerfully heavy corpse, too, and the moonlight, just emerging from behind the clouds, shines over the features of a man of thirty or thereabout, with heavy moustache and clotted hair.

No sign of a bloody encounter is visible at the first glance; but as Bob Dalton turns the body on one side to take a better hold of the man's shoulders, a round, bullet-shaped hole, on the nape of the neck, reveals itself and tells its fearful story. The man has been shot dead from behind—there has been murder here; revolting, cowardly murder.

With a composure far above their years, however, the two lads pursue their dread task and carry across the sidewalk, under the wide, wooden awning that extends all along this side of the street, the remains of the murdered man. They soon lie in the back part of the vast Lang & Lape store, and the proprietor examines them with his usual professional keenness.

He is not long before noticing the mortal wound behind the neck, and without saying a word he looks up toward the brothers, with a precise interrogation in his eyes.

"Know that man?" says Bob, the older one of the couple, answering a question by a question, as if to delay the coming revelation.

"No; never saw him before," is the curt, business-like reply.

"Name of party: Charles Montgomery."

"Well?"

Throwing back the lapel of his heavy overcoat, Bob now displays a U. S. Deputy Marshal's badge.

"Caught him in the act, three hours ago, burglarizing Ted Seymour's stable, close to to the Kansas line."

"But that's in the territory limits, ain't it?"

"Yep."

"A short mile from your father's place?"

"Yep."

"How did you happen to be round that way, tonight?"

"Have had our suspicions, for quite a while; man was no good, anyhow; used to peddle whisky for the Indians, got sentenced a couple of times. A horse-thief besides."

"How do you know that ?"

"We know it, that's all. None of your business, Mister. We are officers of the law and are responsible to the courts only."

"That's all right. But I ain't going to bury a man that's come to his death through a gunshot in the back of his neck, before knowing a thing or two about the whole story. Kind of queer, don't you know ?"

It took no little courage for that unarmed citizen, all alone in his store, in this part of the city left absolutely unoccupied and unguarded, during the night, to thus boldly resist the entreaties,—the orders we might say,—of these two strapping chaps, armed to the teeth and evidently resolved to have their way at any cost. But cool presence of mind has tamed wilder characters than these, and Mr. Lang's interrogatories were finally answered with some sort of impatient respect.

The story, true or not, was simple enough. The brothers had lately enlisted in a regular marshal's posse in the territory; the elder one Bob, just twenty-one years old, had even been entrusted lately with a U. S. Deputy Marshal's badge, and so far, nothing had been said or whispered that could be held as detrimental to the boys' characters.

Now, a few weeks before that eventful night, a tall, lanky Kentuckian had presented himself at a neighboring cattle range, asking for employment. He looked strong and willing enough, and the "boss" being in need of some extra hands gave him a "job" on the spot. He did his work satisfactorily and was soon "one of the boys."

It was not long, however, before—always according to Bob Dalton's narrative—queer stories were set afloat concerning the newcomer. He soon admitted, with a great show of frankness, that he had been engaged in Indian whisky trading, or rather smuggling, and had been "caught at it" a few times and been carried off to Fort Smith jail. But misdemeanors of that kind are so common round about the region that it hardly—if at all—lowered Charley Montgomery in his new associates' estimation.

The U. S. Deputy Marshals round about suspected him, however, of having been connected with various horse-stealings until then unpunished, and

felt sure that he would one day or other get tired of
earning a scant, but honest, living and drop back into
the easier—if more dangerous—avocation he had
once adorned.   So a quiet watch was kept over the
man, and the Daltons, on a visit to their father's farm,
had given a good deal of their time spying upon his
every movement.

That very night, they declared, they had found
him, a crowbar in his hands, attempting to unhinge
the heavy door that led into Ted Seymour's, the rich
cattle man's, stable.   There were half a dozen fast
sprinters located within the premises, and anyone of
them would have been a valuable catch.

According to the unwritten law of the land, a
man engaged in horse-stealing was entitled to a bullet
or two in the body, before even a word of warning.
And this the poor wretch had got with a vengeance.

"It has all been done on the square, Mister,"
Bob said, finishing his terse recital.   "You'll have to
take charge of him, you see; and we'll make our
report to the Marshal and have the court at its
next sitting allow you for your trouble and expenses.
That's all there's about it.   My brother and I are off
to Fort Smith by first train, and we have to get the
thing off your hands, see?"

2

The undertaker thought a while, and then carrying the only lamp, smoky and begrimed, that lighted up this weird scene, to a desk in the front part of the store, he sat down and silently indicted the following document:

"Delivered to Lang & Lape, undertakers of Coffeyville, Kansas, for burial, the body of one Charley Montgomery, who was caught by us last night, December —, 1888, burglarizing Ted Seymour's stable, and was shot by us while committing a crime.

"Expenses to be paid by the Marshal's office of the Indian Territory."

"Coffeyville, Kansas,—December, 1888."

"And you sign here, both of you," Mr. Lang added, having read aloud the contents of this declaration.

Without an instant's hesitation the young men put their hands to the pen and signed boldly:

"Robert Dalton, U. S. Deputy Marshal."

"Emmet Dalton."

"That'll do," the undertaker said; "I don't like that job half too much, but I'll have to do it and that's the end of it. Good-night, boys."

And the three men moved toward the door.

When they had reached the sidewalk and the undertaker had closed the door of his store, Bob said, with a show of cordiality:

"Want a lift to your house, Mr. Lang?"

"Never mind about that, Dalton; it's only a couple of blocks and I have just as lief walk home."

"All right!" was the elder boy's cool answer.

"Now, Em, you get it on the quick; we'll have to catch that 5:00 A. M. train on the Mo. Pac. So let her go."

The two lads were now seated in the wagon and Emmet was gathering the horse's reins.

"A nice, tight little place, this is," cried Bob, looking around approvingly. "You'll see us again, soon. Ta-ta!"

And the wagon rolled noiselessly away upon the snow-carpeted highway.

CHAPTER II.

THE DALTONS AT HOME—A MOTHER OF FIFTEEN CHIL-
DREN—WANDERERS OVER THE FACE OF THE STATES
—TEN SONS AND FIVE DAUGHTERS—A STRONG
FAMILY BOND—LOVE'S OLD, OLD STORY.

———

"Ma! Ma!" a young, not unpleasant voice called
out from inside a shabby, unpainted one-story farm
building, a short distance away from the dusty road.
Near the primitive well close by, a rougher voice
answered:

"What's that you want, Minnie? 's Si complain-
ing?"

"That he is, ma. Ain't the doctor a-coming
soon?"

"Pa's gone for him these two hours. He won't
be long now, I guess. Keep the boy under his
blankets."

"I'm trying to, ma, but the child is that fretful
that I don't know what to do with him."

"Well, tell him I'm coming soon. I'll make him
some lemonade, directly."

And the old woman—she looked older and more bent, whiter of hair and more wrinkled, than her years warranted—pulled up the bucket full of fresh, sparkling water, and poured its contents into the pail by her side.

"Where are they all, I wonder," she soliloquized, moodily, " 'tain't fair to leave an old rheumatic thing like me, and a flighty wench like Minnie, to take care of a house and a sick boy, too. Ah, my! life's harder than it ought to be, by a great deal.—" And heaving a deep sigh, the farmer-wife wended her tired steps toward her homely abode.

Just then she noticed a heavy cloud of dust upon the road leading east toward Coffeyville, the center portion of which could be easily espied at a few miles' distance.

"The doctor, I reckon," she muttered; "it's about time for him and pa to be here. I hope he won't be in a hurry for his pay, for if there is a half a dollar in this whole blessed shanty I'd like to see it.—"

The rhythmical tramp of numerous horses' hoofs soon informed the old woman that her surmises had been wrong. A troop of horsemen were coming up at a rapid trot in the direction of the house. It took her but a few seconds to recognize the new comers.

"Them's my boys!" she cried, with a look of motherly pride lighting up her furrowed features; and in her joy and evident relief, she cried out toward the open window of the house:

"Minnie! the boys, the boys!"

A blushing young face looked out, beaming with delighted surprise. It was easy enough to notice that there was something more than sisterly love in the radiance of the handsome blue eyes. So we might just as well inform the reader right here that Minnie Johnson was the niece, and not the daughter, of old Mrs. Louis Dalton, the old lady we have just seen at the farm well, the mother of the strapping young men and lads known and spoken of, not unfavorably at the time, as the *Dalton Boys*.

For this chapter opens in the late days of the fall of 1888, just six months before this momentous 22d of April, that threw open to the covetous greed of 60,000 settlers the rich plains of the Oklahoma region.

Shortly before that time, a family of eight people had come over from the Indian Territory to take up and rent a small farm in the immediate vicinity of Coffeyville, Kansas, quite close to the tracks of the Missouri Pacific R. R. company. The father was a

gloomy-looking, dull and morose individual, over
sixty-five years old; his name was Louis Dalton, and
his Irish origin could be easily guessed at from the
fact of his having named two of his sons after those
great Hibernian patriots, Grattan and Emmet.

The family seemed to have known better days,
and the old people openly manifested their discon-
tent at their reduced circumstances by having
nothing but gruff and graceless speeches to address
to outsiders or even to their own folks. Their un-
sociable ways cooled off any hospitable intentions on
the part of their new neighbors, and it wouldn't
have been long before complete isolation would
have surrounded the humble Dalton establishment,
had not the young people on the farm made up,
plentifully, by their hearty way and hale-fellow-
well-met demeanor, for the older ones' taciturn and
ill-tempered manners.

Mother Dalton belonged to the famed—ill-
famed rather—James and Younger families, being
herself a half sister of the Younger brothers' father;
she had been blessed with a large brood of children,
fifteen in number—ten sons and five daughters. The
veracious relator of this narration has only been able
to trace the existence of seven among those boys and

of one of the girls. The latter married a butcher in good circumstances called Whipple, now located at Kingfisher, Oklahoma Territory, and of whom anon.

Of the seven boys above mentioned, all alive at the time, Ben, the elder, was his father's mainstay on the little farm by Coffeyville. He had reached already the respectable age of thirty-seven. Next to him a full-bearded, honest and energetic fellow, Frank by name, counted among the best deputies of the Arkansas U. S. Marshal; he was thirty or thereabout. Next to him Grattan, twenty-five, William, twenty-three, Robert, twenty-one, and Emmet, eighteen, were more generally known as *Grat*, *Bill*, *Bob* and *Em*, appellations they were soon to render criminally notorious all over this vast continent, although to Bob, Grat and Em, belong more especially the palm in this competition of evil-doing. Simon, the fourteen year old lad, now lying upon a bed of sickness, closed this list of pillars of the *House of Dalton*.

Of the four boys old enough to be of help to their family or to fight for themselves in the struggle for life, Bob had been recently appointed one of the Deputy U. S. Marshals on duty in the Indian Territory, but reporting to the U. S. Marshal for the State of Arkansas, with residence at Fort Smith.

His young brother, Emmet, who had always been his particular chum and favorite, joined him in his roving excursions through those sparsely-inhabited regions; and Grat and Will fell in with them occasionally, although the latter preferred the Pacific coast as his habitual abode. As a regular business, the two elder boys tried mining, cattle driving, horse buying and selling; anything and everything except the dull but steady occupations, found on a farm or in city life. They were all fond of a free, untrammeled existence, on horseback mostly, with plain but substantial clothing on their back, the rough fare they could find on the road, and the few rather riotous pleasures of an occasional tear-out.

Perhaps had they inherited from their mother, who has been said to have Indian as well as outlaw's blood in her veins, that hankering for a roaming, open-air life, full of exciting variety and which might or might not, according to circumstances, carry them over to a career of open defiance of human law. Whatever may be the case, they had managed so far to remain within the bounds of comparative respectability, and their popularity in those rural districts, and even in the small cities that dot this vast region, had been growing month after month.

No untoward incident had embittered those young, primitive hearts and filled them with a dangerous desire after vengeance under some form or other.

It was not to be long though before just such an incident would throw three of these healthy, energetic and promising youths out of the straight road and turn their destiny into the disastrous and guilty channel, the goal of which was to be ——Death.

As is almost invariably the case, this incident was to have its origin in love, love thwarted, love betrayed, revengeful and merciless Love!

And the culminating point of this dramatic adventure was to be reached within a few short weeks from the day we see the four happy horsemen ride, merrily singing a rollicking refrain, into the farmyard of old man Louis Dalton.

"Hello! Minnie!" cried Bob, who had been scanning the front of the house with marked attention.

"Hello! Bob!" was the joyful reply, while the young girl waved her hand in token of welcome.

The four men jumped out of the saddle and led

their steeds to the rough hewn trough by the well. One of them set himself a-pumping, whistling "Home, Sweet Home," with all his might, while the horses were being relieved of saddle, bags and blankets

"Where is Si?" queried Grat, who had a kind of protective feeling toward the little chap, never in the best of health; the only *puny* one of the family.

We forgot to say that each son had dutifully kissed old mother Dalton with the sincere marks of fond affection that sat well on their bronzed faces.

"In the back room there, in bed," answered the dame, resuming her whining tone which she had left aside for a while to welcome her visiting offspring.

"Poor little chap," said Grat; "is it so bad as that with him?"

"Yes it is; and your daddy has just been out after the doctor."

"Dr. Wood, you mean?" asked Bob, who had finished his task and was washing his head and hands previous to entering in the presence of his well-liked cousin.

"Yes, Dr. Wood; he is a good old man, and won't ask for his money right away, as some of them leeches do."

"Never mind the money, **mother,**" cried Grat,

patting his pocket that gave forth a silvery sound.
"We boys can stand a couple of doctors apiece if
that's to make little Si well and hearty."

Just then a noise of wheels called every one's
attention toward the road. Dr. J. A. Wood's buggy,
with two persons aboard, was just stopping in front
of the house.

The pleasant-featured old physician, with his
long gray beard and his kindly smile, had soon
joined the group around the well.

After a general handshaking, somebody noticed
that "daddy had not come along."

"Oh! he is as perky as ever," cried Mother Dalton, querulously. "I guess he don't care a penny
about any of you, boys. I am sometimes weeks
without getting a word out of him. I say, leave him
alone. If he can stand being cross, so can we; isn't
that so, boys?"

A rather unanimous grunt ratified this somewhat
unwifely sentiment, and not bothering any more
about the head of the family, the whole party ad-
journed inside the house, the doctor and the mother
taking the lead.

They all entered the scantily furnished living
room which, with two small rooms on each side and

a kitchen in the rear, constituted the whole establishment. The door of one of the rooms was wide open, and the excited cries of a small boy were heard within. It called out:

"Grat, Grat, come to me quick!"

With something like a lump in his throat, the tallest and oldest of the four brothers present walked, first toward his little favorite's pallet, and leaning over kissed the emaciated cheek of the feverish child.

"Well, well," he said, mastering his emotion. "What's matter with you, old fellow? I thought I'd find you hopping around the farm happy as a lark."

The little hands pressed the bulky palm of the big brother, while the boy, gasping for breath, said in a voice exhausted by his recent exertions:

"Glad to see you, Gratty. Oh! so glad," and the little fellow broke down, sobbing as if his heart would break.

The good doctor was soon by the bedside, with those soothing and encouraging words that are worth "gallons of choice medicines."

"Never mind, my child; you'll be soon about again; there's nothing much the matter with you, I'll bet. Now, if you, big fellows, will kindly give the boy a little fresh air and leave him to me and mother for a while, we'll see to it that he is up and going in a jiffy."

And with a wave of his hand, Dr. Wood had soon cleared a space around the bed and gradually taken possession of the room. He closed the door behind the last of the visitors, and the mother aiding, began a thorough examination of the wee patient's ailment.

It didn't take him long to discover that the lad had been growing too fast, and was consequently suffering from a general debility, made much worse by the coarse food that was the only nourishment available. Having placed back the little sufferer upon its pillow of rough and not extra clean linen, he stepped out into the sitting-room and said:

"Boys, I guess you'll prove better doctors than I for the little chap. He is somewhat weak from over-growing and he'll have to get, for a while, some better food than cornbread and fried pork. So if you chip in something for to get him a better fare, beefsteaks and chickens, and lots of good eggs, I'll promise that he'll be another boy within a month."

The words were hardly out of the physician's mouth before every son of them had his hand in his pocket and had drawn it out full of coin.

" Here you are, doc," cried Grat, acting the
spokesman; for was not his little chum's life at stake?
"You take the pile and buy what's needed. Mother
might think it money thrown away. Just have the
people at the store send what's needed, and if you
want any more just let us know. We have been
trading profitably of late, and we can't afford to have
little Si die from want of proper food."

"Well said, Grat!" cried a cheery voice. The
door of the other room had just been thrown open,
and Minnie Johnson, arrayed in her best Sunday
clothes, stood there beaming with honest affection,
and applauding with both hands in sign of delighted
welcome.

CHAPTER III.

MAKING LOVE UNDER DIFFICULTIES—BOB DALTON'S
HEART CLEAN GONE—THE WILES AND WAYS OF A
COUNTRY COQUETTE—COURTING BY THE ROAD-
SIDE—AN OUTSIDER THE FAVORITE—THE
MURDEROUS GLEAM IN THE RE-
PULSED LOVER'S EYE—A VIL-
LAGE ROMEO KILLED BY AN
INFURIATED RIVAL.

It has been often and truthfully said that love
acts the same within the bosom of a country girl
and that of a great lady. In both cases it runs its
own, obstinate course, no matter the obstacle, and
perfectly mindless of the sorrows and wraths it does
arouse on its way.

When Minnie Johnson, the only daughter of
Mother Dalton's deceased sister and brother-in-law,
had found a shelter under her aunt's roof, some five
years previous to the beginning of this narrative, it
would not have been a hard thing to guess that one

of her stalwart cousins would be sure to fall in love with the maiden, when her bright country beauty would have reached blooming time.

Nor would it have been overstraining the probabilities to suppose that the said sweet maiden would have returned the sentiment and become, at the right moment, the blushing bride of her tall sweetheart.

Such would have been the *natural* course of things; needless to add that it was all to turn out very differently.

That is, the part played by the girl was to be strangely in variance with the outlined plot.

The part ascribed to the cousin-lover *did* follow but too faithfully the beaten path, and Bob Dalton, for the last six months, had been over head and ears in love with that little heartless coquette of a country lass, the sprightly, saucy, thoughtless Minnie Johnson.

On his duties in the territory, he had now been absent for over six weeks, and during this lapse of time an event of grave import had taken place.

A new suitor had appeared upon the field—or rather within the farm limits of old Louis Dalton—and like Cæsar he had come, seen and conquered.

Minnie Johnson was not heart-free any longer; the massive figure and engaging manners of Charley Montgomery had done their work and driven away whatever affectionate feeling her cousin Bob Dalton had inspired her with.

And it was the first time since that momentous change had taken place in the girl's life, that Bob and Minnie were again reunited in the old place by the Missouri Pacific R. R. tracks.

With the calm duplicity natural to her sex, the girl walked into the room, smiling and cordial as ever, allowing herself to be kissed all round by her four stalwart kinsmen. Bob had his share of the feast, but no more.

After a few moments of desultory questioning and jesting, the lover anxiously awaited an occasion to slip out of doors with his little sweetheart, whom his brothers had always considered as being to a great extent "Bob's girl." She had until then accepted the situation gladly enough and visibly encouraged her cousin's persistent attentions.

But on that day, without putting into it any affectation of coolness, Minnie managed to keep either in the sick room with Si, or in the kitchen with Mother Dalton, or among the men together.

Not a chance did she give Bob for the little tete-a-tete that had made his mouth water, in advance, when riding on the long way home. When evening came on, after the family supper, she spoke of the night before she had spent awake by the child's bedside, and slipping out very soon after entered her own little den and locked the door behind her, with a general "Good-night, boys, and pleasant dreams."

The disconsolate Bob could hardly hide his cruel mortification. He now realized full well that something or somebody must have stepped between "his girl" and himself and caused this painful estrangement. Who it could be he failed to imagine, but his jealousy was of course awakened and he set upon right away questioning his mother.

"What's the matter with the girl?" he brusquely asked, after he had been darkly brooding in his solitary corner for the best part of an hour.

There was a general silence in the living room, for all the brothers were too closely bound together not to take the deepest interest in whatever affected any of them.

"Nothing much, I guess; she is that tired though from watching over Si, day and night, when I am doing the chores about the place. I guess that's all—"

"Then she hasn't been keeping company with any new fellow, since I was here last?" was the next abrupt question. The old woman fidgeted about, visibly troubled.

A voice that had hardly been heard the whole of that afternoon, that of the taciturn, sullen farmer, arose now from his favorite corner near the fireplace.

"What's the use of lying to the boy, mother? Let him have the truth right now and be done with it—"

"Just like you, dad," cried his querulous spouse, "to speak only to bring about trouble. What of it if the girl has been out a few times with that Charley Montgomery—"

"Hold on; is that the man's name?" was Bob's stern question.

"That's the name he goes by, so far as I know," the mother answered, rather sheepishly, "but I tell ye it's just a passing fancy of the girl; nothing to get worried about, Bob."

The boy bit his lips angrily and kept silent. Just then Grat queried:

"I used to know a man by the name of Montgomery who made a living by peddling whisky all through the Cherokee Nation. If he is the same man he has had several months' acquaintance with the Fort Smith jail. He is a tough and a sneak, that's what he is—"

"Remember anything particular about his face?" asked the *pater familias*, who seemed strangely interested in the subject.

"Well, he had a rather promine it nose, with a wart on the left side of it."

"That's our man," quoth Louis Dalton, curtly. "He is working now for Ted Seymour."

"West of the Santa Fe tracks?"

"Yep."

At that moment, Bob rose with an ominous gleam in his eyes.

"Guess, I'll take a walk," he said, picking his wide-brimmed hat that lay on the floor by the side of his Winchester.

Nobody spoke; but every one understood. The boy's untamable temper was well known to all present.

"I'll go along," said Emmet.

"All right; don't you fret mother, we'll be back soon. We'll just take the lay of the land—"

And Bob laughed a loud, dreary laugh.

As the two boys stepped out in the yard, they noticed a light still burning in Minnie's room. The rough wooden shutters were closed but the gleam filtered through the cracks. That set Bob a-thinking.

He walked to the window and knocked at it rather gently, considering his excitement.

No answer came. He knocked louder and louder.

No answer yet. The truth came to him like a flash.

The girl was out. She had gone to meet her lover to warn him to keep away for a while—

Turning about with a smothered oath, Bob said to Emmet:

"Let us get on her trail—we have to find her—and pretty quick, too."

The younger boy nodded silently. His keen look, accustomed for years to the adventures of out-door life, had instantly noticed fresh footprints close to the window. He followed them up across the yard in the direction of the cornfield behind. A brilliant moonlight allowed the young men to keep the trail in clear sight for almost a quarter of a mile. Then a creek came across the track and they had to use their own judgment.

It was not much of a distance to Ted Seymour's place, a large, prosperous-looking group of buildings, on the South side of Coffeyville. This mile or so was covered with incredible rapidity by the excited lover and his faithful chum. When they reached the place, the living house, a two-story building of fair size and aspect, was wrapped up in darkness; evidently every one in it had retired for the night.

Repeated knocking and loud calling finally caused one of the upper windows to be opened and an angry voice shrieked:

"What's this—of a tantrum about? We ain't keeping a hotel, to be waken up at all hours. What you want?"

Bob answered promptly:

"We are two of the Dalton boys, and we have got a pressing message for Charley Montgomery. Excuse the trouble, boss, but we *must* see him at once. It's news that won't keep waiting."

"It is, is it?" was the gruff answer. "Then you better walk over to that big barn, over there to the right, and knock till the fellow wakes up. That's where he sleeps."

"Thanks, Mr. Seymour; excuse the trouble. won't you?"

"I guess I'll have to, anyway. Good-night, boys;" and with a loud, not unpleasant laugh, the master of the place let down his window with a bang.

Two minutes later, the Daltons were executing a regular tattoo upon the big barn door. Inside it sounded as hollow as a bass-drum; but it seemed untenanted by any living being except corn-rats, which were seen scampering away like mad, disturbed in their nightly repast.

Suddenly Emmet discovered that the door was not closed. It had simply been pushed back, and a piece of wood slipped under it from the outside to keep it from turning on its hinges. Around it, recent footprints were clearly visible.

To open the door and rush into the building was but the matter of a few seconds.

Bob leading, the two brothers climbed the ladder at the further end of the barn and reached the hay loft, where they supposed the man they were after to be located.

Through the upper opening the light of the moon threw a white glare of such intensity that every corner of the place was as easily inspected as in full daylight.

And one glance was enough to tell the boy that the loft was empty of its occupant.

But on the floor, just close to the window, there lay a little heap of some red silken stuff.

Picking it up, Bob cried out with a fearful oath:

"G—— —— it! That's the kerchief I gave Lizzie at the last County Fair!"

The girl had been there, notified her lover of the dangers ahead, and now they had both doubtless fled to parts unknown, away from jealous cousins and possible bloodshed.

The bell of a locomotive dragging a heavily loaded train along the Santa Fe track broke the dread silence brought about by this cruel revelation. It was the night Express to Kansas City, just leaving Coffeyville.

And as the boys gazed with excited attention at the line of cars filing but a dozen yards away, fate would have it that Bob's eyes fell upon the form of his faithless sweetheart sitting close to the big burly Charley Montgomery, on her way to undisturbed bliss.

With a curse that almost froze the blood in Emmet's veins, accustomed though he was to the fearful oaths of his habitual associates, cow-boys and scouters, Bob rushed down the stairs like mad, and fired after the flying train every shot in his Winchester.

Then, without noticing the wild disturbance this insane feat of his was creating over Ted Seymour's whole establishment, the boy ran through the fields uttering half in articulate threats of direst vengeance.

Seven weeks later, on a dark December night, stormy and drear, Charley Montgomery, who had come back to his old boss just for a day to get his back pay and his few traps, having been told that Bob Dalton was away in the territory, was shot in the back near the very same barn and fell dead from a single wound.

How the murderers disposed of the corpse has been told in our first chapter. What influence this first crime and the ferocious motive that inspired it were to have upon the Dalton boys' lives will never be clearly elucidated.

Suffice it to know that the treachery of his first love threw Bob Dalton into that criminal existence which was to end in his tragic death, but a short mile from the scene of his first deed of blood.

CHAPTER IV.

THE LAW'S DEFENDERS—OPENING OF THE OKLAHOMA
TERRITORY, APRIL 22, 1889—LICENSE AND CRIME
RUNNING RIOT—HOW WRETCHEDLY UNCLE SAM
REWARDS HIS SWORN SERVANTS—U. S.
DEPUTY MARSHALS AND THEIR ILL-
PAID LIVES OF CONSTANT PERIL
—THE WATCH-DOGS TURN-
ING WOLVES.

On the 22d of Apri., 1889—a day ever to be
remembered by the present generation of settlers in
the glorious Southwest—the bugles, all along the
line of the excited crowd camping upon Kansas
ground, sounded the signal that opened the new
territory of Oklahoma to the incoming of settlers.

In addition to furnishing to the farmer a magnificent soil, unsurpassed even by the Illinois bottoms
in productiveness, and so favorably situated that it
was then and there ready for the plow, being free of
rock, swamp or forest, this superb addition to the

public lands of Uncle Sam is blessed with a climate
so exquisitely balanced between the long winters of
the North and the long summers of the South, that
almost all the products of both North and South
can be successfully cultivated.

And the people far and wide knew of the natural
wealth this new Canaan was to open to the happy
owners of the coveted lands and, for weeks, had
been camping all along the frontier, every son and
daughter of them thrilling with excitement at the
thought of claiming the benefit of the generous
Homestead Law, and of staking valuable claims in
the close neighborhood of the projected cities.

Since other such openings will be offered from
time to time in the same vicinity to those willing to
avail themselves of the privileges so freely granted
by Uncle Sam, we may just as well state here the
leading conditions that render such claims valid and
transferable.

The lands entered in a claimant's name in the
land offices of either Guthrie, Oklahoma City, or
Kingfisher, must be resided upon and improved for
not less than fourteen months, but the settler may
delay making final proof for five years. The extraordinary low price to be paid for such fertile land is

$1.50 per acre, of which amount one-half only has to be paid cash down; the rest within two years. Land office fees for entering 160 acres, $14.00. Final proof fee, $4.00.

When one considers that at the present day, just three years and a half after the reservation was thrown open for settlement, a claim of 160 acres, within the limits of the city of Guthrie, which must have cost to the original owner a total sum (including all fees) of $258.00, part of which he did not even have to pay until April 1891, is worth now all the way from one hundred thousand to a quarter of a million dollars, it is easy to understand with what furious greed the sixty thousand would-be settlers, who rushed in like a living torrent on that memorable day, must have been urged almost to any deed of violence. To take and keep possession of desirable city lots or particularly well situated farm-land; to have one's entries made upon the official records—those two ambitions which might, if successfully attained, make a Crœsus out of a pauper, aroused within this motley and decidedly wild assemblage the worst passions dormant within every human being.

And how was the law prepared to resist and quell

the riotous propensities of this crowd, excited ten-
fold by the rowdy element that is ever sure to be
mixed, in a large proportion, with the peaceful citizens upon business bent?

It may just as well be stated, right here, that *it
was not prepared at all.* In fact *law*, in the usual
meaning of the word, did not *exist* within the new
territory for a full twelve-month, that is, until Congress passed, in March, 1890, a bill establishing a
United States Court, whose jurisdiction was to ex-
tend over the whole of the Indian Territory, Oklahoma included.

Until then, and during this whole year of unprece-
dented excitement, the only guardians of the public peace were a few men of incredible intrepidity,
with U. S. Deputy Marshals' badges pinned to their
coats, and whose indefatigable energy managed to
keep within bounds the thousand and more desperadoes, thieves and outlaws that had chosen to make
the new territory the stage upon which to pursue
their criminal careers.

Of course the early settlements that were to
become within a year populous and thriving cities,
with churches, schools, hotels, brick business blocks
and charming private residences, such cities as

Guthrie, the capital of the territory, Oklahoma City, Kingfisher, etc., were then but large agglomerations of tents or hastily-built shanties, amid which grog-sellers, faro dealers, monte sharp swindlers and lewd women of the worst description thrived and grew fat out of their nefarious traffic.

Promiscuous shooting, either to kill or simply for the amusement of drunken revelers, was heard day and night. Around the tracts of land specially coveted, regular free fights would take place with bowie-knives, revolvers, and even Winchesters, called into frequent and bloody use.

Think of the situation of the honest and respectable citizen who had collected his little whole, and, gathering his wife and children about him, had driven over the limits at a great expense of money and greater expense of fatigue and privations! Now, he was here, on the ground; his troubles ought to have been at an end, and the blessed moment when he would set his foot upon the land that was to be his according to the terms of the law, had come at last. But ruffians had taken good care that his pains should count him for nothing; what they could not pilfer stealthily, they would rob with guns in their hands; and driving him into the wilderness

again, impudently claim ownership over the very
claim he had staked himself. Where was help to
come from for the unfortunate? How was peace
with honor to be restored to him again? All praise
to those noble fellows who threw themselves forward with clear heads, stout hearts and robust mus-
cles to drive away the miscreants! There shall not
be said enough, by half, as an acknowledgment for
those services rendered by that handful of the law's
intrepid defenders. If Oklahoma counts now among
the most prosperous regions of this blessed country
of ours, let it be known far and wide that it is due to
the bravery of those few Deputy Marshals who struggled and fought and won the battle of order over
anarchy waged under its most hated and reckless
form.

Among them the names of Ransom Payne, Geo.
D. Thornton, Ed. Short—those two killed in the
discharge of their sworn duty—Frank Kress, O. S.
Rarick, C. F. Concord, John Swayne and scores of
others who took part, from 1889 to 1892, in this constant warfare for the good cause, ought to be associated with that of U. S. Marshal Grimes and Chief
Deputy Madsen.

We shall have occasion to relate, in connection

RANSOM PAYNE.
The United States Deputy Marshal, who kept on the trail
of the Dalton Gang for over Two Years.

with the criminal deeds of the Dalton gang, many of the feats to the credit of that small troop of noble men.

But, before returning to our "mutton," as the French say, we shall have to make the reader cognizant of one incredible feature in relation with the heroic work done by U. S. Deputy Marshals in the half-settled regions of the Southwest. We refer to the pecuniary compensation those men receive at the hands of Uncle Sam, for their risking their lives in the defense of peace and property.

The figures we insert here, and which can be relied upon as being absolutely correct, are so absurdly small that they are almost sure to bring an exclamation of indignant incredulity out of the reader's mouth. Here they are, though, and Truth itself.

For arresting a suspected or guilty party the U.S. Deputy Marshal receives the munificent sum of *two dollars!* And remember that, out there, he faces death with every arrest, and remains, besides, the marked victim of the arrested outlaw's friends. But let us proceed.

The Deputy Marshal is allowed *six cents per mile* when on the trail after a criminal, all expenses of transportation, board, etc., to be paid by him out of these six cents.

When he returns with his two-dollar prisoner in charge, he is allowed *ten cents*, and has to feed and transport himself, the assistants he may require, and the prisoner himself, all at his (the Deputy Marshal's) own expense.

Now listen; this is not all. When the accounts are rendered, the Marshal deducts thirty-five per cent. of the gross amount *as his fee*. Then the bill is sent to Washington and—sometimes allowed!

In the meantime, the Deputy Marshal has had to advance all the money spent, borrowing it from friends—or usurers; very happy he is indeed if he finally gets in hard cash *just one-half* of what is legitimately due him.

And, mind, the man receives *no salary!*

So that in reality, besides the danger to life and limb he runs, every day the sun rises above the horizon, this valiant protector of the law in the Indian and Oklahoma territories runs another ghastly danger: that of actually starving for want of necessary sustenance.

And now, can any one be much surprised to hear that once in a while one of these courageous men, so

shabbily treated by their own country, falls from
grace and enters the ranks of the malefactors he has
spent the best years of his life hunting down through
the region in his charge? It is an exceptional
occurrence, mind, a most exceptional one; but human
nature is not adamantine; it will succumb when the
tentation of evil-doing grows in the same proportion as the reward for well-doing decreases almost
to nothingness. Then, it's mighty hard, isn't it?
to be month after month deprived of all the com-
forts, even the necessaries of existence, while around
you crowds of loafers, who cleverly evade the
clutches of the law, live on milk and honey pil-
fered right and left. Of course there's no paliating
the dishonor attached to the act of stepping out of
the ranks of the law's guardians to turn out one of
its professional violators. But as He said, in his
tender, merciful way:

"Let he who has never sinned throw the first
stone."

Bob Dalton had for over a year followed in the
honest footsteps of his brother Frank, and seen him,
under his own eyes, fall the victim of desperadoes
he was bent upon capturing. He had liked the
adventurous life of the bold Deputy Marshals,

always on the go, always on the alert, breathing
God's pure air of liberty on the limitless plains.
He had learned then how to exist with little food
and less sleep; how to counterplot the schemes of
the wily criminals; and there was no guilty secret, no
trick of those nefarious trades he had not been taught
to fathom. Just then he was ready to graduate as a
full-fledged defender of the peace, or a most dangerous enemy of society. The knowledge acquired
could serve him both ways, and had he found in the
career of an officer the wherewithal to satisfy, within
certain limits, the love of pleasure lads of his age
cannot escape, doubtless that he would have finally
settled down as a man to be trusted and to be even
proud of.

But the $2.00 for each captured prisoner, the *six*
cents traveling money, and the *ten* cents return sub-
sidy, seemed to grow smaller and smaller as his
appetite grew larger and larger. Around him
abounded the occasions for illicit gains; as an officer he could hope for a while to escape discovery,
and he doubtless succeeded more than once in sup-
plying the Indians with the whisky the law forbids
selling to them. This was his first downward step.
Already the deed of blood of the preceding fall, the

consequences of which he and his brother had almost miraculously escaped, had given him a foretaste of the fascination of outlawry. He felt like the lion-whelp which has tasted human flesh for the first time; it thirsts after more warm blood, and generally gets it.

An incident we are about to relate, trifling in appearance, but decisive in its consequences, was the last drop that caused the glass to overflow.

CHAPTER V.

BOB DALTON RECRUITS HIS GANG—THE BRAWL IN THE
GAMBLER'S DEN IN KINGFISHER—SHOOTING TO
KILL—A BROTHER OFFICER LEFT BEHIND, A
CORPSE—BOB A BORN LEADER OF MEN—
HORSE STEALING AS A LIVING—"ON
THE SCOUT" FOR GOOD.

About that time, Ben Dalton, the eldest of the
ten brothers, who had always stuck to the legitimate business of farming, although with only
moderate success, settled down with his mother
upon a claim he had staked in the vicinity of the
new city of Kingfisher. He is living there yet and
attending faithfully to the duties of his calling.
Father Louis Dalton, who had always proved a
steadily unsuccessful man, and whose temper had
been soured to such a point that he had turned a
regular man-hater, did not linger long upon the new
plan but soon returned to Coffeyville, where he lived
for a while doing odd jobs about the country, finally
dying in the early part of 1890.

Ben, although disapproving the roaming disposition of his younger brothers, had of course no
authority to hinder them from shaping their lives
according to their own fancies. He, kindly enough,
kept a home for them to visit at times and recuperate,
and the mother stuck steadfastly to her great love
for "her boys," whom she doubtless remembered as
wee little tots, in tattered garments, gambolling
about her in the old, happy days of her comparative
prosperity.

The Kingfisher farm was of course a very primitive building, but it was prettily located near a
green-encased creek, and was sheltered from view
by a number of full grown trees. The causeway
was over two miles away, and, taken altogether,
the place was retired and quiet enough. Perhaps
when Bob and Grat had selected the spot, at the
time of the general invasion, they had shrewdly surmised the possibility of the place becoming for
them, later, a safe temporary refuge, when hardly
pressed by pursuers.

Be it what it may, one morning, almost at dawn
of day, toward the end of summer, 1889, three riders
were seen approaching cautiously the vicinity of
the Dalton farm. Their horses seemed jaded and

nearly ready to break down, and steeds and riders were bespattered with mud; for it had been raining heavily for several hours and the waves of dust had been transformed into mire pools. The men wore wide-brimmed slouch hats and had big boots on their feet. Winchesters and heavy revolvers constituted their visible weapons, and they formed altogether a pretty formidable troop. One of them, a beardless fellow, looking hardly more than twenty, but who seemed by common consent to be the leader, stopped the horses short, saying in a quiet voice:

"Here is the place—now you stay there, boys, under cover, and I'll reconnoiter. If the family is alone, will stop in for an hour's rest. The poor beasts need it;" and he patted affectionately his horse's neck. The brute seemed to like it and half turned its head in recognition. Bob and his horse—for the young man was none other than Bob Dalton himself—were evidently fond of each other.

"All right," said Grat, the oldest of the trio, getting off his steed and leading it to the creek near by. Emmet, also on foot, followed him silently, holding Bob's bridle, for his favorite brother had already wended his way toward the house.

A slender smoke above the trees indicated where the habitation was located and was sufficient evidence that somebody about the place was already up and doing. In fact, Bob had hardly reached the outskirts of the small clearing that surrounded the frame building than he noticed his mother standing in front of the open door, milking a cow.

A low and peculiar whistle on the boy's part caused the old woman to raise her head and gaze intently in the direction the well-known voice came from. The familiar form of one of her best-beloved children loomed up but a few rods away. She lost no time calling to him to come forward, and well knowing the ever cautious ways of his mother—she was not for nothing the aunt of the Younger brothers —the young U. S. Deputy Marshal now approached fearlessly.

After a hearty kiss to the "old woman" and a few words of hurried explanation, Bob retraced his steps in quest of his brothers, and, a few moments later, the three of them were gathered within doors and enjoying the first hearty meal spread before them for many hours. The horses, of course, had received their first and best care.

The story of their stealthy visit was told in a very

few words. They had taken part, the night before, in a bloody affray in which, for the first time, they had taken sides with some of their new friends among the territorial outlaws and against the officers of the law, their former associates; the latter had been driven back, leaving behind one of their number, shot dead through the heart. The constable had attempted, on that night, raiding a well-known lair of robbers and whisky peddlers, and had met with utter routing

The worse of the case was that the Daltons had been recognized in that most objectionable company and were now constrained to throw the mask and to give up serving two masters: Uncle Sam, that paid them so ill, and the outlaw gang who offered them such alluring inducements.

Some of the toughest characters in the region were taking part in last night's revelry, that terminated in actual murder, and the Daltons had been plainly recognized and even called by name with amazed indignation by several of the officers who later had made good their escape. So that they must now be counted among those after whom the marshal and his posse would be starting, that very morning, in hot and revengeful pursuit.

The die was indeed cast; the bridges cut down
behind the trio; they were to bloom now into full-
fledged desperadoes, and, all other means of living
being thus rendered unavailable by their own fault,
they would have to find their subsistence as open
and daring violators of the law.

With tears streaming down her wrinkled cheeks,
did the poor mother listen to that terrible revelation.
Ben stood by, sternly gazing at those once so promising lads who had decided to become the shame
and grief of the family.

What was the use reproving them? Their bed
was made, they had to lie on it now, and the first
consequence of this awful night's work was to render
them vagabonds upon the face of this great republic.

And so, the meal hastily eaten, and the horses
barely rested, fed and watered, the boys kissed their
afflicted parent, shook the hand of the bewildered
eldest brother, and off they went toward one of
those many out-of-the-way camping grounds they
had often noticed when riding about as officers of
the law.

Shortly afterward, large and systematic stealing
of horses from the herds became more frequent than
ever, and the new gang of thieves gained rapidly a

reputation of audacity unequaled in these parts. The rapidity of their movements and their surprising faculty of raiding one place while being almost seen at quite a distance from it, became the object of general fear and bewilderment among the cattle men and unfeigned admiration among outlaws and their ilk.

That admiration rendered, of course, very easy the recruiting of the troop of depedators soon dubbed "the Dalton Band," and which had instinctively and unanimously recognized for its chief and leading spirit Bob Dalton, the beardless youth hardly of age then. His shrewd and inventive genius, backed by an unbreakable spirit of intrepid determination, was a quality of such capital value to all men of his kind that they granted him enthusiastically the absolute obedience he expected from all men in his band.

His clear blue eyes had the steel glance before which everything and every one seemed to bow unwittingly. His riding was fearless and indefatigable; his shooting so sure that his marksmanship was the boast of all his friends. He could live on less food and less sleep than any brigand or law officer in these parts, and finally he possessed that mysterious

mastery over his fellow-beings which has been the
vaunted privilege of but a few famous men. Besides,
his courage awakened the enthusiasm of his "boys"
who would have followed him—and did follow him,
many and many a time, to death's door.

Three of them even fell by his side, without a
hesitation or a murmur, when came the dread hour
of final retribution—

Among the spots chosen by the new gang, which
had rapidly grown in number, power and daring, for
disposing of the products of its thefts, Baxter Springs
was the settlement most generally selected; and so
cleverly did Bob organize his raids that the robbers
generally managed to get rid of their ill-gotten
spoils before the first rumor of the raid had gained
much headway. Besides, there are always in the
territories and the bordering states of Kansas,
Texas, Arkansas, people of doubtful honesty ready
to drive any specially good bargains without too
close inquiry. All they want is to be safe against
any legal complication; and, as they pay their queer
customers but a very small fraction of what the
goods are worth, the profits compensate them
plentifully for the risk they run, as *de facto*, if not
openly, receivers of stolen property.

After each particularly successful and productive raid, the boys would disperse for a while and spend a few days or weeks in some of the small border cities, where they could find all those low pleasures just made for them and their ilk. Most of them, of course, were wildly dissipated fellows, drunkards and gamblers to the core and addicted to every species of vice.

But to Bob Dalton's praise be it said, he seldom plunged into those reeking abysses of iniquity, and always took good care to keep his young brother Emmet away from them. The leader had understood, from the start, that no such enterprise as the one he was managing at the peril of his life, could last for any time, with the ghost of a chance of success, if the chief and inspirer should have his brain habitually muddled by fiery drink and riotous living. So he decided to remain within bounds and to keep his head clear and sound on all occasions. To that pledge he remained true to his dying day.

The band had passed without much trouble through the winter of 1889-90, and the few fellows dropped on the way either through capture or desertion, had been quickly replaced by just as stout and determined chaps. For the ground over there,

in the territory, was, especially in those days, fertile in all kinds of outlaws, from the city-thief and
burglar too well known by the police of the
larger towns, to the miners and the cowboys " on
the scout," that is, having abandoned their regular,
honest trade, to pick up their livings in a life of wild
and criminal adventure.

But the spring opened disastrously for the Dalton gang, for Grat, one of its most trustworthy
members, fell into the clutches of the law—not
while acting in consort with his pals, but when
caught prowling about the large range of Charles
McLelland, a prominent cattleman of the territory,
evidently with a view of preparing some gigantic raid.

The U. S. Marshal was so elated by the capture
of so valuable a prize that he ordered a strong posse
to take the man to Fort Smith, Ark. The force thus
employed was so numerous and so vigilant, that the
gang who dogged their footsteps, day and night, until
they reached the Fort, failed to find an opportunity
to rescue their chief's brother. An attempt of the
kind not followed by success could only gravely
compromise the prisoner, against whom, after all,
stood only charges of a general nature as being one
of the members of the gang.

The fact is, that after keeping Grat three months in jail at Fort Smith, no true bill was found against him; and in spite of his detestable reputation, the horse thief, not yet grown to his full stature as one of the most dangerous bandits of the age, was allowed to go scot-free, and was soon ready for more distinguished feats in the annals of crime.

Only, this time, Bob and he and Emmet thought prudent to make themselves scarce for a while, on the theatre of their recent outrages, and obeying some mysterious invitation—perhaps one from their brother William, settled at the time in California—disappeared suddenly this side of the Rocky mountains, and were heard and seen no more about their habitual haunts.

CHAPTER VI.

THE TULARE COUNTY RAID—AN EXPRESS TRAIN HELD
UP AT ALILA, ON THE MAIN LINE OF THE SOUTH-
ERN PACIFIC—POOR FIREMAN RADLIFF KILLED
BY MASKED ROBBERS—FIVE MEN IN IT; TWO
ARRESTED BY DETECTIVE WILL SMITH
AND HIS POSSE—THE REST ESCAPE—
NINE THOUSAND DOLLARS REWARD
OFFERED BY THE COMPANY—THE
CONVICTED GRAT DALTON LEAPS
FROM A RUNNING TRAIN

————

The Southern Pacific Express, which runs
through between San Francisco and New Orleans
and leaves the Golden Gate City at 9 A. M. daily, is
due at the small station of Alila, Tulare county,
about 9 P. M. In winter it is crowded with passengers for the famed resorts of Southern California,
and especially for the prosperous city of Los
Angeles, which it reaches at 7:45 the next morning.
The express car run by the Wells-Fargo Express

Company is generally freighted with valuables, money packages, etc. The line has the reputation of being secure from high-handed robberies, and there is really but a few spots where such attacks could take place with even a possibility of success, for of late years all this region has grown marvelously in wealth and population.

Tulare county, though, and especially the portion south of the city of Tulare, is mountainous and ill adapted to cultivation. Hence, its settlements are insignificant and rather far apart.

However, when the Atlantic Express left Tulare, on the night of February 6, 1891, no one on board felt the least apprehension on account of the few lonely canons the train would have to cross before reaching the plains of Kern county.

The porters in the sleeping cars had attended to their nightly duties, and all the passengers, with the exception of a few jovial fellows making merry in the smoking compartment, had retired within their berths, when the train which was to have passed the station of Alila without stopping slowed up gradually, and finally came to a standstill but a few rods from the little depot.

The conductor, an old hand ready for any emer-

gency, immediately stepped out to find out the motive of this unusual occurrence, but a dozen oaths of
choice calibre and the random firing of a couple of
Winchesters drove him back into the cars with a
rush.

There was no mistaking the incident; it was a
bona fide hold up; the train had been stopped for
the purpose of robbery.

Stopping the train had been easy work.   A
red light had been procured from the frightened
station agent; the wires, both ways, cut down to
prevent any communication ahead or behind, and by
waving the light in front of the incoming train, in
accordance with the railway regulations, the engineer had reduced speed and finally stopped.

A second later, two men, wearing long black
masks, had jumped on board the engine and covered
both its occupants with their Colt revolvers.

Then, by a dodge rather new at the time and
which seemed to have been the pet invention of
Bob Dalton, another couple of robbers seized the
fireman, ordered him to take down his coal pick, and
placing him in front of the Express car door, had
him notify the messenger within, that the door
would be broken open at once if he did not open it

willingly. He was warned not to shoot as he might, and probably would, hurt the fireman and not the assailants.

No answer from the besieged man being vouchsafed the attacking party, the work of destruction began without delay, and the door, battered and broken, was soon a useless protection.

Then this gruesome thing happened—

Poor Geo. Radliff, the fireman, his task under dire threats accomplished, made a gesture the robbers doubtless interpreted as an attempt to join the messenger and defend the burglarized car. Instantaneously a shot through the head threw the unfortunate fireman on the ground, while a second shot killed him on the spot.

Then the work of pillaging began. The messenger, however, had managed to jump out on the other side and to take to flight in the underbrush. With him went the combination that would have opened the safe, and the iron chest was too solidly fixed to the floor to be moved one inch. Crowbars broke in the attempt to force it open and the robbers had not supplied themselves with dynamite.

So that after all the attacking party had to content themselves with a few parcels, comparatively valueless, and not caring probably to visit the inmates of the cars now thoroughly aroused and doubtless prepared for systematic resistance, they called away the engineer's guard, and firing in the air a few disappointed volleys ran away in the darkness, leaving behind them the corpse of poor Geo. Radliff, murdered in cold blood and without even the shadow of an excuse.

The victim of the bloodthirsty wretches was tenderly picked up by the engineer and by the messenger who had been hiding but a short distance away, and the train started again, in mourning for the honest fellow wantonly butchered.

The next few hours carried the news of this gory outrage all over the country, and the Southern Pacific R. R. Co.'s chief detective, William Smith, was, before morning, on the theater of the daring attack, with two carloads of horses and officers.

Aggregate rewards to the amount of nine thousand dollars were offered by both the railroad and the express companies. A hot pursuit began within eight hours of the perpetration of the crime, and by an unheard-of streak of luck two of the probably guilty parties fell into the hands of the police before the week was ended.

They proved to be a Californian gentleman of political prominence in those parts, by name William Dalton, and his brother, just fresh from the Indian Territory, and whose recent exploits were soon exposed—Grat Dalton himself.

Grat's horse had met with a severe fall shortly after the attack, and his master had been much bruised in the accident. Thinking himself absolutely unsuspected, since this was the very first raid attempted by his gang that side of the Rockies, he had boldly taken refuge upon his brother's place, in the same county of Tulare. A chain of circumstantial evidence traced him from the Alila canon to his present shelter, and the messenger and engineer both declared under oath that they had heard his voice on that eventful night of the 6th of February, and that his size and general outlines corresponded exactly with that of the robber left in charge of the engine.

This fact, of course, saved Grat from the gallows, as the shots that had killed poor Radliff had been fired by the men that stood about the express car.

On the other side, Will Dalton's political pull helped him, undoubtedly, to establish the alibi which made him an apparently total stranger to the

Alila hold-up. The fact of his sheltering his wounded brother, even coming to him under suspicious circumstances, could hardly be counted against him.

So that finally the Tulare county jury acquitted William Dalton, but found Grat Dalton guilty of complicity in the Southern Pacific R. R. robbery at Alila.

The judge sentenced Grat Dalton to twenty years in the state penitentiary.

And the convicted robber was about reaching his destination when another extraordinary occurrence changed once more the course of events, and set Grat one step nearer to the terrible death he was to meet twenty months later at the hands of the infuriated Coffeyville citizens.

Two deputy sheriffs had been entrusted with the task of bringing over Grat Dalton from the Tulare county jail to the state penitentiary. Knowing the man to be an athlete and a fearless desperado, they had decided to have his feet tied together with a leather thong, allowing their prisoner to take short steps only, while by turns each of the deputy sheriffs would link one of his wrists to one of the man s wrists by means of a double manacle. Thus it seemed that no possible escape could be effected. By using a day-train full of people there was no danger of an attempt at rescue by Grat's confederates.

So the trio started on its trip on a fine morning in early April, 1891. The temperature was very hot, as it usually is at that time of the year all over southern California, and the window next to which sat the prisoner had been thrown open. While the train was running at full speed—forty-five miles an hour— between Fresno and Berenda, the deputy sheriff who was tied up to the prisoner felt so drowsy that he let his head droop upon his breast, while he sunk in a delightful doze. His companion was having a chat and a smoke with a friend at the further end of the car.

Suddenly Grat Dalton rose from his seat with a jerk that awoke his bewildered neighbor. By a magic that has never been explained to this day, the bracelet around the prisoner's wrist fell upon the seat, while the man himself pitched headforemost and with lightning rapidity through the open window. A great noise of water was heard outside, and the excited passengers, now all shouting and crowding to that side of the train, could just see the form of the escaped prisoner swallowed up by the blue waters of a running stream.

The whole thing had not lasted five seconds, and the officers were gazing at each other with comic desolation, without even thinking of having the train stopped, when it slacked speed upon the conductor's spontaneously pulling the bell-rope.

The deputy sheriffs started out in hot pursuit, but their search was fruitless.

All they found on the river bank, close to the point where this incredible plunge had taken place, was the leathern thong and the fresh hoofprints of a couple of horses that had evidently been kept waiting for the prearranged escape of Grat Dalton.

PART THE SECOND.

CRIMINAL MEN.

CHAPTER I.

THE GANG'S LAIR—IN THE INDIAN TERRITORY AGAIN—
RANSOM PAYNE ON THE TRAIL—A HOT CHASE—
TIGER JACK'S DISCOVERY—THE OUTLAWS'
CAMP FIRE FOUND SMOKING YET—A NAR-
ROW ESCAPE FROM A SURE AND TER-
RIBLE DEATH—FOILED AGAIN.

The trial of Grat Dalton and the precise circumstantial evidence which had connected him with
the Alila, Tulare county, hold-up on the S. P. R. R. revived at once in the minds of the police force in the
Indian and Oklahoma territories the remembrance
of the various depredations traced to the Dalton
brothers during their last month's stay in the Southwest.

Although Grat had kept stolidly mum as to his
accomplices' names, decided as he was to face the

highest penalty of the law rather than peach upon his pals, the detectives in charge of the case reached rapidly the following conclusions:

Grat's brothers were with him in the Tulare county outrage;

And if the trio, now reconstituted through Grat's successful escape, were ever to be found and arrested, they must be looked for through the Indian Territory they knew so well, and where hundreds of friends, among the outlaws and the Redskins, would be only too proud to supply them with shelter and assistance.

Will Smith, the official entrusted by the Railroad Company and by Wells-Fargo's Express Company with the task of bringing the raiders to retribution, communicated at once with the Marshal of the Oklahoma Territory, and, as a consequence, the skilled, indefatigable and intrepid Deputy Marshal Ransom Payne was put in charge of the case, and directed to scour the country to get the three Daltons dead, or alive, into the clutches of the law.

Ransom Payne was already well known about the land as a fearless enemy of evil-doers and a shrewd discoverer of apparently lost trails.

He was a tall, strongly-built man of about forty.

with a fine, clean-cut face and a blonde moustache of no mean proportions. He was born in 1850, in Kappolo county, Iowa, but had been raised in the state of Kentucky, where he had received an excellent common-school education. At the time of the Tulare county outrage he had already resided in the Southwest for about eight years, having been quite successful as a real estate agent in the city of Wichita, Kansas.

Since 1888, however, the attractions a life of exciting activity always exerts over the minds of brave men, had induced him to enter the ranks of the territorial force as U. S. Deputy Marshal, and as such he had acted during the extraordinary period that immediately followed the opening of the Oklahoma reservation—April 22, 1889.

The presence in the region of thousands of outlaws of every stamp and description, mingled with the toughest kind of rumsellers, gamblers and fast women, rendered almost superhumanly difficult the task of the sixty men entrusted by Uncle Sam with the charge of keeping a semblance of order amid the sixty thousand new citizens of this extemporized community; especially so on account of the staking out of claims bringing about constant and bloody affrays between citizens otherwise respectable.

Two cases followed up to a successful issue by Ransom Payne and his chosen assistants attracted much attention at the time and deserve more than a passing notice in these pages, as they are typical of the state of semi-anarchy that reigned over the whole territory until Congress, in March, 1890, promulgated laws for the protection of property and its owners,

A veteran soldier, by name Captain Couch, was murdered by one J. C. Adams, the crime being the direct upshot of a disputed claim extending over part of the present city of Guthrie, capital of the territory, this piece of land being now valued over $250,000.

The murderer was tracked by Ransom Payne, arrested and brought to trial. The case cost the United States the snug sum of fifteen thousand dollars. Adams was convicted and sent to the Columbus, O., the nearest United States penitentiary, for a long term of years.

The details of this eventful pursuit and the recital of the deeds of extraordinary bravery to be placed to the credit of Ransom Payne and his posse would suffice to fill a volume.

Another case of mysterious and enthralling interest is that of the murder of Charley Grant by one Eddie Belden, on a farm near Edmund, Oklahoma Territory. Grant owned a valuable claim close by, which his chum and bosom friend, Eddie Belden, insisted he should sell to him. The young man persistently refused, and one night the two had a quarrel about it, and Grant was shot dead. His corpse was hidden under a pile of manure, and his disappearance was plausibly explained by Belden, who produced a document pretending to be signed by Grant and transferring to him, Belden, the fee-simple to the above-mentioned claim. The crime had been committed on the farm of a man named Holley, a brother-in-law of Belden. It was not long before Payne had ferreted out the guilty party, acting upon the well-known principle: "Look out for whomsoever is benefited by the crime."

Both Belden and Holley were arrested, not without the former showing fight. The body was discovered, recognizable yet, although in a fearful state of putrefaction, under the growing heap of manure; but the brother-in-law's complicity could not be established, as he protested his absolute ignorance in the matter. Eddie Belden, however, was convicted of murder in the first degree, and sentenced to be hanged. The President of the United States commuted the dread penalty to imprisonment for life.

Ransom Payne, who had, pistol in hand, arrested the accused murderer, himself brought the sentenced man to Columbus, Ohio.

These are but two of the many dramatic incidents in the busy life of U. S. Deputy Marshal Payne; they are quoted only as displaying on his part, besides an unusual amount of intrepidity, a cool and discerning spirit that made him a sure and shrewd leader among the defenders of the law.

It explains how the marshal of the territory chose him, out of a number of reliable and courageous men, to trace the Dalton gang and bring it to book for its first railroad outrage and the wanton murder of poor George Radliff, the fireman of the S. P. R. R. Express.

After conferring with Will Smith, the California detective, who had come all the way to Guthrie to start the searching party on its work, Ransom Payne recruited with the utmost care a posse he could depend upon, and having laid in a sufficient supply of horses, guns, ammunition and provisions he started on the trail.

In the party thus formed were found such c ol-
headed and determined men as Dodge, of the W₁lls,
Fargo & Co.'s squad of officers; Hec. Thomas, an
experienced posse man; Burl Cocks, a tried U. S.
Deputy Marshal, and a faithful and intelligent full-
blooded Indian, Tiger Jack by name.

One day those five men, who had been for seventy-
two hours in hot pursuit of Bob Dalton, Emmet Dalton, and their most daring associate, Charlie Bryant,
stopped for dinner at the entrance of a canon in the
vicinity of the Cimarron river, also known as the
Red Fork of the Arkansas river.

It was early in May, 1889, the weather was beau-
tifully clear; there were plenty of trees about, afford-
ing a cooling shade, and the men, cracking jokes
and exchanging anecdotes about their various experiences, went on preparing their meal according to
the customary camp method. They hurried through,
as they knew the trail to be fresh and their objective
enemies but a few miles distant at most.

When they were about saddling their horses
again and starting on their man-hunt again, they
noticed Tiger Jack, the Indian follower they had
taken along with them, wildly running from the
mouth of the canon, his arms playing the windmill

act in a half insane fashion. He kept mute, though, until he had come up with them, and they cautiously imitated his silence.

His tale was a startling one and showed how narrowly the party had escaped wholesale slaughter. Without trying to imitate Tiger Jack's queer lingo, we'll just give his story as follows:

"I thought," said the man, "that while you were finishing dinner, I would go around a little and see how clear the trail was through the canon. I walked on, in the underbrush, very slow and quiet like, until suddenly I thought I smelt horses to windward. You know I can smell them a couple of miles ahead when the wind blows the right way. True enough, as I crept a few yards farther, now flat on my belly, I discovered three men grouped behind a stone ledge, to the right of the path we should have been sure to follow. We couldn't have seen them, you know, until passing a few feet from their hiding place."

"Then our fate was settled, boys," said Ransom Payne; "we should have been shot down like rabbits, every son of a gun of us— I guess Jack saved our lives, that's what he did."

The men were too startled yet to properly manifest their gratitude. Burl Cocks asked:

"And while you were watching them, did you notice that they were aware of our presence?"

"No doubt about that, captain; they must be kept posted along by some of those d— friends of theirs. But I think they were preparing to go, for the horse I saw was ready saddled and there was some cautious moving behind the ledge—"

"The best way to find out, without letting them have the fun of shooting us down from their vantage ground," suggested Dodge, "would be to climb the hill just above their camping place, instead of kindly passing under fire of their cursed Winchesters."

"Right you are, Sam," said Payne; "let us follow your plan; Tiger Jack and I shall precede, the party about one hundred and fifty feet. We'll soon find out."

The party did not linger any longer around their smoldering fire, and proceeded on their march, in the order indicated. Some hard climbing amid the brush and loose stones brought them under cover directly above the spot where Tiger Jack had discovered the robbers' ambuscade.

But as their eyes plunged down upon the clever hiding place, they discovered at once that it was deserted—

The birds had flown; doubtless finding retreat the better part of valor, the possibility of the posse coming down upon them from above not escaping their practical judgment.

And when Ransom Payne and his men, after searching the woods with systematic caution, had come together again, just behind the ledge where their mortal foes had stood in wait for them, they found there, besides the remnant of a hearty meal and the hoofprints of several horses, two packages of cartridges, an overcoat and, stranger still, a live but maimed horse, with his saddle and trappings all complete—

Once more the courageous representatives of the law had been foiled by their dangerous adversaries —poor Geo. Radliff's death remained yet to be avenged.

CHAPTER II.

The village of Kingfisher, one of the creations of
the recent settlement in the Oklahoma reservation,
has grown already to the dignity of a full-fledged city.
A United States Land Office is located there, and a
great deal of visitors having business with it are found
in its neatly kept hotels. Stores and amusements
such as are appreciated among this class of people,
are found here in plenty, and the tone of the popu-

lation is rapidly growing better and steadier. The rowdy element has had to give up the struggle and make itself scarce, although of course, it is represented there yet by tough characters and a strong heavy drinking and gambling element.

Among the business men themselves, a few may be found who tolerate, if they don't openly sympathize with, whatever there is left of rampant lawlessness. Half out of fear, half on account of the pecuniary benefit they derive from having those men as regular customers and often enough sharing their illegal profits, they will at times be caught in rather doubtful transactions which place them under the law's hand. It is especially so when they happen to be related by family ties with some of the desperadoes who still infest this otherwise highly prospelous section of the country.

As was stated in one of our preceding chapters, Mother Dalton's only surviving daughter had been married for some time to a well-to-do butcher of Kingfisher, a man called Whipple. When the attention of the officers began to be directed toward the Dalton boys' criminal operations, and especially after the Tulare county hold-up, and the murder of George Radliff and the daring escape from custody

of Grat Dalton, a very strict, although secret, watch
had been established, not only around Ben Daltons'
farm, upon which, as we know, resided, and resides
to this day, the boys' mother, but also upon the
movements and surroundings of Whipple, the
butcher, married to a Dalton girl.

Nothing, however, of a particularly suspicious
nature warranted, for awhile, the police's interference in the brother-in-law's affairs, until, one day,
this worthy returned from a business trip riding a
horse nobody in town knew him to possess. He
declared that he had bought this horse during his
trip, and nothing more would have been thought of
it, if, shortly afterward, Fred Carter, a cattle man of
Beaver county, happening to pass in front of Whipple's store, had not recognized in the horse tied to a
hitching post and awaiting his new master, a horse
stolen from him, with several others, a couple of
months earlier by Bob Dalton's gang. He had even
been told that Bob was particularly fond of the
beast, and had sung its praises over and over again.

Having called at the U. S. Deputy Marshal's
office, to have a talk with him concerning the
matter before asking a justice of the peace for a
writ of replevin, Fred Carter met there Ransom

Payne, on a searching tour, down from Guthrie, his
home. The men compared notes, and the officers,
clearly remembering the version of the purchase as
given by Whipple to his friends and the public, concluded that there was here something that needed
immediate explanation and might lead to a series of
startling and most useful discoveries.

A cautious inquiry was set on foot, Fred Carter being recommended in the meantime to keep his
own counsel and not allow any one to know of the
proposed proceedings.

The information collected proved sufficient
to establish a *prima facie* case against Whipple,
of receiving and keeping stolen goods knowing the
same to be stolen; and later on, the same night,
the two U. S. Deputy Marshals, who had sworn
the necessary warrants, pounced upon Whipple as
he was returning to his home, a short distance from
the city, riding the very steed Fred Carter claimed
as his own. That same night, the prisoner, the com-
plainant, the two officers and the horse, were carried
over the Rock Island R. R. to Wichita, Kas., the
nearest United States jail, where Whipple was soon
securely locked up.

The arrest had been made with such secrecy and

with such lightning rapidity, that the population of Kingfisher was absolutely dumbfounded when they heard of it.

Mrs. Whipple, *nee* Dalton, was alone in the store, weeping violently and protesting her husband's absolute innocence. She received the condoling visits of her neighbors and friends, and soon decided to proceed with business with the help of her assistants, proposing later in the day to start for Wichita, bringing to her husband the necessary money to fight the case to the bitter end.

Doubtless the Dalton brothers must have been just at that time in hiding but a short distance from their mother's farm, or the telegraphic news of their brother-in-law's arrest must have reached them almost as once, for a written, although unsigned message, clearly emanating from the redoutable trio reached, within twenty-four hours, the Kingfisher civic authorities.

It read as follows:

"You are making d—— fools of yourselves if you think you can tackle any of our people without putting yourselves in a —— of a fix. That Ransom Payne 'll have to swing for it, sure, or to have so much lead pumped into his d—— carcass that his own mother won't know him. Let those that are called as witnesses beware!"

And underneath, they had rudely drawn a skull and cross bones with these words in big red letters:

"WE SHOOT TO KILL!"

The mayor and police captain of the village found it useless to rouse the frightened anxiety of the population by allowing this scurrilous epistle to be generally known. They simply increased the precautions generally taken by them to prevent any outrage against the lives and property of the citizens to be perpetrated, and kept a close watch upon gambling dens, groggeries and houses of evil-resort where the Daltons counted numberless friends but too ready to help them in any pillaging or burning of houses.

The Kingfisher officials were soon relieved, however, of this new load of anxiety by the news that Whipple had been let go scot free, his wife's active interference having caused the withdrawal of the complaint.

But the very same day this announcement was made to the public, thus removing the probability of a revengeful and murderous attack upon the city on the part of the Dalton gang, the telegraph wires flashed the astounding news that the desperadoes had resumed their railroad holding-up operations, and, true to their oath of getting even with Ransom Payne, had combined "business with pleasure" and stopped the very train upon which the faithful officer was returning from his Wichita trip, en route to his Guthrie home.

And in the saloons of Kingfisher that night, the ruffian element, enthused by the proud record their favorites were making, were crying out boastfully, speaking in the absent desperadoes' name:

"Don't you see, they are 'fraid of us!"

CHAPTER III.

THE WHARTON HOLD-UP ON THE SANTA FE LINE—
THE SOUTH BOUND PASSENGER TRAIN ROBBED
BY THREE MASKED MEN—AN OATH AND A BOAST:
"WE DONE IT!"—A POSSE INSTANTLY
FORMED, RANSOM PAYNE AT THE HEAD
—BOB, EMMET AND CHARLIE BRY-
ANT THE GUILTY PARTIES—THE
THREE OF THEM RECOG-
NIZED BY THE TRAIN
HANDS.

———

In the councils of the band, Bob more in control than ever, it had been resolved to strike a great and resounding blow, in the midst of the region that knew them so well but had never seen them yet at work upon any really startling affair.

A hold-up of the first class taking place upon the territory itself would place their gang right away in the front rank among those associations of malefactors, the very name of which inspires terror

BRODWELL   BOB   GRAT   POWERS

JOHN J. KLOEHR
The heroic liveryman who shot dead
Bob Dalton, Grat Dalton and Bill Powers

and secures for their members a success based on other people's cowardice. In other words, they would be able, henceforth, to stop trains, raid banks and march, in broad daylight, through closely-inhabited settlements, without any one even daring to raise a finger or pull a gun.

Just then occurred the Whipple arrest, and Bob declared that now was their opportunity to spread a wholesome terror in the camp of the enemy.

First, they would boldly proclaim their intention of getting even with those who had dared molest the friendly butcher, their relative by marriage.

Then, they would manage to hit two birds with one stone in holding up the very train containing their arch-enemy, Ransom Payne, taking both profit and revenge at one fell swoop.

This tremendously risky move was agreed upon enthusiastically and an approximate date fixed some time after the ending of the expected trial of Whipple at Wichita. That left the band several days, weeks perhaps, for other minor business, and they dispersed on their various criminal errands bent.

Only Bob, Emmet, and Charlie Bryant remained together on the watch, full arrangements having been made to notify the rest of the band, in due time.

But things having turned entirely differently from what the gang expected, that is, Whipple having been released almost at once, Bob was notified, just a few hours ahead, of Ransom Payne's departure from Wichita, and of his being on board train No. 403, the Fast Texas Express of the Santa Fe R. R., en route to Guthrie. The Deputy Marshal was to leave at 5:45 P. M. that very night, and if he was really to be captured on his way home, the operations must be conducted with almost lightning rapidity.

The bold desperado was up to the emergency though, and he decided, on the spot, to "face the music," that is, hold up the train, rifle the express messenger's safe and secure possession, or shoot down in his tracks their indefatigable and unconquerable enemy, Ransom Payne. He would do it all with the two associates that were with him at the time—his brother Emmet and their trusted partner, Charlie Bryant.

An hour after the above information reached them, the three robbers had saddled their horses and were fleeing at their top speed toward the station on the Santa Fe road, chosen by Bob as an appropriate point for a successful night attack.

It was the small Wharton depot in the Cherokee strip—about twenty miles from where the three men had been camping on the banks of the Red Rock creek, one of their favorite hiding places— that was selected by Bob; and toward it the men rode in post haste.

The time tables of the Santa Fe R. R., indicated that the Texas Fast Express would pass Wharton station at 10:13 P. M., but only stop there if properly signaled. For Wharton is not a center of population by any means, the whole agglomeration consisting of a small frame station and one or two general stores, with postoffice attachment.

However, the Wells-Fargo Express Company is represented there in the person of the station agent, and the Indian farmers and cattle men around patronize the station occasionally.

That night everything was more than usually quiet around the depot, when, toward 9:30 P. M., three horsemen rode to the door, and tied their horses to the hitching post.

It was Bob Dalton, Emmet Dalton and Charlie Bryant. Bob entered the station alone, the lower part of his face muffled up, and his broad brimmed slouch hat brought down over his forehead. He stepped up to the solitary agent, and putting up his Winchester, said in a low but distinct voice:

"Get out on the platform and put up the signal for that train to stop."

The man opened his mouth and eyes wide in frightened stupefaction, then, closely followed by the desperado, walked out and fixed the signals as told.

He was then marched back in short order within the station, bound and gagged solidly in his little office and left to his own, not overpleasant, meditations.

In the meantime the two other robbers had patrolled the neighborhood and found everybody sound asleep and the couple of houses closed tight. No risk of any interference on the part of the baker's dozen of inhabitants, if they indeed counted up as high as that.

Then the trio prepared operations in earnest. The horses were led about a quarter of a mile back and tied there, while black masks came out of the men's pockets and were carefully placed over their features. Guns and revolvers being carefully in-

THE WHARTON TRAIN ROBBERY.—PAGE 97.

7

spected and found in prime order, the gang was now ready for the coming event.

All this had needed but a few minutes' time, and when the fast Texas Mail slowed up speed in obedience to the regular signals, its assailants stood ready to receive it.

But now we will let Ransom Payne himself, a passenger, as we said above, on board this unfortunate train, tell the story of the hold-up and the concomitant robbery.

"I had been slumbering for some time in the last car, in the rear, utterly fagged out by the preceding week's exertions, and truly delighted at the thought of reaching in a few more hours my cheerful home and my comfortable bed, when a sudden jerk told me that the train was stopping at some way station. There had been no hold-up in this neighborhood for a long while and my first thought was not one of alarm. However, I recollected at once that this night express, which I very frequently patronized, was but very seldom signaled to stop between Arkansas City and Guthrie. This stoppage awoke therefore my apprehensions and I tried to look out of the window to discover what the matter was. Suddenly a couple of shots sounded in the stillness of the night.

"It was all clear as a bell now. The Dalton boys had learned somehow that I was on the train and, true to their boast, they were coming on to "pump lead" into my unworthy—but decidedly precious— frame.

"Not a minute was to be lost. The fact of my having chosen the last car probably saved my life; for I could reach unnoticed the end of the car, which was at the same time the end of the train; and pulling out my trusty Colt, I slipped on the ground and walked noiselessly and under protection of the train, which lay between me and the robbers, toward the underbrush close to the track.

"There I stopped and stood in calm expectancy, resolved to sell my life dear if I should come to be discovered by the bandits.

"From the distance I could now hear the yells and the dreadful oaths of the scoundrels as two of them went through the cars, at breakneck speed, searching for me. I was told later that, according to the system they had practiced in Tulare county, they had taken the fireman down from the engine and had him act the coerced burglar.

"They soon gave up finding me, especially when conductor McTaggart swore, with a great deal of well-assumed sang-froid, that I had missed the train and was not to leave Kansas before morning.

"The brigands then concentrated their efforts towards rifling the Express car. I was told since that they only got $1,600 out of the safe and over-looked a sack containing over $5,000 in silver.

"This time there was no bloodshed, and the whole performance did not occupy thirty minutes. I could see no trace of horses in the vicinity, although the moon was so clear that one could have almost read a newspaper by the light of its rays.

"The passengers, perhaps thirty or fifty in number, half of whom were located in the sleeping car, had been awakened of course by the noise of the shooting; but obeying the conductor's advice, which they doubtless did with great alacrity, they remained quiet and hardly spoke above a whisper until the train had been released by the gang.

"It was hardly eleven by my watch, when the train steamed on, leaving me behind and alone in this deserted spot. The situation was not so criti-cal though, after all, for the desperadoes, who had no idea of my being so near them, were not long joining their horses—by the way, they passed just a few feet from me—and I soon heard the hoofs rapidly striking the dry ground.　They were away and I was free to act.

"It did not take me two minutes to realize what to do next.　I ran to the station, released the poor agent from his bonds and gag, and having repaired the north wire as best we could, I set him telegraphing to Wichita a short but pithy narrative of the hold-up. I asked for men and horses to begin a hot pursuit, and proceeded at once toward Orlando, the next station and a village of some two hundred people to gather among the brave fellows there the first elements of a posse.

"The next morning, at daybreak, a carload of men and horses reached Orlando from Guthrie; and having selected a set of men whose courage and indefatigable activity I could fully trust, I started before noon, on that day, on a furious chase that lasted over six weeks, and among the leading incidents, of which undoubtedly the most extraordinary was the death of Charlie Bryant, killed by poor Ed. Short, the best and truest of friends, in the discharge of his **sworn duty.**"

CHAPTER IV.

BOB DALTON IN LOVE AGAIN—HIS FAME GAINS HIM THE
HEART OF DAISY BRYANT—HE BUYS HER A FARM
NEAR HENNESSY, O. T., WHERE THE GANG CARRY ON
RIOTOUS LIVING—THIS NEW LAIR DISCOVERED
BY RANSOM PAYNE—HIS APPROACH MADE KNOWN
TO THE DALTONS—THEY VANISH IN TIME,
LEAVING BEHIND CHARLIE BRYANT SICK
IN BED—THE TRAGIC END OF THE
CAPTURED AND HIS CAPTOR.

———

The sensation caused all through the Indian and
Oklahoma territories and the neighboring states
of Kansas, Missouri and Texas, by the hold-up of
the Santa Fe Express at Wharton, Cherokee strip,
on the night of May 9, 1891, is yet in every one's
memory. It revived in the older folks the remembrance of the James Brothers' and Younger Brothers'
deeds of blood, and coupled with the Tulare county
outrage it gave rise to the gravest apprehensions.

It was useless to deny it any longer; a new gang.

under a leader of unusual daring and executive
ability, had come to the front, and would be sure to
attempt any crime to equal, if not surpass, the terrible fame left behind them by their predecessors.
The Daltons grew, almost in a week, to the proportions of full-fledged bandits of the most dangerous
stamp, and United States Marshal Grimes, in charge
of the Oklahoma Territory, realized that he must
send his best force on the trail and crush this new
power for evil that threatened to assume such re-
doubtable importance.

In such, not yet fully established communities, the
vigilant officers of the law are well aware of the
evil influence a few successful, unpunished crimes
of this particular stamp exert upon the imagination
of the younger, somewhat wild, element, not con-
taminated yet but too prone to be carried off by the
recital of deeds of extraordinary recklessness. The
tendency to instinctive imitation is rampant in the
human nature; especially so with young people accustomed to the open-air life and the rough existence of the cowboys and farmhands in the Southwest.   If a gang of depredators be allowed to grow
in reputation, and manages, for a prolonged period,
to escape the clutches of the law, it either increases

and develops in enormous proportions, or it causes
other similar gangs to be organized about the land
with the avowed boast of throwing all past exploits
into the shade.

And another very serious evil arises from the
continuous existence of such bands of malefactors.
As their deeds of blood are narrated about and of
course magnified, from village to village and from
insolated farm to lonely cattle range, the peacefully
inclined citizens cannot help being filled with an increasing dread. The possibility of a raid haunts
their sleep; and if by chance, the scoundrelly gang
happens to call upon them for ammunition or vic-
tuals, they not only get the goods without paying
for them but are often sheltered for a time against
the pursuing posses. The excuse for such cowardly
conduct evidently is, that the officers once gone and
the small settlements left to themselves again,
any refusal of help or any indication as to the
whereabouts of the robbers is sure to bring
down the bloody and prompt vengeance of the
gang.

So, it comes to pass that the prolonged prosperity and impunity of any band of train robbers
increases the amount of lawlessness rampant about,

and renders the citizens less and less of a help to the police force.

U. S. Marshal Grimes, alive to the gravity of the situation, telegraphed to his trusty lieutenant and deputy, Ransom Payne, pressing orders not to spare any effort to overtake the assailants of the Texas Fast Express and to gather in those other well-known members of the gang who did not happen to be present at the time of the Wharton outrage.

Such capital officers as George E. Thornton, E. D. Short, Frank Kress, Joe P. Jennings, George Orin Severns, were sent along to assist Payne, and, during those forty days of hard riding in pursuit of the desperadoes, other men were added to the posse, or took the places of the worn out ones.

But Ransom Payne went along, apparently impervious to exhaustion and collecting, on the way, with shrewd judgment, a mass of valuable information concerning the Daltons' habits and habitual rendezvous.

Love was again to play a part in this exciting frontier story, Bob Dalton a second time the hero of an amorous intrigue, but the triumphant hero, this time; no longer the rejected swain of a fickle little country lass.

"His girl," in this occurrence, was the tall, shapely, diamond-eyed sister of his chum and accomplice, Charlie Bryant.

She was a full blown beauty, and was said to be a grass widow from one of the Northern States. An expert on horseback; she handled a Winchester or a Colt with unfailing accuracy. Attracted by Bob's dash and imperious manner, she had thrown herself in his arms, so to speak, and, since his return from California, shared frequently with him the perils of his criminal enterprises.

But she soon found out that she could be of much more use to her lover and his companions, by keeping for them, always ready and well supplied with reserve horses, ammunition and provisions, a retreat which could be shifted from one corner of the county to another when the territorial police would get an inkling of its whereabouts.

Recently, that is a couple of weeks after the Wharton hold-up, Daisy Bryant, under the name of Mrs. Harry Jones, and with the demure ways of a Dakota widow in quest of a milder climate, had invested quite a snug little sum buying out an abandoned claim, a few miles west of Hennessey, in the Oklahoma Territory. She had found there a house of some size, and the approaches of the place were such as to allow of an easy and far-reaching watch over all approaching visitors.

There had Bob, Emmet and Charlie Bryant found their devious way, and, remaining well under cover, managed to keep a riotous sort of a "good time." This lasted for three weeks at a stretch, and the funds were getting low again, and something had to be done soon to replenish the depleted exchequer. So Bob and Emmet started on a still hunt to pass the word to their principal associates, leaving behind, under his sister's roof, Charlie Bryant, who had not recovered yet from a first-class fit of delirium tremens, the consequence of long habits of inordinate intemperance.

We may just as well repeat right here, although we have mentioned the fact once before, that Bob Dalton had never been a heavy drinker, and had never allowed his younger brother to become one. That kind of prudence he had, to always keep his wits about him, at his and his pals' command.

The Daltons were already gone two days, and Charlie was feeling so much better under the careful nursing of his sister, who had strict orders to keep the whisky bottle away from him, that he was thinking of joining the boys on the very next day, when, in the middle of the night and without any warning whatever, the whole force of Ransom Payne's posse surrounded Daisy Bryant's house.

The Indian male-servant, whom the fair widow had trained to be both deaf and dumb on all such occurrences, opened the door promptly at the first knocking of Payne, who always ventured at the head of his men in any such particularly dangerous occasion.

Obeying preconcerted orders, the officers invaded every room in the house almost at the same time, not indulging in any parleying whatever, but just taking possession, as they would have stormed a fort under fire.

In one room, already half-dressed and her hand on a Winchester she had had no time to use, Daisy Bryant was discovered and provisionally hand-cuffed.

In the garret, in a very ingeniously contrived retreat, which contained a shake-down and other such primitive conveniences, Charlie was pounced upon, also unprepared to resist so rapid an attack.

He was made a prisoner, and a squad being left in the house to prevent Daisy Bryant or her Indian

help from communicating with the outside, Charlie,
pretty tightly hand-cuffed, was placed in Ed Short's
charge and marched in prompt order as far as the
Henessey station of the Rock Island R. R., there
to await the passage of the next train. It had been
decided to have Charlie Bryant conveyed to
Guthrie by way of Caldwell, Arkansas City and,
down south, by the Santa Fe R. R. as far as the
capital of the Oklahoma Territory.

This memorable trip was undertaken August the
23d, 1891. While traveling over the Santa Fe, Ed
Short had gone to sit with his prisoner in the Express car, the messenger being an old friend of his.
The train having stopped at Enid, a way station,
some time in the afternoon, Ed Short felt like
straightening his legs by a little walk on the platform. The prisoner seemed quiet enough and had
been fairly cheerful the whole day, protesting his
innocence and making sure to be set free by the
first judge who would have cognizance of his case.

Still, in spite of appearances, the handcuffs had
not been removed, and when Ed Short stepped
down he placed his revolver in the messenger's
hands with a sign of warning. The Wells-Fargo
man was a fellow of little experience, and he had

failed to recognize the true nature of the brigand who sat so demurely a few feet from him. So, heedless of Ed Short's silent warning, he laid the revolver by his side on the floor and began arranging a few packages just delivered him by the station agent.

Quick as lightning, the prisoner lowered his two hands, tightly bound together, within reach of the revolver, and picking it up noiselessly, glared with shining eyes toward the open door.

Just at that minute, he espied Ed Short on his way back to the car. Bang! bang! went the revolver!

Hit in the breast, then again in the neck, Short staggered and cried out:

"I am done for!"

But his indomitable pluck did not forsake him in this horrible moment. With a hand already trembling with the approaching agony, he pulled out his second revolver, and once, twice, thrice, fired at the crouching form of his murderer.

Without a word, without even a gasp, Charlie Bryant tumbled headforemost out of the car—a dead man.

And rolling by his side, still clutching his revengeful weapon, poor Ed Short, faithful to his trust even unto death, fell down, vomiting his life's blood.

Captor and captured had met together before their Maker's judgment throne.

CHAPTER V.

THE SUMMER OF 1892 SEES THE GANG REORGANIZED —
THE RED-ROCK HOLD-UP— A SECOND ATTACK ON
THE SANTA FE ROAD— ONLY A FEW MILES
FROM THE THEATER OF THE WHARTON
ROBBERY— ANOTHER POSSE IN FULL
PURSUIT— BUT RANSOM PAYNE IS
NOT THERE TO LEAD— THE
DESPERADOES ESCAPE
EASILY AND ARE
SOON READY
FOR ANOTH-
ER HAUL.

Poor Ed Short was dead, shot down in the most cruel and cowardly manner by the chief accomplice and pal of the Dalton brothers, Charlie Bryant, the sister of Bob's paramour, Daisy Bryant, the dashing Hennessey grass-widow. For a time, it seemed as if this deed of blood, followed, like a flash of lightning, by the murderer's death, would cow down the indomitable spirit of this band of desperadoes and disrupt their criminal league.

Ransom Payne's efforts had been so far successful that he had unearthed the gang's principal refuge, captured one of the leading spirits among those brigands and caged the fascinating creature whose clever dodges were of so great a help to the Daltons' comfort and security.

In the task, one of his trusted lieutenants had fallen, faithful to the last; but this was one of the forfeits to be paid whenever risking one's life in the dangerous career of defender of the law.

And it seemed as if this heavy sacrifice of a noble, unselfish existence was to put an effectual stop to this era of extraordinary lawlessness the Daltons had inaugurated, in boastful imitation of their predecessors and kinsmen, the Jameses and Youngers.

For months after this eventful twenty-third of August, 1891, when this bloody drama took place in front of the Express car of the Santa Fe train, the country that had trembled under the criminal sway of the Daltons was left surprisingly undisturbed.

It seemed almost as if the earth had swallowed up the whole gang, consigning it doubtless to that place in the lower regions where it truly belonged.

8

The place near Hennessey had been closed up, and remained so, all through the winter of 1891-92 and the following spring, although Mistress Daisy Bryant had been released from custody, no clear case of receiving stolen goods or harboring outlaws having been established against her. Of course Charlie was an outlaw, and there were several true bills found against him by various grand juries. But then he was undoubtedly her brother and she would never have been convicted if brought to trial for hiding her own flesh and blood from the pursuing officers.

So the fair and wily creature went off scot free, but not unwatched, however; for Ransom Payne and the Logan county district attorney's office felt certain that she would be sure to establish, sooner or later, some communication with the vanished Bob Dalton, and had great hopes to thus be able to reach and secure the remaining members of the most successful criminal association the Southwest had known for years.

Mistress Daisy was, however, too much even for Ransom Payne's experienced and vigilant foresight. After apparently settling down to a life of thrifty labor, as a dressmaker, under the very eyes of her watchers, in the city of Guthrie, she, one cool morn-

ing in early April, 1892, disappeared as if by magic.
Not the faintest clue did she leave behind her, and
during the winter months her mode of life had displayed no mysterious features.

So far, therefore, the officers of the law stood
baffled. But the continued in activity of the gang convinced them that they must have disbanded or settled
down in some populous eastern town, away from
those who knew too much about their past career.

The fact is that, in a cosy little house built by
some early settler who had soon tired of the lone-
some neighborhood, away in Greer county, that
section of the Indian Territory claimed both by
Texas and Oklahoma. Daisy Bryant had finally
joined her beloved Bob, who had been living there
in clover all winter long with his inseparable chum,
Emmet, and in the company of two other men who
counted among his most reckless pals, "Tom Evans"
and "Texas Jack."

They had received their supplies through trusted
friends, and had kept all along so quiet and undemonstrative in a locality far distant from railroads
or causeways, that the presence there of this small
colony of strangers was hardly known at the nearest
settlement, over twenty-five miles away.

The purpose of Bob in thus remaining in absolute inaction for so long a time was evidently two-
fold: He found it necessary to put to sleep the
lynx-eyed watchfulness of his arch-enemy Ransom
Payne, and he wanted to gather about him a phalanx
of such redoutable fellows as would throw terror
in every village of the territories and border states.
These two objects—the first especially—could not
be attained in a week or a month. Payne would
keep up his posse a-going all over the country until
far into the winter season, or as long as the funds
would allow him. Then some other case would
be placed in his charge and the Dalton gang cease
to become his sole and foremost consideration.
Then, and then only, would the time come to re-
sume operation.

And to do so "with a startler" as a first move,
was now the goal of Bob Dalton's insatiable ambition. The man's peculiar trait never was either
cruelty or greed—so much we must be allowed to
say in his favor. But an inordinate vanity ruled his
every action, a vanity before which everything and
everybody had to bow, and which would lead him
to any amount of bloody work if it could be satisfied in no other way. To surpass the record of every

robber in this country and time, and in all countries and times, was the stubborn aim of Bob's every thought and action.

In death, if not in a prolonged and disastrous career of crime, the young desperado's insane ambition was to find itself satiated, for the Coffeyville tragedy may be counted among the most extraordinary dramas of the age.

Winter had gone, spring had gone, fields and trees were alive again with verdant vegetation, farm life had resumed its activity, and still nothing was heard of the Dalton gang. They were getting among the old stories, in that super-active Southwest where months do the work of, and count for, years.

But the warm breeze of June had hardly begun raising the dust upon the highways, when this startling news ran through the country, with the exaggerated details that are sure to be added in such cases:

"Another train hold-up! The Daltons are out again!"

And so it was. Bob's forces had gathered again, and played their old game for a third time.

Ransom Payne to the rescue! Your arch-enemies are in the field!

Singularly enough, the theater of this new and
daring outrage was but a few miles distant from the
scene of the one immediately preceding.   Apparently satisfied that nowhere else could his gang find
an easier escape, their crime once committed, Bob
Dalton had selected the Red Rock station, in the
Oklahoma Territory, and on the Sante Fe road, just
twenty-six miles from Wharton, as the point where
he and his pals would stop and pillage the southbound express that steams past this small depot in
the early part of the night.

The Fast Texas Express on the Atchison, Topeka
& Santa Fe R. R. was due on Thursday night, the 2d
of June, 1892, at 9:40 P. M., past the Red Rock station, but was not to stop there unless signaled to do
so. The settlement there is unimportant, and the
depot is used almost exclusively for the loading of
cattle to be carried northward. Night trains have
very seldom occasion to stop there, except to receive
some instructions from the train dispatcher at either
end of the section, announcing some change in the
movement of the trains.

So when the engine slowed up in answer to the
signal, there was immediately some alarm manifest
among the crew and those of the passengers who

were somewhat familiar with similar experiences. Their worst fears were soon to prove true.

For hardly had the train slacked speed in front of the wooden shanty used as the depot of Red Rock station, than six masked men rushed silently toward the engineer and had him bring the train to a standstill, their Winchesters significantly pointed where they could do the most harm.

Then the usual tactics, which might be called "the Daltons' own," were faithfully followed. The engineer being kept under watch, some distance from the locomotive, his fireman was directed to take his pick-axe and smash the door of the Express car, which the messenger declined peremptorily to open. A few shots fired in the air were sufficient warning for the train hands and passengers to keep quiet and undemonstrative within the sleepers and cars, and the threatening and revolting oaths of the robber in command soon caused the Express safe to be opened and its contents revealed. They were not by any means satisfactory to the gang, who expected a very different kind of a haul. They hardly got two thousand dollars for their trouble, and swore their choicest curses when thus disappointed.

They did not feel though like facing the possible resistance of the passengers, and their plunder gathered, they ordered the engineer and fireman back to their engine, and firing a final volley, this time through the windows of the passenger cars and sleepers, they disappeared through the night.

For the third time the robbers had got away without a scratch.   One more of their crimes, had proved as easy of execution as its predecessors.   It was time indeed that something should be done.

Be it said to the credit of the railroad company and the territorial authorities, not an hour was lost before starting in pursuit of the daring brigands.

Before dawn of the next morning, Wednesday, the 3d of June, sixteen men, well mounted and armed to the teeth, commanded by the indefatigable and determined Ransom Payne, were in full chase of the desperadoes, and for a couple of days seemed on the point of tracking them to their retreat.

The place in Greer county was discovered and raided.

It was absolutely empty of its inhabitants, however, Mistress Daisy having made good her escape But the signs of long occupancy by the band were easily detected and many valuable points collected by the shrewd U. S. Deputy Marshal.

After covering an immense amount of ground, in an amazingly short time, the posse had to be dismissed and a few select men only kept at work, in a more mysterious manner, tracking, to the best of their abilities, each of the men supposed to be associated with Bob, Grat and Emmet Dalton in the commission of those repeated outrages.

The trains crossing the territory were now guarded with jealous care, the least rumor of a possible hold-up sufficing for a number of armed men being taken on board and carried along for a long distance.

Thus it was hoped to discourage any further criminal attempt of the kind. And this proved correct enough—for just *forty-two days*, that is, from June the second to the memorable Thursday, the fourteenth of July, 1892.

CHAPTER VI.

THE FAMOUS M., K. & T. ROBBERY.—EIGHT BOLD OUT
LAWS OVERCOME NINE ARMED DETECTIVES—THE
ROBBERY OF THE MISSOURI, KANSAS & TEXAS
TRAIN AT ADAIR SURPASSES ALL PREVIOUS REC-
ORDS—ARMED GUARDS DRIVEN BACK INTO
THEIR CAR AND THE BOOTY HAULED OFF IN
TRIUMPH—ONE MAN KILLED AND FOUR
OTHERS WOUNDED—NO ONE EXCEPT
THE EXPRESS OFFICIALS AND THE
OUTLAWS KNOW HOW MUCH MONEY
WAS TAKEN—AN EYE-WITNESS'
STARTLING TESTIMONY.

As was stated before, after weeks of persistent
and exhaustive researches following immediately upon the Wharton hold up, Ransom Payne, having
been placed in charge of other business, had to give
up, for the present, his favorite occupation of tracking the Daltons. He had made it hot for them dur-

ing the whole time he was instructed to continue on their trail, the capture of Charlie Bryant not being the least important of his exploits.

But now, for some reason or other, probably because a general feeling of security had succeeded months of bewildered apprehension, Payne had only accidently busied himself with the Dalton case, and it was more and more apparent that only his untiring vigilance and his determined, fearless attitude had kept the rascals at bay. He out of the way, their city· friends notifying them of the fact, the Daltons' reckless spirit had again full sway.

The Red Rock hold-up was a success; and through the country a rumor ran like wild fire:

"The Daltons are about yet; they 'll be heard of soon again."

The Indians, although generally friendly to a degree toward their suppliers of fiery liquids, the outlaws, and keeping mum, with national taciturnity, concerning their whereabouts, had been heard to say between themselves that the Missouri, Kansas & Texas railroad would be the next line attacked by the gang, and this very soon.

Finally the territorial police was notified that the Daltons were encamped at or near Pryor creek, a petty station on the M., K. & T., located forty-five miles north of Muskogee, in the Oklahoma Territory, the stations between being but of very insignificant importance.

It was decided, therefore, to have every train on the main line carefully guarded by a special force of men until full information should be received as to the capture or dispersion of the gang.

This wholesome precaution proved to be absolutely useless, as there was indeed a wide and radical difference between the fellows comprising this troop of police and the sturdy, indomitable fellows Ransom Payne had led through perils innumerable.

Here are the details of this incredible, and, in many respects, highly farcical encounter.

Adair is a small and lonely station on the Cherokee division of the Missouri, Kansas & Texas railroad. It had been rumored for two weeks, as stated above, that the Daltons were encamped near there between the town and Pryor creek. On the evening of July 14, 1892, at about nine o'clock, the gang, more numerous than ever before—eight of them, bad men, heavily armed—came to town. They went right to the depot and proceeded to business.

Although some of the houses in the small settle-

BOB   AND   GRAT]

The two Dalton Brothers Photographed after their Death

ment were still lighted and people seen, grouped in friendly conversation, the men, carefully masked, entered the little station.

The depot agent, under menace of Winchesters, was made prisoner. Then the gang looted the place, taking all the money and valuables to be found. They bound the agent and put him in a corner.

This took but little time. The northbound train No. 2, the one which the men had come to rob, was not due until 9:45. So the eight robbers sat down on the platform and calmly waited for the train to come.

It was on time. When the engineer slowed up at the platform, there was a detachment of the eight waiting to claim the attention of Engineer Glen Ewing and his fireman.

They were both put under cover of Winchesters and were requested to keep quiet.

Others of the robbers formed a reception committee to greet Conductor George Scales and his porter when they stepped off the train, and they were made captives before they knew what was stirring.

In accordance with the Daltons' invariable custom, the fireman was told to come down out of the cab, and bring his coal pick along. He was conducted to the door of the Express car and ordered to make ready to smash it.

The messenger, George Williams, refused to open the door. One of the robbers announced in a loud voice that he had just put a big stick of dynamite under the car, and some of the others fired a few shots through the windows just to notify Messenger Williams of the extreme gravity of the situation. The door was opened.

In swarmed the greedy robbers with their guns aimed at the messenger. They made him unlock the safe and they pulled everything they could lay hands upon out of it and piled it upon the floor of the car. Then the three robbers in the car took away the messenger's watch, bound that unhappy wight and dumped him in an out of the way corner. From out of the darkness there appeared a spring wagon driven by one of the robbers. It backed up to the door and the heaped-up plunder was shoveled into it. Then the business-like Daltons prepared to depart.

It would doubtless interest the reader to know what kind of attitude was that of those valiant guards, carried free and well paid by the railroad company for the special purpose of fighting and bringing to bay those very brigands who had just been looting the train they were in.

The nine good men and true, headed by a certain J. J. Kinney, their worthy captain, had taken possession of the smoking car, and, surrounded by their many weapons, announced to the admiring passengers that they were on their way to signal victory over those —— —— scoundrels and brigands—the Daltons.

Having stated their bloodthirsty intention and looking every inch, in looks and costume, the twin brothers of these very desperadoes they were sent to meet, capture or kill, they proceeded "to imbibe" and to exchange jocose and boasting remarks.

It was noticed, however, that the nearer the northbound train No. 2 came to the notorious Pryor creek, the quieter and visibly uneasier grew the bellicose crowd.

But when Pryor creek was passed without unpleasantness, and also the next station, Perry, the drooping spirits of the "brave" police revived marvelously, and a festive drink was absorbed in honor of this narrow escape, which the men boisterously qualified of "——bad luck."

Just seven minutes later—for Perry and Adair are but three and a half miles apart—the engine slacked speed and finally came to a full stop with something more than ordinary suddenness.

There was a rumor outside.

The train hands were noticed running about, lanterns on their arms.

The guards looked at each other in silent dismay, but not a son of them budged an inch. Talk had died on their lips, and so had whatever meager measure of courage they might have even possessed. Mice are not more discreet when they hear the steps of the housewife—

The chiefs, Captain Kinney and Captain La Flore, the latter a Cherokee half-breed and chief of the Cherokee Indians' special police force, stood up alone and began an animated but whispered conversation at the further end of the car.

"How many are there, do you think?" said Kinney

La Flore ventured his head out of the window, but brought it back in a hurry, for a regular salvo from the enemy's Winchesters was fired as a threatening warning.

"I saw seven of 'em," he whispered. "Might be a dozen more for what I—know."

"Well, boys," called out Kinney, feeling that the situation was growing critical, "shall we go out and fight them—?"

This singular way of commanding his men to do their duty met with the expected answer—that is, no answer at all. They were not going to hazard their precious skins, not they, and the captain had better understand it right away.

Still it would never do to reach the next station and have to acknowledge themselves such arrant cowards; so, about the time the robbery was all over, these guards consented to become dimly aware of what was going on, and, rising cautiously from their seats, they opened a rapid fire at the freebooters through the car windows. The robbers replied with promptness and much vigor. Bullets whistled everywhere. Somewhat emboldened now, and the two captains not being after all such absolutely despicable funks, a few of the guards followed their lead out of the smoking car down on the side of the track where the robbers were not and began shooting between the cars at the retreating forms of the bandits. Undaunted though and briskly firing back, the robbers, none of whom seemed to have been hit by the wild firing of their pusillanimous adversaries, loaded their wagon and drove merrily off towards the woods, firing as they went.

After the robbers had disappeared in the dark, it was found that their fire had been deadly.

In a drug store near the depot Doctors W. L. Goff and Youngblood had been sitting comfortably, exchanging remarks about the day's work. The noise of the fight soon told them what the trouble was; a few stray bullets tore through the frame wall of the building and both of the men were struck by them.

Dr. Goff died in a short time.

Dr. Youngblood's condition was so serious that he was long at death's door.

The robbers' bullets wrought injury among the guards, too. Captain Kinney was slightly wounded in the shoulder and La Flore received a superficial wound on the arm, while a guard named Ward was slightly injured.

Thus was the honor of the Indian police saved from absolute and unredeemable ruin.

All this shooting created a great panic, of course, among the passengers, who were frightened almost into a frenzy. But none of them were harmed; the Daltons, as usual, confining themselves to express safe pillaging whenever they went on a business tour.

As the reader may not feel like believing the whole of our positive statement concerning the extraordinary conduct of Captain J. J. Kinney's guards, we beg leave to insert herein the very words in which one of the passengers on board train No. 2 narrated the actual facts and stigmatized the fellows' behavior.

Mr. J. T. Hearn, of St. Louis, arrived on July 16th at Coates Hotel, Kansas City, from the Southwest, where he had been on a business trip. He was one of the passengers on the Missouri, Kansas & Texas train that was held up at Adair, I. T., on that eventful Thursday night. He was awake and witnessed the entire fight and has some very strong opinions about the detectives and Indian police on board the train. He characterized their conduct as cowardly in the extreme and deserving of universal condemnation. In speaking of the very exciting episode Mr. Hearn said:

"It was about 10 o'clock and every one in the sleeper had retired excepting myself. We were bowling along right merrily on the other side of Adair, and on stopping at that station I glanced out

of the window. I saw some rather uncertain figures
and a wagon standing near. Then came a few scat-
tering shots, and then the batch of detectives piled
out of the coaches.

"Inside of ten minutes there were no less than
200 shots exchanged and, during that time, the passengers were secreting their valuables or crouching
low to escape the rain of bullets from all sides.
Then the firing let up a little and the valiant detectives came tumbling in pellmell, any way to reach
shelter. Chief Detective Kinney had a slight
wound in the fleshy part of the left arm. There
seemed to be about fifteen of the detectives, and
early in the evening I had noticed them and remarked what fearless looking fellows they were.
Every one looked the typical "bad man" and they
were armed to the teeth.

"A passenger asked the chief if the men were
gone and he answered that they were in the express car. Then some one asked why the detectives
were not outside trying to prevent the robbery, and
they made scant reply. Several suggested that they
could waylay the robbers as they emerged from the
car, as by actual count there were only seven, or at
most eight of them; but the detectives only replied

by finding safe shelters behind the seats and on the rear platform. I had placed my watch and pocket-book under the edge of the carpet on the floor of the sleeper, but there were so many detectives on the floor that I thought the valuables would be safer in my pocket, so I returned them to their proper places.

"After awhile the robbers dumped all the stuff they wanted from the express car into the spring wagon, got up on the seats, and drove twice around the entire train, firing as they went. All the time the detectives were in their holes with the exception of one man about fifty-five years of age. He was fighting all the time until he received a wound in the shoulder from one bullet, while another plowed a furrow across his breast. Another man was shot through the left forearm, the bullet passing on and striking his watch. That stopped both the bullet and the timepiece. Afterward he laid the watch out on a piece of paper. It was in so many pieces that it could be gathered up and sifted through the fingers.

"A stray bullet struck a physician in a drug store up town, cutting an artery in the thigh. They thought when we left that he would bleed to death.

"That batch of detectives was on the train in the expectation of an attempt being made at robbery, and they were very brave until the time came for action."

DEAD CRIMINALS.

CHAPTER I.

RANSOM PAYNE TO THE RESCUE—POSSES AGGREGATING
OVER ONE HUNDRED MEN ORGANIZED BY THE BRAVE
UNITED STATES DEPUTY MARSHAL—HE LEADS THE
MOST DETERMINED BAND OF THE LAW'S DEFEND-
ERS—LARGE REWARDS OFFERED BY THE M., K.
& T.—THE BRIGANDS ARE TRACKED AND
FORCED TO DISPERSE—THE EL RENO BANK
OUTRAGE WRONGLY ASCRIBED TO THE
DALTONS—BOB'S PLANS FOR ROBBING
THE COFFEYVILLE BANKS MATUR-
ING—HIS NIGHT VISITS TO THE
CITY — DRUGGIST BENSON'S
STARTLING ADVENTURE.

The news of the Adair hold-up, the incredible
details about the cowardice displayed by the Indian
police, and the startlingly easy success of the Dal-

tons' bold raid in the face of armed forces they
must have known to be on board the northbound
train of the M., K. & T., on that eventful Thursday,
the 14th of July, 1892, caused an immense emotion
all through the territories and the border states.

It seemed, indeed, as if there were no security
left for railway passengers, and as if the moneys in
transit were to be henceforth at the mercy of this
reckless band of robbers.

The time had come for a gigantic effort that
would wipe out this triumphant band of outlaws, and
restore some tranquiilty to travelers and express
companies.

Besides, the pitiful conduct of the Indian police
showed but too clearly that the citizens would have
to depend on themselves only and on their fearless
efforts to protect the peace and good name of their
region. A general cry came up from among all
those who had kept posted concerning the criminal
annals of the couple of years preceding, and it
was:

"Call Ransom Payne and his men to the rescue!"

And the Missouri, Kansas & Texas R. R. caused
it to be publicly announced that large rewards, aggregating six thousand dollars, would be paid for the

MISSOURI, KANSAS & TEXAS RAILWAY COMPANY.

Parsons Kas — July 15th 18 2

$ 5000 Reward !

The Express Car on the north bound
train of the M. K. and T. Ry. was
robbed by masked men at Adair
Indian Territory Thursday night July 14th
A Reward of Five Thousand Dollars will
be paid by the undersigned for the Arrest
and Conviction of each of the men engaged in
this Robbery to an amount not exceeding
Forty Thousand Dollars.

Signed { M. K. & T. Ry. Co.
by Alex C. Purdy.
Second Vice President.

Pacific Express Co.
by L. A. Fuller.
Superintendent.

capture and conviction of the robbers who had so successfully raided their northbound Express. We have picked up in one of the way stations of the company one of those hand-written posters, and we reproduce it here.

But the plucky and shrewd U. S. Deputy Marshal and the brave and true men gathered around him were this time to be the mainstay of pursuing justice, and it took but a few hours for the posses, three in number, and including over one hundred well-armed and determined men, to be set on the different trails left behind them by the Adair robbers.

For the Daltons and their pals had dispersed almost at once, not specially caring to attract by their number the attention of the settlements they would have to cross to reach their various destinations.

The wildest rumors concerning the lightning rapidity and secrecy with which Bob Dalton conducted his operations were now spreading all over the territory and the bordering Kansas towns, and every act of particularly bold outlawry was placed to his credit.

So it came to pass that hardly had the first emotion succeeding the Adair robbery died out when robbers appeared in El Reno, on the Choctaw Coal and Railway Company's lines, one morning, and when the streets were crowded with people and teams entered the leading bank of the city.

The only person in the bank at the time was the wife of the president, who fainted at the first sight of the revolvers. The bandits leisurely took all the money in sight, and remounting their horses rode away. The raid netted them $10,000, which was such a severe loss to the bank that it was forced into liquidation.

To this day the raiders in this case were not discovered and it has always been the general, although probably erroneous opinion, that the Daltons tried their hands bank-robbing at the expense of this little Oklahoma community.

" I have no doubt," Superintendent C. H. Eppelsheimer, of the Pinkerton detective agency, said, in in an interview with a Kansas City reporter, " that many crimes have been laid at the doors of the Dalton boys that they were not guilty of. I am not defending them in the least, but in this respect they resembled the James boys. In their time every robbery and crime committed in this section was laid to them, while it is an unquestioned fact that they knew nothing of many of the occurrences. So it was with the Daltons."

We only mention this well worded opinion because we think it backed by facts, and also because we earnestly believe that the first time the Dalton gang ever attempted bank robbing was on the tragic fifth of October, which our narrative is now approaching.

For by that time, that is six weeks and over after the Adair hold-up, the ground was indeed becoming too hot for the boys. The systematic search undertaken by Ransom Payne and his faithful followers, the wholesome excitement generally spread all over that region could not fail, within a very short time, to end in the capture of the robbers. The only refuge left them was flight, disappearance, dispersion of the gang, and all this needed money, a good deal of it, for Bob well knew that in other parts of the country he would have to lay low for quite a while until a new band could be formed and new connections created that would facilitate his escape after each criminal attempt.

And thus germinated in his mind the audacious scheme of raiding some wealthy village bank, and with the funds thus gathered in to vanish for a time,

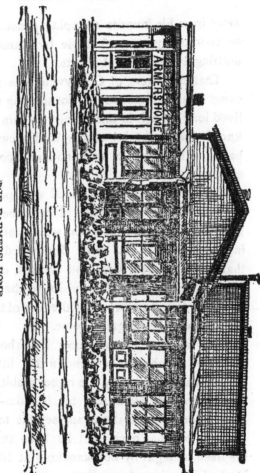

THE FARMERS' HOME.

In the smallest building, at the left of the picture, lay the wounded Emmet Dalton, until he was taken by the sheriff to the County Jail, at Independence, Kansas.

away from his favorite stamping grounds, rendered so thoroughly uncomfortable by Ransom Payne's untiring and intelligent efforts.

That the name of Coffeyville was the first to come to him seems natural, considering that he had lived long enough in this vicinity to gain a thorough knowledge of the lay of the land, securing for his band, as he thought, an unnoticed access and an easy exit.

Besides, he had kept himself well posted about whatever changes had taken place in the prosperous little city, and since the event we are about narrating happened, it has been discovered that more than once had Bob, Grat and Emmet, either alone or separately, paid nightly visits to the place they had but a few years before, in the time of their honest youth, made their regular home.

The landlord of the queer little hostlery, the sketch of which is to be found in this little volume and which was called by the rather ambitious name of the *Farmer's Home*, told his friends,—since the destruction of the Dalton gang set his tongue free —that, more than once, had he been awakened in the dead of night by Bob knocking at his window. He had been forced, on those occasions, to admit

the robber chief and those of his men that were
with him. The landlady had been called upon to
prepare a warm supper for the "gentlemen of the
highway," and to accept their thanks—instead of
their money. At the time, the terror those precocious
bandits inspired was such that there was no thought
of refusing them anything, or any imprudent talking, the next day, over the incident.

But another visit of Bob within the precinct of
Coffeyville took place, very shortly, in fact within
the week preceding the famous raid of October 5th.
It was curious enough to deserve a detailed account.

On Walnut street, just a few doors from the postoffice, there exists a drug store conducted by Frank
Benson, manager and partner of the firm of George
Slosson & Co. About a week or ten days before
the raid, a little before midnight, a man knocked
a long while at the door of Mr. Benson's home for
admission.

Awakened from his sleep, Mr. Benson cried out,
"Who's there?"

The stranger replied, calling Mr. Benson by name
and urging him to come down.

Another demand as to his identity was met as
evasively, and, moved by the man's persistence, Mr.

Benson at length partially dressed himself and opened the front door, leaving the latched screen door between himself and his visitor.

There stood Bob Dalton, upon whose head a great price was set, a revolver in his hand, the pearl handle of another gleaming at his belt, filled round about with cartridges.   Mr. Benson had not seen him for a great length of time, but he recognized him immediately.

Dalton threateningly demanded that Mr. Benson sell him a gallon of alcohol.

They don't care much for whisky down in the fire nations. They drink alcohol down there—a gallon of it will go as far as a barrel of whisky.

Benson said that he did not sell alcohol, that he had none in his store, and that the sale of it was against the law.   Bob was not to be moved, though, from effecting a purchase or exacting a free gift, and he insisted that Benson go to his drug store and make the sale.

At length Benson managed to partly convince the outlaw of the truth of his statement and sent him off upon another track by directing him to Rammell Brothers, druggists, on the opposite side of the square, on Union street, next door to the First

National Bank, as a firm which kept alcohol in stock.

"Did he get it there?" Mr. Benson was, later asked by a reporter.

"I don't know whether he did or not."

When Mr. Benson closed and locked the door on the departing desperado, he felt a ton lighter. The longer he thought of the visit the luckier he felt himself to be.

Next day he confidentially told his friends of the visit he had received. He did not go publicly about proclaiming that Bob Dalton was in the neighborhood, for that would be an indiscretion that such outlaws as the men who now lie dead in their graves, in Coffeyville, frequently rebuked with knife and bullet with murderous promptitude.

Mr. Benson's friends could scarcely believe his statement. They did not doubt his integrity, but it seemed impossible that a man for whose capture so many thousands of dollars had been offered would dare to return to a locality where his identity was so generally known and where his capture would not be a matter of that bloody difficulty which attended pursuit of him in his fastnesses in the country.

10

So they mocked at Benson as a dreamer of idle things, as one who walked in his sleep and saw impossible visions, and as one fond of being the hero of imaginary adventures.

This brings us within these days of the great tragedy. Other sources of information, and especially the statements extracted from the wounded Emmet, furnish sufficient evidence as to the careful and business-like manner in which Bob Dalton had been preparing the great robbery that was to make him the most famous brigand of the age.

CHAPTER II.

ON THEIR WAY TO COFFEYVILLE—THE MEETING WITH
EMMET—BOB DALTON'S LOUD BRAGGING—"I'LL SEE
JESSE JAMES AND GO HIM ONE BETTER!"—WHAT
THE MEN DID ON THE EVE OF THE RAID—THE
GANG IS MET APPROACHING THE VILLAGE—
WERE THERE SIX ROBBERS OR FIVE?—THE
NOW HISTORICAL FENCE WHERE THE
HORSES WERE TIED—MARCHING IN
SOLDIERS' STEP AND ARRAY—
RECOGNIZED!

It is universally admitted that the extraordinarily bold attack upon the two banks of Coffeyville, Kan., that took place, in broad daylight, on
Wednesday morning the 5th of October, 1892, that
the thrilling fight, the courage displayed alike by
bandits and citizens, make up the most wonderful
story the border has ever furnished. Such a chapter
of western life has not been written since the ro-
mance went out of the rough riding, bank robbing,

train wrecking career of the James boys and the
Youngers in that disastrous raid of the Minnesota
village of Northfield.

Probably the easily gotten wealth obtained from
the express car of the northbound train of the M.,
K. & T. R. R., on the 14th of July, took swift wings;
probably the delights of easy moving circles of
Denison and Fort Smith, where it is said the members of the hunted Dalton gang disported themselves even under the federal eye were expensive.
More probably yet, the necessity of escaping,
by an immediate exile from their usual haunts,
the close hunt of the persistent, indefatigable Ransom Payne, made itself more strongly apparent day
after day. Whatever may have moved the band to
fresh action, certain it is that when some two weeks
ago Emmet Dalton was working on a ranch twenty
miles south of Tulsa, in the territory, he received a
letter sent by his daring brother Bob from his safe
point of hiding in the nation. Bob wrote that he
had found a plan of profitable action on lines of
endeavor quite distinct from those which had heretofore engaged his professional attention; would
Emmet join him?

Emmet answered the letter in person. Where

that place of rendezvous may have been he refuses
to tell. His statement speaks of a fortuitous meeting between him and Bob, but denies all regular,
preconcerted appointment. Doubtless there are yet,
in that lair, spoils well worth the hiding.

With Bob Dalton were the men who aided him
in the train robbery on the Missouri, Kansas &
Texas at Adair. There was Grat Dalton, whose
life sat so lightly upon his consciousness that he
was fattening out of the recollection of men who
knew him a year before. There was Dick Broadwell, whose father lives in Hutchinson, Kan., and
who had become so experienced a desperado in so
astonishingly short a time that men thought "Texas
Jack" was with the gang; finally there was Bill
Powers, of the Three D ranch, the equal in daring of
that Tom Hedde whom Coffeyville took him to be.
Bob Dalton's plan, when unfolded to his youthful
brother from the Tulsa ranch, was the robbing of
the Coffeyville banks, but both of them at the same
time, an exploit amazing enough to throw in the
shade the most famed raids of Jesse James, the
Youngers and their imitators.

In Coffeyville, as we narrated at some length,
the Daltons had long lived. There, in the Daltons,

lot in the cemetery, lay buried Dalton, the father, a
man of gruff disposition, but whose laziness and
love of ease smothered a viciousness which lacked
determination to become assertive. There, too, was
buried Frank Dalton, a brother, who died a U. S.
deputy Marshal in 1889; when across the Arkansas from Fort Smith he pumped his Winchester
valiantly to the last, fighting criminals against
great odds. Every by path and road in the country
hereabout the surviving Dalton brothers knew
minutely, every place of concealment, every avenue
of escape; the people of the town and the neighborhood they were also fully acquainted with, for
their last stay was but three years old.

Bob Dalton formed the plan, and the others
accepted it without question.

Later, when interrogated, Emmet Dalton, then
lying upon a bed he probably thought his death-bed,
made a long rambling statement which our readers
will find given in full in these pages and which con-
tains the following lines, easily explained when one
remembers that the wounded brigand thought himself about to be lynched by the infuriated population:

"When Bob explained his plans to me, saying
that he could discount the James boys and rob two

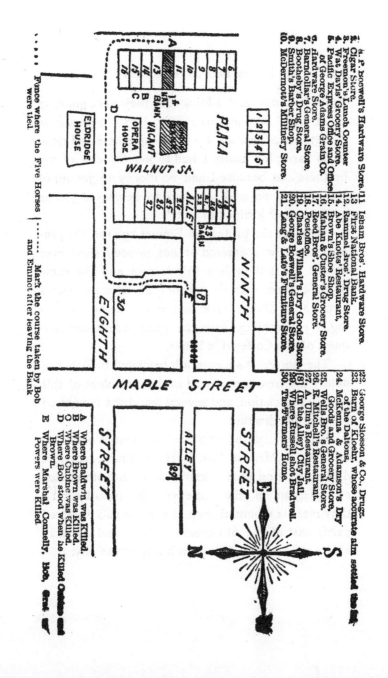

1. A. P. Boswell's Hardware Store.
2. Cigar Store.
3. Freeman's Lunch Counter.
4. Wat Davis' Grocery Store.
5. Pacific Express Office and Office of George Adams Grain Co.
6. Hardware Store.
7. Barndollar's General Store.
8. Boothby's Drug Store.
9. Smith's Barber Shop.
10. McDermott's Millinery Store.

11. Isham Bros.' Hardware Store.
12. First National Bank.
13. Rammel Bros.' Drug Store.
14. Abe Knotts' Restaurant,
15. Brown's Shoe Shop.
16. Mahan & Custer's Grocery Store.
17. Reed Bros.' General Store.
18. Postoffice.
19. Charles Withell's Dry Goods Store.
20. George Boswell's General Store.
21. Lang & Late's Furniture Store.

22. George Slosson & Co., Drug.
23. Barn of Kloehr, whose accurate aim settled the fat.
24. McKenna & Adamson's Dry Goods and Grocery Store,
25. Wells Bro.'s General Store.
26. R. Mitchell's Restaurant.
27. A. Ulm's Restaurant.
A. (In the Alley) City Jail.
28. Where Russell shot Bradwell.
29.
30. The Farmers' Home.

A. Where Baldwin was Killed.
B. Where Brown was Killed.
C. Where Cubine was Killed.
D. Where Bob stood when he Killed Cubine and Brown.
E. Where Marshal Connelly, Bob, and Powers were Killed.

. . . . . Fence where the Five Horses were tied.

------ Mark the course taken by Bob and Emmet after leaving the Bank banks in a day, and adding that they were going to do it, right here in Coffeyville, *I tried to prevail on the boys not to come up*, for the people here had done us no harm; but finally I had to join for love of my brothers and because I had no money to get out of the country on, and was sure to be chased just as hard whether I joined or not."

Whether the protest of Emmet against the proposed raid was entered or not, nobody shall ever know. He fell in line, this is sure, and the same night camped with *the boys* not far from the Davis farm, in the Onion creek bottoms. The next morning, Wednesday the fifth, the gang rode to the conquest of the Coffeyville banks.

The horses, it appears, all belonged to Bob, evidently the treasurer as well as the president of this unholy association, and several had been bought on purpose for this raid.

Between 9:30 and 10 o'clock on that Wednesday morning, as Mr. and Mrs. R. H. Hollingsworth were driving west on what is known as Eighth street (see our Diagram of the Coffeyville Business Center), they met six mounted men at a point two hundred yards east of the old cheese factory, and less than half a mile from the western limits of the city.

They were both attracted to the men by the peculiar appearance of the party, and the fact that they were all heavily armed. They agreed that there were six men and six horses in the party.

Within a hundred yards east of where they passed Mr. and Mrs. Hollingsworth, the same party was met by Messrs. J. M. and J. L. Seldomridge, who were driving west on the same road. They, too, were attracted by the appearance of the riders, and were led to remark that the men were undoubtedly on some strange mission, as they were armed to the teeth and apparently disguised. These gentlemen are also firm in their declarations that the crowd consisted of six persons and the same number of horses. Persons residing on Eighth street, east of what is known as the Hickman property, saw the party pass their residences. Of the large number of other people who observed this troop of horse-men, every one, however, asserts that there were only *five* riders in the party when they passed over that thoroughfare. They were seen by parties all along the street up to where Maple street crosses Eighth, and no one counted more than five horsemen. It is presumed that one of the party either backed out as they were about to enter town, or else diverged his

course into a cross street and made a circuit through
the southwestern portion of the city, in order to
reach the plaza from the south and aid in stamped-
ing the citizens from that point in case of an attack.

Anyhow, he was never seen since met by the
Hollingsworths and Seldomridges.

The five men rode boldly and at a swinging trot,
raising a cloud of dust which literally enveloped
them as they passed down Eighth street. They
turned into Maple street and passed alongside of
the Long-Bell Company's office and entered the alley that runs from Walnut street, at Slosson's drug
store, to Maple street and thence to the western
boundary of the city.

There were a number of persons in the alley at
the time and several teams were hitched in the rear
of Davis' blacksmith shop. An oil tank of the Consolidated Company, with two horses attached thereto,
was standing near McKenna & Adamson's stables,
almost in the center of the alley.

The party hitched their horses to the fence in the
rear of Police Judge Munn's lot, and within a few
feet of the temporary residence which he is at present occupying. [See Diagram.] A stone-cutter,
who was examining some rock lying near the city

ARRIVAL OF THE DALTON GANG AT COFFEYVILLE.—PAGE 155.

jail, observed them riding into the alley and dismounting.

All of the robbers were cleanly shaven except Powers, who retained his heavy, dark brown moustache ; Emmet, who could not sacrifice the down upon his young lip ; and Grat, who kept his scraggly little moustache. No one knows whose razor went over those five faces within two hours of the raid.

Dismounting from their horses, Bob and Grat Dalton and Dick Broadwell ineffectually disguised themselves with black beards. Meanwhile the town rested unconscious of their coming and unprepared for the attack. There had been some talk of the possibility of a raid, as there had been in all the towns along the border, but such unconcerted preparation as may then have been made to meet such an emergency had been quite forgotten

The desperadoes had quickly formed into a sort of military line, three in front and two in the rear, and walked closely together. The stone-cutter mentioned above walked closely in the rear of the crowd as they passed from their horses through the alley, until they reached the street, when he turned north to his work at the other end of the block.

The alley opens upon the public square about

THE DESPERADOES ENTERING THE CONDON BANK.

which is clustered the whole business of the thriving town directly in line with Condon's bank and almost directly across the street from the First National bank. The robbers came out on the street in a close bunch at a dog trot, their Winchesters hanging in their arms ready for use. Alex McKenna stood on the steps of his store at the alley's mouth.

"There goes the Daltons," he said, in alarm. Black beards hid no identities from McKenna's eyes, but there was no wish in McKenna at that moment to make himself conspicuous.

After silently passing Alex McKenna's store the men quickened their pace and three of them went into C. M. Condon & Co.'s bank at the southwest door, while the two in the rear ran directly across the street to the First National bank, and entered the front door of that institution. The next thing that greeted Mr. McKenna's eyes was a Winchester in the hands of one of the men, and pointed toward the cashier's counter in the bank. He realized the situation at once, and called out to those in the store, that "the bank was being robbed."

The cry was taken up by some others who had been attracted to the men as they entered the bank, and quickly passed from lip to lip all around the square. Persons in the south part of the plaza, the open space between Walnut street and Union street, could plainly see the men as they moved around through the bank.

The two men who entered the First National bank were observed by a number of parties, but their presence did not attract any particular attention at first.

The scenes that took place in the two banks were wonderfully exciting and must be described in detail in order to be understood.

CHAPTER III.

ROBBING TWO BANKS IN ONE DAY—THE GREATEST FEAT
OF THE KIND EVER ATTEMPTED—GRATTAN HEARD
THE PARTY TO THE CONDON BANK—THE CASHIER'S
MARVELOUS PRESENCE OF MIND—THREE MINUTES
GAINED SAVED THE BANK—BOB AND EMMET
RAID THE FIRST NATIONAL—$20,000 STOWED
IN A BAG—COOL AND COLLECTED, BOTH
PARTIES BEGIN THEIR RETREAT
LADEN WITH SPOILS

———

The five robbers now reached the door of the Condon bank. Emmet and Bob stood without and for a minute or so, lent the tenor of their silent presence. The others went within. There behind the counters, with interposing panels of glass and wickets of brass, were Charles Ball, the cashier, with brains in his head, and Charles Carpenter, one of the proprietors of the bank.

In the safe in the vault was $18,000.

Grat Dalton addressed himself at once to business. Broadwell took his stand at one door and Powers at the other. With oaths and threats they demanded that the cashier place all the bank's money in a two-bushel wheat sack, which was produced, and fingers trifled with triggers with menacing carelessness.

"The time-lock doesn't go off until 9:45 o'clock," said the cashier, blandly conscious the while that the safe stood unlocked.

As he spoke, there was across the street short, fat, gray-bearded John D. Levan, the money loaner.

There was no stranger in sight as he crossed the street from the west. Emmet and Bob Dalton had passed over to the First National bank when they saw the Condon bank officials caged. He had heard that the Daltons were coming, and he meant to warn the bankers. He opened the door, and as he did so his arm was grasped by a muscular hand, and he was jerked prisoner within.

"The time-lock doesn't go off until 9:45 o'clock?" said Grat Dalton, interrogatively, as he looked at a gold watch, which was the souvenir of some gay exploit, and then he swore famously.

"Well, time'll be up in three minutes; we'll wait"

Those three minutes cost the members of the Dalton gang their lives and treasure. The men of the town awoke in that length of time to action. The delay was fatal, and it was the lie of the quick-witted cashier which occasioned it.

Dry Goods Clerk James leisurely crossed the street. He had a draft to be cashed, and his mind was on ribbons, not robbers. Like Levan, he, too, opened the bank door, and he, too, was grasped as he entered and held prisoner at the Winchester's muzzle, but the robbers did not fail to improve the three minutes' wait to the utmost. They compelled Cashier Ball to put in the bag all the currency in the drawer. Some three thousand dollars in silver they rejected as weighty and useless.

And they were men of business, these robbers.

"How much cash did the books show to be on hand the night before at the close of business?"

"Four thousand dollars," said the cashier, making little of the eighteen thousand dollars in the safe. "The money for the day's business will come later by express," he explained agreeably.

Luther Perkins, the capitalist, who owns the bank building, hearing the noise below and seeing from his window armed men enter the First National

bank across the street, took a pistol in each hand
and went down the back stairway. There he opened
the rear door of the Condon bank and Broadwell
had his Winchester upon him before he could move
a step. Mr. Perkins could fairly see the ball moving toward him, and shutting the door hastily re-
treated with his pistols up the stairway to his office.

There was hurrying about of men from store to
store in search of arms and confused preparations
for attack on all sides of the square, and before the
expiration of that three minutes wait it was learned
that the Dalton gang was at work in both banks.

On the east side Iceman Cyrus Lee spread the
alarm. He was on his wagon in front of the First
National bank when Emmet and Bob Dalton passed
before him and entered the money changer's house.
Despite a false beard he knew Bob at once. He
jumped from his wagon and rushed into Isham's
hardware store, next door to the bank.

"The Daltons are robbing the bank!" he cried,
and Cattle Dealer J. H. Wilcox knew the robber,
too, and called out from his office above the Condon bank. Folks in the stores laughed at Lee, but,
nevertheless, he ran with his warning to every store
on the east side of the square.

Just as he reached the south end of the block, Harness Maker Miller opened fire on the robbers in the Condon bank with his Winchester.

After the first shot he gained a station on top of the awning and pumped bullets quickly through the window of the bank eighty yards away. The first shot pierced the plate-glass window front and slightly wounded Broadwell.

" I'm shot," he said composedly, and then patronizingly suggested to Ball and Carpenter that they go into hiding under the counter, "or else you will get killed by some of these people," he added.

Miller was joined by others in the attack. The patter of bullets became a shower and then a storm; but the desperadoes bided their time and made no present attempt to fight or flee, though bullets hustled in from all parts of the square before them.

Meanwhile all went well with Bob and Emmet Dalton, and their visit at the First National bank had proceeded most favorably, as far as *their* interests were concerned.

When the two men entered the bank, Cashier Thomas G. Ayers and W. H. Shepherd, the teller, were in the front room behind the counter, and J. H. Brewster was transacting business with the former.

They covered all three of these gentlemen with their Winchesters, and addressing Mr. Ayers by name, directed him to hand over all the money in the bank.

At the same time one of the men, keeping his Winchester at ready command, ran into the back room and drove Bert S. Ayers, the bookkeeper, into the front part of the building where the vault is located.

Cashier Ayers very deliberately handed over the currency and gold on the counter, making as many deliveries as possible, in order to secure delay in hope of help arriving.

The bandit then ordered Mr. Ayers to bring out the money that was in the vault.

The cashier brought forth a package containing $5,000 and handed that over. About this time the fellow who was behind the counter discovered where the money was located, and proceeded to help himself to the contents of the burglar-proof chest, all of which, together with the money taken by the first burglar, were stuffed in a common grain sack and carefully tied up.

They then undertook to put the three bankers out at the front door, but a shot from the outside, just as Mr. Ayers reached the pavement, evidently changed their plans, for the terrible fusillade of lead which swept up the square, made sheer madness any attempt to cross it in safety to their horses in the alley beyond.

Bob and Emmet accordingly turned and went out of the rear entrance of the bank, intending to go north in the alley to the first street, upon which the engine house fronts, then west to the business houses fronting the square from that direction, and then unperceived south to their horses in the alley.

The Ayers, father and son, and Shepherd they let go.

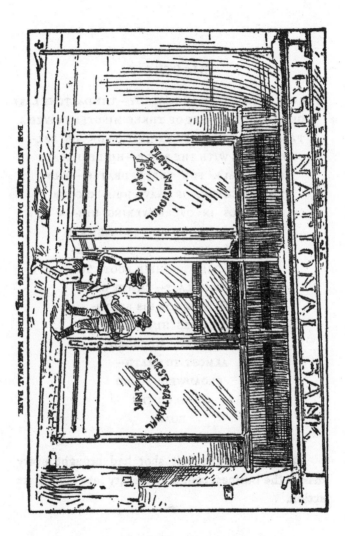

BOB AND EMMET DALTON ENTERING THE FIRST NATIONAL BANK.

CHAPTER IV.

THE GREAT COFFEYVILLE TRAGEDY—THE DALTONS' LAST
FIGHT—HOW THE WAIT OF THREE MINUTES PROVED A
FATAL ONE—FEARFUL EXHIBITION OF BOB DAL-
TON'S SKILL WITH THE RIFLE—HIS DEADLY AIM
ACCOUNTABLE FOR THREE DEATHS—ONLY
THE QUICKNESS OF BRAVE JOHN KLOEHR
SUCCEEDS IN OVERPOWERING HIM—A
TOTAL OF FOUR CITIZENS KILLED AND
THREE WOUNDED—THE DESPERA-
DOES CLING TO THEIR BOOTY TO
THE VERY LAST—EMMET DAL-
TON'S LOVE FOR HIS BROTH-
ER CAUSES HIM TO BE
CAPTURED, WOUNDED
ALMOST TO DEATH—
BROADWELL FOUND
DYING ON THE
ROAD.

The noise of the first shot had brought every
man in the business center of the city into immediate
action.

From every advantage point a rifle or pistol sent lead hurling at the robbers now caged in the Condon bank, but Bob and Emmet Dalton were not forgotten.

It had been their plan, as the wounded Emmet confessed, to rob the banks without losing or killing a man.

"Bob wanted to show Coffeyville what he could do," gasped Emmet in explanation—and he did.

The brother desperadoes had no sooner gained the alley than they met Lucius M. Baldwin, a twenty-two-year-old clerk, whose widowed mother lives in Burlington, Kan. Baldwin had gone to Isham's hardware store at the first alarm and there snatched up a pistol, for all the hardware dealers of the city made free to all comers their stocks of firearms.

Baldwin hastily ran through the store, out in the alley behind, with the intent to take the Daltons in the rear.

One of the robbers ordered him to stop, but Baldwin, as he stated in his dying moments, did not hear the command, and mistaking the parties for men who were guarding the bank, continued to advance toward them.

Just then one of the robbers drew up his Winchester and exclaiming, "I have got to get that man," fired. The ball entered Mr. Baldwin's left breast, just below the heart, and he fell dying on the spot.

Several persons who were in the alley without arms, seeing the condition of affairs, took refuge in an adjoining building, while the men ran northward in the alley to Eighth street and thence west to Union street near Mahan & Custer's store, the one with the sack keeping in front of the other, the latter carrying his Winchester at a ready.

Bob's plan of escape was working well so far.

Quickly ejecting the shell, Bob joined his brother Emmet in a run and they soon gained the north end of the alley, the rattle of firearms in the square lending their heels swiftness.

Going west they ran in the center of the street upon which the Eldridge house is built and looking south. When they reached the square they saw up and down its sidewalks hastily armed men pouring lead into the Condon bank in a noisy stream. They hoped to cross unseen, and might have done so had it not been for the awaking within their breasts of the irresistible instinct to kill.

George Cubine, who worked in the shoe-shop of

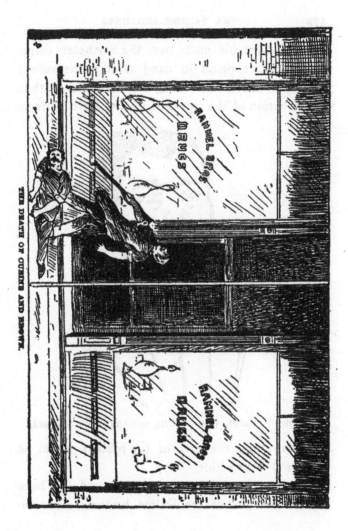

THE DEATH OF CURRY AND BROWN.

D. W. Cubine, his uncle, near the northeast corner of the square, pistol in hand, stood in the walk in front of Rammel Bros.' drug store looking south in the direction of the entrance to the First National

GEORGE CUBINE, ONE OF THE COFFEYVILLE HEROES.

bank, awaiting the exit of the robbers, whom he supposed to be within.

By the side of Cubine, who had in old days been a personal friend of the Dalton brothers, stood unarmed Charles Brown, a fellow shoemaker and an old, harmless man. Cubine's back was turned to the Daltons, but Bob could not resist the temptation to stop in his unperceived flight and shoot.

CHARLES BROWN, ONE OF THE COFFEYVILLE HEROES.

Straight from his Winchester flew the bullet to Cubine's heart, and the man dropped dead on the walk.

Brown stooped to pick up the revolver from his companion's nerveless hand, and straightened his body and there whistled another bullet from that same deadly Winchester, and prostrate on one dead body fell another.

Bob Dalton's aim was fatally unerring and he needed never to shoot twice. The delay, though short as it was, cost him a moment of time and drew on him the attention of the citizens which had chiefly been directed to the robbers in the Condon bank.

As soon as Cashier Ayers, Bert Ayers and Shepherd found themselves in the street, driven out of the bank by the robbers, they ran into Isham's store adjoining. There the cashier caught a rifle from the hands of a man whom he remembers not, and just as the two Daltons ran across the street, north, he caught sight of them from the door of the store.

At that very minute poor Cubine fell mortally wounded, followed almost instantly by old man Brown. Seeing this, Cashier Ayers knelt to shoot, that he might shoot more accurately. He was within the door and almost hidden from observation by articles exposed for sale.

But Bob Dalton's quick eye spied him out—the

only thing in all that multitude of things that flashed in general view, hidden behind a wheel and harness, yet Dalton saw the head above the concealed body. The distance was fully seventy yards. Ayers had already aimed, yet in an inappreciable space of time that deadly Winchester came to the villain's shoulder and Ayers fell forward helplessly on the floor, a bullet in his head, his unused rifle in his sprawling hand. Blood spurted from the wound as if from a fountain.

Dalton laughed, and with his brother ran westward to the rear of the buildings, which there face the square, and turning to the south they ran to the alley, where their horses were tied, Bob Dalton carrying on his arm the sack which held the stolen treasure.

Meanwhile, the three desperadoes in Condon's bank had kept silent, though the fire was terrific. With dogged tenacity they were waiting for the expiration of the time which the cashier said the time lock had been fixed for.

Dalton's first rifle shot was to them the signal for escape. Boldly they prepared to sally out with such money as they had. All the town was firing at these robbers behind the plate-glass windows.

As soon as the shooting had begun, Liveryman John Kloehr, the best shot of the town, seeking a rifle, was given one by Barndollar from his own store. Gun in hand, he crossed to the southwest corner of the square and opened fire.

To silence the general fire and escape under cover of the confusion, through the plate glass windows the outlaws sent bullets back.

Boyish Harry Lang, Undertaker Lang's son, on the east side of the square near the alley, had a shotgun loaded with bird shot. He offered it to a man who declined to shoot when he was told what the gun was loaded with, whereupon the boy himself joined in the general conflict, although his bird shot merely flattened on the plate-glass window.

The storm of bullets raged heavily, and twenty bullet holes in the windows and their casings attest the vigor of it.

With a shout the three outlaws ran from the entrance, and Powers caught sight of Charlie Gump, a laborer, with a pistol in hand. Crack went his Winchester; the pistol dropped, and a hole in Gump's wrist marked the bullet's course.

That in the hail of bullets which then swept up the square all the flying robbers, who ran toward the

COFFEYVILLE GANGS SHOOTING AT THE GANG FROM ISHAM'S STORE

alley where their horses were, were not killed seems miraculous.

A squad of men was gathered on the porch in front of Isham's store, from whence across the square, to and up the alley to where the horses stood, the field was clear. Volley after volley chased the fugitives. Mat Reynolds fired at one squad and wounded Powers. The man turned in his flight, made a face at Reynolds and returned the fire, wounding him in the foot. Joe Uncapper, from above the bank, wounded Broadwell with a bullet, but the man kept on and ran up the alley.

Bob and Emmet Dalton, approaching from the north in the rear of the business block facing the square, met Grat Dalton and his associates just as they all reached the barn where stood their horses. From the east up the alley came the flight of bullets, but they paid little heed. Bob Dalton tied the stolen $20,000 to the pommel of his saddle and said:

"We've got the swag, boys, and we'll keep it;" but the attack came closer. The squad on Isham's porch across the square kept their Winchesters hot.

John Kloehr, running to the south of the block on the west side of the square, passed through his stable and came out behind a board fence on the alley, not fifty feet from where the Dalton gang came together.

Marshal Charles T. Connelly, taking the same course, had borrowed a rifle from Swisher's gun shop and came out upon the alley west of the robbers. He ran boldly- out, looking westward and ignorant of the fact that the desperadoes were not fifty feet behind himself and Police Judge Charles Munn.

Grat Dalton raised his rifle, though wounded himself at the time with a bullet, and Connelly dropped dead with a bullet in his breast. Then Grat wheeled about to face the increasing storm.

The firing was so brisk that the outlaws did not dare to mount their horses and attempt escape. Bill Powers shot and killed two horses attached to an oil tank because their plunging disturbed his aim.

From his position behind the fence near by Kloehr took aim at Bob Dalton, just as he was ejecting a shell. Dalton caught sight of him and worked with such incredible rapidity that when he fell with a bullet from Kloehr's rifle in his bowels he discharged his reloaded gun. The bullet sped harmlessly in the air. There was a convulsive motion and Bob Dalton was dead.

Grat Dalton caught sight of the assailant behind the thin fence. He lifted his rifle, but again Kloehr's Winchester spoke first and Grat Dalton fell dead with a bullet hole exactly in the center of his throat.

Emmet Dalton jumped to the saddle on Red Buck, his big bay racer, and transferred the money to his saddle. Bill Powers tried to mount his horse, when a shot from the squad on Isham's porch caught him in the breast, and tossing his gun up with a convulsive motion he fell dead near his leader.

Dick Broadwell reached his saddle in safety and led Emmet Dalton in the race for the western end of the alley. A hail of bullets flew up the narrow alleyway. Broadwell reeled and blood spurted from his mouth, but he kept his saddle, crossed Maple street, and spurred his horse toward safety.

Then Emmet Dalton, boy as he was, with the down of his twentieth year on his lip to mark his youth, did as incredible a thing as men ever looked upon.

He reined his horse in before he had reached the exit from the alley, and in all that terrible, constant

CITY MARSHAL CHARLES T. CONNELLY.
The Dead Coffeyville Hero.

fire which fed the narrow crossway with leaden bullets, he deliberately rode back the whole distance to
where his brother Bob lay dead, dismounted and
tried to lift him upon the saddle of his horse that he
might bear him away.

A bullet from a Winchester shattered his right
arm near the shoulder, making a mere mass of
splinters of the bone.

Bob's body dropped and Emmet, holding the
rein as best he could, sought to use his left hand.
A load of buckshot struck him in the back and side.
Carey Seaman, a barber, fired the shot. When Harris Reed told him, "of course that's one of the robbers, let him have it," there was a flash, a flame, a
cloud of smoke, and Emmet Dalton fell uncon-
sciously by the side of his brother, his arm shattered, his thigh broken, and a dozen buckshot in his
back.

Dick Broadwell rode on and on into the country
half conscious, bleeding from a dozen wounds and
swaying in his saddle. The direction of his flight
was soon discovered. A mounted posse gave chase.
A mile from the scene of the fight, near the gate
of the creamery on the Independence road, they
found him dead on the roadside, the bridle of his

LIEUT. DALTON, UNDER FIRE, TRYING TO SAVE HIS BROTHER BOB

mounted horse in hand.   How he came to his death is told in the following chapter.

We desire to state here, in order to contradict some unfounded reports that have been sent out by excited newspaper correspondents to the effect that the citizens were prepared for the attack, that when the robbers were discovered in the bank, there was not a single, solitary armed man anywhere upon the square or in the neighborhood.

Even Marshal Connelly had lain his pistol aside, and was totally unarmed when the alarm was given. Every gun that was used, with the exception of that brought into action by George Cubine, was procured in the hardware stores and loaded and brought into play under the pressure of the great exigency that was upon the people.

The firing was rapid and incessant for about three minutes, when the cry went up: "They are all down."

In an instant the firing ceased. Several men who had been pressing close after the robbers sprang into the alley, and covering them with their guns ordered them to hold up their hands.

One hand went up in a feeble manner.

Three of the robbers were dead and the fourth helpless.

Between the bodies of two of the dead highwaymen, lying upon his face, in the last agonies of
death, was Marshal Charles T. Connelly, the bravest
of all the brave men who had joined in resisting the
terrible raiders in their attempt to rob the banks.

Dead and dying horses and smoking Winchesters on the ground added to the horrors of the
scene.

It took but a few minutes to discover who the
desperadoes were. Tearing the disguises from their
faces, the ghastly features of Grattan Dalton and
Bob Dalton, former residents of Coffeyville and
well known to many of our citizens, were revealed.
The other dead body proved to be that of Bill
Powers, whilst the wounded man was Emmet Dalton,
the youngest brother of the two principals of the
notorious gang.

The wildest excitement prevailed. Marshal Connelly breathed a few moments, when his brave spirit
went out without a struggle. Emmet Dalton was
carried to Slosson's drug store, and subsequently to
Dr. Wells' office. At first he denied his identity,
but realizing that he was recognized and likely to
die, he admitted that he was Emmet Dalton.

It is simply impossible to describe the scenes

that followed. Excited men, weeping women and screaming children thronged the square.

A few cool-headed citizens kept disorder from ensuing. The dead and dying citizens were removed to their homes or other comfortable locations. The dead raiders' bodies were thrown into the city jail. Guards were thrown out, and the city sat down in sackcloth and ashes, to mourn for the heroic men who had given their lives for the protection of the property of their fellow-citizens and the maintenance of law in their midst.

CHAPTER V.

AFTER THE FIGHT—MOURNING FOR THE DEAD—THOU-
SANDS OF VISITORS POURING INTO THE CITY—MORE
DETAILS ABOUT THE KILLED DESPERADOES—YOUNG
T. N. RUSSEL THE SLAYER OF BROADWELL—THE
GHASTLY SIGHT WITHIN THE CITY JAIL—BURY-
ING THE BANDITS IN THE POTTER'S FIELD
—TALK OF LYNCHING EMMET NOBLY SUB-
DUED—THE CITIZEN-HEROES COMMIT-
TED TO THEIR GRAVES—THE DALTON
FAMILY ARRIVES—ALSO BROAD-
WELL'S RELATIVES—A TRUST-
WORTHY STATEMENT FROM
THE LIPS OF EMMET DALTON
—THE WOUNDED ROBBER
OFF TO INDEPENDENCE
UNDER CLOSE GUARD.

The smoke of the terrific battle with the bandits had blown aside, but the excitement occasioned by the wonderful event soon increased, until it reached fever heat.

The trains over the four principal roads leading to Coffeyville brought thousands of visitors to the scene of that bloody conflict between a desperate and notorious gang of experienced highwaymen and a brave and determined lot of citizens, who had the nerve to preserve their rights and protect their property under the most trying circumstances.

Shortly after twelve o'clock, noon, on that eventful Wednesday, that is, as soon as the telegraph had carried the news over to Parsons, Supt. Frey, of the M., K. & T., at the head of fifty heavily armed men, came down on a special train that ran over the thirty-one miles between Parsons and Coffeyville, in thirty-two minutes. When they reached their destination, however, they found that the brave little city had, unaided and alone, conquered and laid in the dust its criminal invaders.

Telegrams and letters offering assistance and extending condolence to the four stricken and bereaved families were received in great numbers from all parts of the country.

Those of the citizens who were not in the fight felt justly proud of those who were, and the latter meekly bore their laurels and assisted in restoring order and preserving the peace.

CAREY SEAMAN.

The heroic barber who shot down Emmet Dalton.

By comparing watches, it was discovered that less than fifteen minutes had elapsed from the time the Dalton boys entered the banks until four of their party were dead and the remaining one grievously wounded and in the hands of the officers.

Not over fifteen guns were actively engaged in the fight on both sides and the engagement lasted about ten minutes. Eight persons were killed and three wounded. The percentage of loss was greater than in any battle of the great war of the rebellion.

There were no "stray shots," either, no "accidental shootings." The fellows who held the guns were cool and collected.

The citizens of Coffeyville who were killed in the terrible engagement were each one engaged in the fight, and were not innocent bystanders. They are quiet and steady people in those southwestern border towns, but they are also adepts in the business of resisting law-breakers, and they know how to do their duty, though it costs blood.

The true inwardness of Broadwell's slaying was only fully revealed later in the day. It gave a new proof of the courageous blood that runs through the veins of the Coffeyville citizens, young and old, and it places on the roster of honor one more name, be-

T. N. RUSSELL.
The brave lad who shot the fleeing Broadwell.

sides those of the dead heroes, Connelly, Baldwin, Cubine and Brown; of the wounded ones, Gump, Reynolds and Dietz; and of those who escaped unscathed, John Kloehr and Carey Seaman first and foremost. This name is that of young T. N. Russell, whose experience, related by himself and corroborated by several eye witnesses, has its legitimate place in these pages.

It appears that when Broadwell—the only one of the desperadoes who managed to leave the fated alley, astride of his horse—rode on at the top of his mount's speed toward safety, he had to pass the back of G. W. Russell's lot, on the same alley, west of Maple street.

Just at that moment, the young son of Mr. Russell had run to the fence, a heavy Colt revolver in his hand, intent upon doing his share in the fight that was raging but a few yards away.

He espied the rider rushing toward him, urging his horse like mad and flourishing his trusty Winchester; and as the man passed him, not five feet distant, the lad let go his revolver, once, twice, thrice—

The robber uttered a yell as if touched in a vital part, but continuing his break-neck riding, contenting himself with discharging his Winchester behind his back, without even turning his head.

Not half a mile farther, the pursuing posse found him dead on the roadside, still holding the bridle of his faithful horse.

The young fellow's aim had been true, and the size of the wound in the man's abdomen was clear evidence of the kind of weapon that had done the dread work—a Colt revolver of the very same calibre as the one in the hands of T. N. Russell.

The body was brought back to town, and the four desperadoes, after having lain for a couple of hours piled up promiscuously in the narrow little city jail, found common lodgment in four black-varnished coffins.

They were laid out side by side in front of the barn near which their horses had been tied. They looked very ghastly and unheroic.

Here they were photographed, and from these photographs have our sketches been drawn.

There were hundreds of morbid ones who came to gaze and stayed long.

Some handled the bodies in the coffins, and whenever Grat Dalton's right arm was lifted a little spurt of blood would jump from the round black hole in his throat.

So they remained all night, and the morning

13

dust lifted by the feet of crowding bystanders
settled thickly on the corpses and open coffins.
Myriads of flies, called out by the warmth of the
sun and the smell of blood, gathered on the living
and the dead, but the crowd took no heed of the
time until noon, when there came an undertaker
who closed the coffin lids.

Early that afternoon the bodies of the robbers
were given burial, and although the Dalton family
own a lot in the cemetery there, they were buried,
two coffins in a grave, in the potter's field, within a
stone's throw of the grave of poor Charley Montgomery, the first of the victims of their murderous
guns.

Shortly after his surrender, Emmet Dalton had
been removed to a barely furnished room over Slos-
sin's drug store. There was much talk of lynching
and Sheriff Callahan, of Montgomery county, who
had arrived at once from Independence, the county
seat, was watchful during all the night.

Once there was even a pretense of an attempt at
action, but, let it be said to Coffeyville's great honor,
it came to naught. Still, during the first days of
intense excitement, any move on the part of the
sheriff to have the wounded desperado transported

THE CROWD IN FRONT OF THE COFFEYVILLE JAIL, WHERE THE BODIES OF THE FOUR DEAD BANDITS LAY.

out of the city's jurisdiction would have been stub-
bornly met with determined resistance. What saved
the boy's life, however, was the well-substantiated
rumor that he had but a few hours to live; and in
fact, the doctors' verdict was that Emmet's chances
of surviving were about five to a hundred against.

In spite of his terrible exhaustion and loss of
blood, Emmet had already made some rambling
kind of a confession, very contradictory in its details. He denied his participation in any other
affairs, but admitted that Bob, Grat and their two
lesser associates were in the robbery of the Missouri, Kansas & Texas train at Adair, in the robberies of the Santa Fe trains at Wharton and Red
Rock, and in the California robbery. At first, he
tried to deny his identity and said that his name was
Bailey, but so many came who knew him that he
abandoned it. Those of the desperadoes who had
been killed were brought before him and he identified rightly, his two brothers, but said that Dick
Broadwell was Texas Jack and that Bill Powers was
Tom Evans, alias Tom Hedde. Afterward he admitted that he had lied, and the identity of every
member of the gang was fully established. Others
disputed Grat Dalton's identity, but there now re-

mains no question but that the outlaw is one of the dead.

Emmet Dalton passed this first night in continuous pain. Amputation of his arm was suggested, but he would not consent. At noon of the next day, he was removed to the Farmers' Home, the little frame boarding-house the Dalton brothers used to patronize on their nightly excursions, and there he lay in the front room of the smaller building, for the next five days, exposed to the gaze of hundreds.

It was there that Ransom Payne visited him on the following Saturday.

He found the wounded lad surrounded by his aged mother, wrinkled and bowed down beyond her years by unspeakable sorrow, and her eyes dim with continuous crying; by his sister, Mrs. Whipple, a comely young woman, with dark energetic features; by honest Ben Dalton, the type of the sturdy farmer of those parts, and finally by Will, the whilom Californian, suspected of, but finally acquitted from, guilty participation in the Tulare county hold-up.

As soon as Emmet, who had by this time surprisingly rallied and showed undoubted signs of recovery, saw the stalwart form of Payne approach his bed, he stretched his hand, which the officer kindly pressed, and cried:

"So you have got us in, after all!"

Then, feeling that he could talk freely in the presence of a man who knew so thoroughly every detail of his criminal career, he made the following statement, which has certainly the appearance of un-garbled truth. He said:

"On the first of Oct., 1892, I met the boys south of Tulsa, and they asked me how much money I had. I told them about $20. I asked them how much they had, and they said about $900. I asked them what they were going to do and they said this town, Coffeyville, had been talking about them, and some of the people had been trying to get them captured. I told them I knew it was a lie, that they used to have lots of friends here.

"Bob said he could discount the James boys' work and go up and rob both banks at Coffeyville in one day.

"I told him I did not want any of it at all. He said I had better go along and help and get some money and leave the country; that if I stayed around here I was sure to get caught or killed.

"On the morning of Oct. 3rd we saddled up north

of Tulsa in the Osage nation and rode about twenty miles toward Coffeyville, and we talked it over that day. I tried to prevail on the boys not to come up, for the people here had done us no harm. They said all right, if I didn't want to come that they four would come and give the town a round up. I told them if that was the case I might as well come with them. I came for the love of my brothers, and I knew that I would be chased just as hard if I didn't come as I would be if I did, and I had no money to get out of the country on.

"We camped in the timbered hills on the head of Hickory creek, about twelve miles from Coffeyville, on the night of the 4th, and in the night we saddled up and rode to the Davis farm in the Onion creek bottoms, and this morning (the 5th) we fed our horses some corn. I asked them if they were still coming up here. They said they were. I told them it would not be treating the people right, as they had always befriended us.

"I asked them how they were going to do it. Bob said that we would ride in about half past nine o'clock in the morning, saying that there would not be so many people in town to hold up, and he wouldn't have to hurt any one.

"He told me he would like to have me go with him, because I was quick on foot, and that he and I would go to the First National bank, and let the others go to C. M. Condon's. He said we would ride in and hitch at the old C. M. Condon building. He said we would hitch there so that people would not see us until we got right into the banks.

"When we got to the lumber yard we saw that the street was all torn up, and he said: 'Let us ride down in the alley and hitch.'

"All the five horses belonged to Bob. He bought one on the 2d, and others next morning. I am a first cousin of Bob and Cole Younger. My mother is a sister of Cole Younger's father."

Later in the day, Ransom Payne had a long talk with Ben Dalton, who showed no hesitancy in expressing himself concerning his brothers. He spoke somewhat in this wise:

"I was sick in bed at our home on the farm, four miles north of Kingfisher, when we received the news of this awful affair, but managed to come with mother and the others. We had not seen the boys for a long time, and I had no idea where they were or what they were doing. I never had much in common with the ones who lie here dead and badly

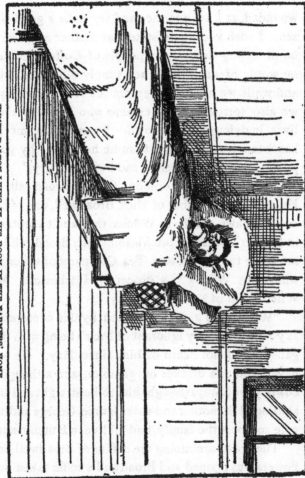

EMMET DALTON LYING IN HIS ROOM IN THE FARMERS' HOME

wounded, as I am a farmer and try to be a good citizen. I wish you would state that mother and I have no ill feeling against the people of Coffeyville and no words of censure. They simply did their duty, and while we naturally deplore the loss of our boys, we also sorrow for the citizens who gave up their lives in defense of the town. Emmet tells me he has been treated better than he hoped for by your people, and we are feeling sad but not angry."

On that same afternoon, George Broadwell, of Hutchinson, a brother of Dick Broadwell, one of the dead outlaws, and E. B. Wilcox, the bandit's brother-in-law, arrived from Hutchinson. Mr. Broadwell is a salesman for the Boston Tea Company of Chicago, while Mr. Wilcox is a grocer in Hutchinson. Mr. Wilcox said of the dead man:

"We were as greatly shocked by this occurrence as you, and entirely ignorant of Dick's being with this gang. Had not heard of him since May. He was never wild or a drinker or gambler, and although a cowboy, we always thought him to be straight and law abiding. His mother and sister Jennie, George and my wife compose the family, and all live in Hutchinson."

The grave containing the coffins of Broadwell and Powers was opened and Broadwell's coffin taken out.

The body was then clad in a new suit of clothing, placed in an expensive coffin and reinterred. It was thought at the time that the bodies of the other bandits ought to be exhumed and a careful examination made of their clothing, as there might have been money or valuables sewn in the lining of the garments, but the idea was not acted upon.

Mr. Broadwell endeavored to obtain his brother's horse, which had been neither killed nor wounded, and the $92.40 found on his person, but those who held the property refused to turn it over, although an indemnifying bond was offered. None of the friends of Bill Powers, alias Tom Evans, put in an appearance, nor have they been heard from.

The body of Lucius M. Baldwin, the first victim of the outlaws and a most worthy young man, was shipped to his mother at Burlington, Kan., on the following morning. George Cubine was buried that same afternoon, and all the stores of the town were closed and draped in black. The funeral was very large and most impressive in its simplicity. Mr. Cubine was a member of the M. E. church.

The Missouri Pacific Railway Company kindly furnished two coaches, free of charge, and placed them at the disposal of the family and friends of the dead Marshal Connelly, for the purpose of conveying them to Independence, where the funeral occurred on Friday.

Charles T. Connelly, the dead hero, was born in the state of Indiana, November 25, 1845, where he resided until he moved to Kansas in 1885. He enlisted in the Ninth Indiana Battery at the age of seventeen years and served his country gallantly until the close of the war. In the year 1867 he was married to Mary McCord. Two children, Bert and Grace, blessed their union. His wife died in 1874. Two years after her death he was married to Sarah Alexander. This union was also blessed with two children, but one of whom is living, Miss Jessie. As a teacher in Coffeyville city schools, Mr. Connelly was ever faithful and efficient, and enjoyed the confidence and esteem of his pupils. As city marshal he discharged his duty with great courage and absolute fidelity to the best interests of the city. He gave his life freely in defense of the lives and property of the citizens, and his faithfulness to duty will ever be held in grateful remembrance by the people of Coffeyville. The deepest sympathy of the entire community and the people at large went out to the bereaved wife and children as they mourned the loss of a loving and devoted husband and father.

The remains of the courageous old shoemaker, Charles Brown, were sent to Harley, S. D., where his wife resides.

All the wounded citizens, including Cashier Ayers, who was thought to have been fatally shot by Bob Dalton's unerring Winchester, have recovered from their injuries.

Finally, at a very early hour on the Tuesday following the great tragedy—the 11th of October it was—Emmet Dalton was taken to Independence to jail by Sheriff Callahan, without any objection by the citizens. William went along. Now that all the Dalton crowd had gone the citizens felt relieved, as their presence kept the town full of undesirable visitors who were apt to cause trouble. It was thought then that Emmet would recover, and so he did.

With his capture and the certainty of his being sent to the penitentiary for life (since the death penalty is never enforced in the state of Kansas), the Dalton gang is practically annihilated, and whatever remains of it is deprived of the bold and intelligent leadership of Bob, so strongly backed by the devotion and reckless intrepidity of his brothers.

For a while—for a long while, we hope the terri-tories and border states are to be freed from the constant terror which the Dalton gang had contrived to spread through this prosperous country.

Ransom Payne had not toiled in vain.

Driven to extraordinarily desperate acts of crimi-nality in their anxiety to obtain resources enough to flee the vicinity, the Dalton boys and their pals had run head foremost into the jaws of death

CHAPTER VI.

THE SCATTERED REMNANTS OF THE DALTON GANG
THREATEN DIRE REVENGE—"THE WHOLE CROWD AIN'T
DEAD, BY A—SIGHT!"—HEROIC JOHN KLOEHR RE-
CEIVES A "SKULL AND CROSS-BONES" WARNING—
THE COFFEYVILLE PEOPLE READY FOR THEM—
UNIVERSAL SYMPATHY FOR THE VICTIMS AND
THE INTREPID DEFENDERS OF THE LAW—
THE BANKERS ALL OVER THE COUNTRY
SUBSCRIBE LARGE SUMS—THE R. R. COM-
PANIES URGED TO PAY THE RE-
WARDS—A GOLD MEDAL PRESENT-
ED TO JOHN J. KLOEHR BY HIS
CHICAGO ADMIRERS—A TRAGE-
DY NOT SOON TO BE
FORGOTTEN.

A week had hardly elapsed after the terrible
events of the 5th of October, 1892, had taken place,
than an alarming rumor gained ground all over
Southwestern Kansas.

"The Dalton gang had not been wholly extermi-
nated; the survivors were coming on to wreck their
vengeance upon valiant Coffeyville!"

The report started from the robbing of the Missouri
Pacific train at near Caney, a small place a few miles
from Coffeyville, during the night of October 13th.

Just as the train drew up at Caney at 10:15
o'clock that night, two masked men, heavily armed,
climbed on the locomotive tender from the front
of the combination baggage and express car and
covered Engineer Eggleston and his fireman with
their rifles.

The locomotive engineer was ordered to pull
slowly to the switch, where there was no danger of
molestation.

At the whistling post the outlaws ordered the
engineer to stop and made the fireman uncouple
the express car from the rest of the train. This was
done so quietly that no one in the coaches was disturbed.

The engineer then pulled ahead with the express
car. When a deep cut half a mile farther on was
reached the engine was halted.

Express Messenger J. N. Maxwell, who had witnessed the uncoupling, had in the meantime blown

out his lights and barred and barricaded the doors.

The order to open the car elicited no response, and the robbers began firing into the sides of the car.

Maxwell answered the shots with his revolvers for a few minutes, but finally received a bullet in his right arm, which disabled him. The robbers ordered him to light his lamps and open the car door, and as soon as he had done so they entered the car, with the engineer in front of them as a shield. Maxwell was then forced to open his safe and deliver his watch and personal property. The men backed off the car and disappeared in the darkness.

Messenger Maxwell declares that the robbers secured less than $100 all told. The men engaged in that night's work were thought immediately to be those pals of the Daltons who had not reached Coffeyville in time to take part in the tragic raid on the fifth.

It was understood to be sufficient evidence that the gang was being rapidly reorganized and was moving upon Coffeyville with the avowed purpose of avenging the death of their pals.

Couriers arrived in Coffeyville at an early hour

14

the next morning, bearing this important news, the word was passed around, and in the shortest possible time the people were armed and ready to defend their homes against the invasion of the threatened mob. Since the Dalton massacre many persons have been noticed in Coffeyville, openly condemning the manner in which this notorious gang met its death, and several sympathizers have even been arrested and confined in jail.

All of the rifles in the town were in readiness, and every man stood waiting for an attack. A car from the M., K. & T., at Parsons, stood at the depot barricaded and armed.

In the Coffeyville homes, women and children were frightened over the outlook for another bloody encounter with the bandits. Still, the mayor of Coffeyville, after having conferred with the railroad officials, wired to Parsons that the people here could care for themselves, as the number of the attacking party was greatly magnified, and that a matter of a few hours would result in their capture.

"Coffeyville people," said he, " have shown their ability to care for themselves."

Ben and William Dalton, and many of their sympathizers, had been loitering about Coffeyville for days. When Emmet Dalton's wounded body was removed to Independence, Ben and William and their mother accompanied him. Since then nothing had been heard from them. That evening a bonfire was started on the plaza of the town to furnish a reassuring illumination.

The information of the approach of the Daltons had been conveyed to the people of Coffeyville by the force under Detective Dodge, of the Wells-Fargo Company, who is scouring the Indian Territory for members of the gang.

One of his men heard it and wired the mayor of Coffeyville, who asked for help from Parsons and had it kept there in readiness. The plan was for one of the surviving Daltons and forty whites and half-breeds, completely armed, to ride into Coffeyville at 9 o'clock on that night and wipe out the place. No mercy was to be given, according to Dodge's information.

Since then, of course, the town of Coffeyville has been a pandemonium of excitement, yet no braver set of men ever shouldered a gun than the gallant and fearless citizens of this little Kansas town.

There is every reason to believe from the actions of some of the men who have visited Coffeyville

that if Emmet Dalton recovers, some steps will be
taken by his friends to liberate him. The people of
Coffeyville will see to it that he gets his just deserts,
even if they again have to resort to arms.

The following letter, received by John Kloehr,
the man who is most justly credited with having
killed three out of four of the Dalton gang, shows at
least that all of the gang is not dead:

"ARKANSAS CITY, Kas., Oct. —, 1892. To John
Kloehr—Dear Sir: I take the time to tell you and
the citizens of Coffeyville that all of the gang ain't
dead yet by a —— of a sight, and don't you forget
it. I would have given all I ever made to have been
there the 5th. There are five of the gang left, and
we shall come and see you all some day. That day,
Oct. 5, we were down in the Chickasaw Nation, and
we did not know it was coming off so soon. We
thought it was to be Nov. 5. We shall have revenge
for your killing of Bob and Grat and the rest of
them. You people had no cause to take arms against
the gang. The bankers will not help the widows of the
men that got kill d there, and you thought you were
playing —— when you killed three of us, but your
time will soon come, when you will have to go into
the grave and pass in yo' r checks for the killing of

Bob and Joe Evans and Texas Jack, so take warning. We will leave you in the hands of God for this
time. Yours truly,   DALTON GANG

"And sympathizer of this gang of outlaws."

This letter, which bears new testimony to the
great courage displayed by John Kloehr in thus
jeopardizing his life, not only in the fight but for a
long time after, renders doubly opportune the token
of high esteem presented to this brave man by bankers and citizens of the city of Chicago.

The First National Bank of the western metrop-
olis, aided by contributions from nearly all the
banks in that city, ordered an elegant badge, which
was recently placed on exhibition at Chamber &
Co.'s store. It has since been sent by express to the
courageous defender of Coffeyville.

A semi-circular plate of gold bears the name of
"John Joseph Kloehr." Below this is a gold ribbon
on which is engraved: "The Emergency Arose. The
Man Appeared." Suspended from this by three
gold links at each end is the badge proper, a gold
circle two and one-fourth inches in diameter, with a
narrow raised band on the outer edge. Next within
this is an open scroll-work, then another raised band
of bright gold, and within this a laurel wreath. A

third raised band of bright gold incloses an eight-
pointed bright gold star, in the center of which is a
large diamond, the star being three-quarters of an
inch in diameter.

JOHN JOSEPH KLOEHR

THE EMERGENCY AROSE,
THE MAN APPEARED.

Badge presented to John J. Kloehr by the Banks of Chicago.

The entire badge is four inches in length and
cost $350. On the reverse is the inscription: "Pre-
sented by friends in Chicago, who admire nerve and
courage when displayed in defense of social order."

We give herein an exact reproduction of this
beautiful badge.

Neither have the families of the victims of Bob

Dalton's and his pals' Winchesters been forgotten either in their own city or through the country at large.

A mass meeting of the citizens of Coffeyville was held on the Friday following the tragedy, for the purpose of taking action in respect to the matter of aid for the families of the men who died in defense of the property of their fellow-citizens, or were wounded in the fight with the Dalton gang on the Wednesday preceding.

Thomas Scurr, Jr., president of the First National bank, presided, and D. Stewart Elliott, editor of *The Journal*, a most excellent weekly paper that does the greatest honor to its editor and publisher, was made secretary. It was resolved to immediately prepare and send out an appeal circular to the banks, monetary institutions, railroad and express companies, asking contributions for the purpose above stated.

The following committee of prominent business men was appointed to issue the circular: Charles T. Carpenter, Dr. T. C. Frazier, J. J. Barndollar, William McCoy and H. W. Read. The First National bank and the bank of C. M. Condon & Co. were designated as the custodians of the funds received. The committee met and organized after the adjournment

of the meeting when the paper was prepared and
the following subscriptions received:

First National Bank..$500

C. M. Condon & Co..$500

The committee was directed to make weekly re-
ports of amounts received through the city papers.
C. T. Carpenter was made chairman and Dr. T. C
Frazier secretary of the committee.

On the day preceding, the president of the Union
National Bank of Minneapolis had already sent a
message to William B. Green, Secretary of the
American Bank Association in New York, asking
why it would not be a good idea to call upon all
members of the American Bank Association to con-
tribute each $5 to $10 for a fund for the members of
the families of the men shot down in Coffeyville,
Kan., in the Dalton bank robbery raid.

His appeal was heeded, for, on October 20th, the
Kansas State Bankers' Association meeting at
Topeka took action regarding the fund for the slayers of the Dalton gang. This fund then reached nearly
$18,000 from all sources. The Bankers' association
required all members to forward their individual
subscriptions and added $137. The association also
organised a protective association with $2,000 in the

treasury, for the purpose of hunting down and prose-
cuting all persons who defraud or attempt to defraud any of its members. The sum is to be kept
intact by assessments whenever rewards and prose-
cuting expenses have used any portion of it.

There gathered in Coffeyville during the days
immediately following the tragedy from fifteen to
twenty railway and express company officials. These
gentlemen unanimously requested their companies
to pay the full rewards to the families of the dead
citizens, and all expect favorable responses to their
requests.

It is to our personal knowledge that the rewards
offered by the Southern Pacific R. R. Company
and by the Wells, Fargo Express Company, after the
Tulare county outrage, are still *alive* and will be
most probably paid to those entitled to them or their
heirs.

As to the reward offered by the M., K. & T. R.
R., after the Adair hold-up (July 14, 1892), they
have been officially withdrawn, on September 15th
last.

So much about the rewards, which, in our opinion, will not be paid to any one, dead or alive, for
there is no absolute evidence as to who the actual

slayers of the bandits may be, as the latter all died of many wounds. The Daltons and Bill Powers ought to be credited to Kloehr and Seaman, and Broadwell to young Russell. But it would have taken a much more thorough examination of the bodies before interment to reach the indisputable truth in the matter.

Corporations are known to be heartless. There is hardly any hope that they will show themselves different in this particular occasion.

Speaking of money, the two following items are not without some interest.

It appears that the money secured from the First National Bank amounted to $20,240 and that from Condon's $3,000.

The amounts turned over to the banks exceed this amount and serves to verify the statement by Emmet Dalton that they had $900 when they came to the town.

And, now, just as this final chapter is going to press, we hear that the surviving Daltons propose suing the city of Coffeyville for that very amount of $900, although it be, without any manner of doubt, the proceeds of some anterior and successful robbery, the Adair hold-up most probably.

Let us now close this minute record of one of the briefest but most bloody careers of crime ever heard of in modern times, and give in full the valuable opinion of Superintendent Murray concerning those gangs of train robbers who have made traveling in the Southwest much too picturesque for absolute comfort.

After praising as it behooved the valiance of the small Coffeyville community, the superintendent added:

"The Dalton gang were desperate, reckless men. They never hesitated to shoot. Their character was known all over the West. It was one thing to talk about facing them and another to do it. The Daltons did no work in the East. They seldom, in fact, got very far away from the lairs in the territory. The Coffeyville people made a clean sweep of the worst members of the gang.

"There is a certain bravado that glorifies characters such as the Daltons in the minds of tough men, and they are easily rallied around a leader bent on crimes that involve daring. The 'bad men' in the country who are liable to rob trains are narrowed down to Chris Evans and John Sontag. Under the leadership of George C. Contant, alias Sontag, they robbed the Southern Pacific train between Visalia and Fresno, August 4th. Four people were killed in the fight which occurred. Chris Evans and John Sontag got away and are in the mountains back of Visalia. There is a reward of ten thousand dollars offered for their capture. It was this gang that committed the famous express train robbery at Western Union Junction. Their depredations have been many.

"The other celebrated train robbers are either dead or in prison. Captain Bunch, Rube Burrows, Jim Burrows, and Rube Smith are dead. The Pegleg gang in Colorado are in the penitentiary. The Cooleys, who were graduating from henroost robberies into much more serious crimes in Pennsylvania, have met with a check in the killing of one of their number.

"But none of those gangs ever equaled, in such a short space of time, the daring criminality of those four young men who are now lying stiff and stark, in their coffins, in the Potter's field by Coffeyville, Kan."

[THE END.]

BLACK JACK KETCHUM

LAST OF THE HOLD-UP KINGS

BLACK JACK
KETCHUM

Last Of The
HOLD-UP KINGS

AN AUTHENTIC BIOGRAPHY
OF THE OLD WEST

by
Ed Bartholomew

Title Page Designed and Hand-Set by
Jack D. Rittenhouse

Book Design by John Scardino, Jr.

Photographs from the N. H. Rose Collection
Owned by the Author

1000 Copies Were Printed by Scardino Printers,
July, 1955, at Houston, Texas

Bound by Universal Book Bindery,
San Antonio, Texas

CHAPTER I

Born For Hell

If ever there was a mortal born for hell, Thomas Edward Ketchum certainly held a claim for a first class ticket on the parlor car of that train which was to transport all maleficient spirits to their audience with the angel of the bottomless pit!

From his early teens to his very death at the age of thirty-five, the man who was to become the most noted highwayman of the late ninteenth century, was forever obcessed with the fear, or the gleeful acknowledgement that he was headed for the infernal shades below, and only fate could change this hellish direction. Throughout his reckless life in Texas, New Mexico and Arizona, he often expressed the belief that he was headed for the habitation of the fallen angels, with a down hill shove and it is said that when the rope guillotine severed the head from his dying body at Clayton, New Mexico in the spring of 1901, he had just uttered a last request for his executors to hurry up their job for he was already late for his first lunch in hell. But when his head rolled under the gallows that April day, his fear of tormenting hell-fire and brimstone, came to an end, unless "the hue of dungeons and the scowl of night" was his actual destination.

Tom Ketchum was born on Richland Creek in western San Saba county, Texas, shortly after the end of the War for Southern Independence. Among the early residents of the valley were the families Hall, Ketchum, Harkey and the Duncans, with whom this story shall touch, in time. During the boyhood of the Ketchum

5

boys, Berry, Sam and Tom, listed in order of age, Tom being the youngest, Richland Springs was hardly any different than other Texas towns of the times and the area. Lampasas was the nearest railroad station. San Saba offered the nearest bank. There were three churches, one school, a sawmill, a grist mill and a cotton gin. There were three stages weekly to Brady and San Saba. The population when Tom Ketchum was in his late teens was about a hundred and fifty souls. They had a tri-weekly mail, brought on the stages: the postmaster was P. W. Johnson. The three stores were run by Barretts, Browns and Johnsons. There was the Saunders Hotel and the Taylor drug store. Tandy Mills ran the grist mill and gin.

For San Saba county, Joe M. Harkey was sheriff and Dee, his brother, was his deputy. When folks came to the county seat they stopped at the Bostwick Hotel or the Munger Hotel, had their horses shod at Austin Bros. blacksmith shop. They bought their staples from J. M. Pool's general store and drank their bourbon or beer at Wiley Williams' saloon. The weekly paper in San Saba was the News.

It was here, around Richland Springs on the northeastern border of Edwards Plateau of southwest central Texas that the Ketchum boys grew into young manhood. They were at work and play in the cedar brakes, the mesquite and live oak flats, the black and gray limestone hills and the sandy loam valleys of the San Saba river. Their home was located near where the first settlement was established in 1847, then known as County Seat. This was long before San Saba county had been organized and which was created from Bexar county, February of 1856. Other early settlements were Bolts, Rochester and Sulphur Springs. Later there came Richland Springs, Harkeyville and San Saba, the county seat. In 1875 an irrigation company had been formed and the success of the canals made the valley areas fine farming country. As youths the Ketchum boys learned the back breaking work on the farm, the never ending fight

6

against the rocks and stones that seemed to continually grow themselves out of the soil. The years of their boyhood was spent toting the stones to the field boundaries, making stone fences with the stone fruit of the fields.

Of the Ketchum boys there were three, Berry, Sam and Tom, who was the youngest, Berry the oldest. Things were bad on the frontiers of the county during the early years of the Ketchum boys. Indians often made raids into the valley and minute men were organized to trail and fight them and among those young men who went out against the Indians were Berry Ketchum and Joe Harkey. Of the Harkey family there were thirteen children, eight boys and five girls, and who were orphaned in 1869 when both parents died. Joe was but seventeen when he took over the running of the farm and the raising of the large family. He was later sheriff of the county, his younger brother Dee, born in 1866, the same year as was Tom, his deputy. In time three of the Harkey boys were shot to death, each when he was twenty-one years of age. The Duncan boys, Dick (Jack), and Bige, were cousins of the Ketchums. Dee Harkey, when a deputy for Joe Harkey, was to handle Tom Ketchum later as an officer of the law: his first arrest having been that of young Jim Miller, a wild youngster who had drifted into the San Saba country and who was the same age as was Dee and Tom, later to become a badman in his own right.

When Tom was a young boy the Texas badmen were running up and down the state, robbing stages, stealing cattle, killing folks, and raising hell in general. As Tom Ketchum entered his teens he went to work for the Hall outfit at Richland Springs. When Tom was but five years of age the three Hall brothers, Jim, Nathan and Will, had taken herds out to the Cimarron River country of northern New Mexico, some fifty miles north of where the town of Clayton was later to be located. From their home ranch at Richland Springs they had driven twenty-five hundred Texas longhorns and had organized

7

the Cross L Ranch there on the Rio Cimarron Seco, just a few miles south of the Colorado line. Ketchum worked for the Halls at Richland Creek, as well as the Tankersly outfit. Two of the Harkey boys also worked for Tankersly and perhaps the Halls. Tom Ketchum had made drives from San Saba county out to the Cimarron country but it is doubtful if he had made the trail drives before 1881 when the Halls sold out to W. R. Green for around half a million dollars. The Prairie Land Company had ranches in Colorado, New Mexico and the panhandle of Texas. It is believed that Tom Ketchum first went out on the trail to the Prairie Land Company about 1890.

It has been said that Tom, the youngest, was the smartest of the Ketchums. A tall lanky, boy, somewhat pampered by the older boys and who tried their best to look out for their younger brother, he did not do well at school. Like most young cowboys, at thirteen he was almost forced to go to school. In 1880 Joe Harkey was elected sheriff of the county and two years later, when Dee Harkey and Tom Ketchum were sixteen years of age and both young cowboys, Dee was named deputy to his brother and in this position he served until he was twenty years of age. During this time Tom was working as a cowboy on ranches in San Saba county. In 1948 when Dee Harkey was an old man, with many years behind him as a peace officer in Texas and New Mexico, he had this to say about those times in the county: "San Saba County was full of criminals and outlaws and Joe kept his jail full of those kinds of fellows all the time. Jim Miller and Bill White and the three Renfro brothers were a hard gang, and they were making a rough house of the town."

It seems that there had been some trouble over an arrest the sheriff had made and Jim Miller and the others had gathered at Wiley Williams' saloon. Sheriff Harkey came to the jail and told his brother Dee for him to help take the men. He instructed Dee to rush the saloon door with him: Dee was to kill Jim Miller and Joe White and

8

Joe the others. However, the men gave in and Miller was the first man that Dee arrested. He said the five men were jailed.

The Duncan boys and the Ketchums ran together and living only some six miles west of town were often seen in San Saba. It has been said that Tom was first arrested there for disturbing the peace and that the Duncans were arrested by Dee Harkey when he found "two flour barrels full of bells, harness, and hobbles", hid in a smoke house and Harkey said that later "they made bond and left the country". It has also been said that Dick (Jack) was later arrested in Presidio county for murder, tried and hanged at Eagle Pass. Dick was in the cow camp on the Gano G4 ranch in Presidio county, when Rangers Outlaw and Reynolds were forced to kill a man known as Dick Saunders in a gun battle when he resisted arrest. The other brother later moved to Tom Green county, was always a well respected citizen: it was Bige who went to Santa Fe in 1899 to identify his cousin, Sam Ketchum. Dee Harkey said that next Sam and Tom were indicted in San Saba county for horse theft and were holed up at Cow Valley, in McCulloch county and he was sent on their trail but they escaped.

CHAPTER II

A Cowboy For To Be

It was about this time that Doctor Ketchum decided to move his family to Tom Green county, settled at a small settlement some twenty miles southwest of San Angelo, near the Irion and Tom Green county line, named Knickerbocker. A small community then, it is now a small school and church settlement, with a post office, several business houses and about forty inhabitants. When they settled there near Dove Creek, the nearest railroad station was a hundred miles, Abilene. The nearest bank was in San Angelo. The population was about twenty-five and there was a semi-weekly mail. E. M. Grennel was postmaster. Just to the west of the Ketchum place there is a mountain named Ketchum Mountain: this is near the Middle Concho river. About this time the older brother, Berry, reliable and usually trying to look out for his younger brothers, started a ranch in Sutton county, some fifty miles to the southwest. Sam and Tom went to work for their brother, later for L. B. Harris, again for the Tankersly outfit near Knickerbocker.

Somewhere down the line Tom may have gotten into serious trouble for Father Stanley, in his book, Desperadoes of New Mexico, said that while at Richland Springs Tom had shot and killed a man known as Jap Powers, and "escaped" to the Chisum ranch in the Pecos country. I have found no documentary information on this matter. Sheriff Gerome Shields of Tom Green county, later said that Tom was arrested in San Saba in 1892 for disturbing the peace, and it seems that if he had been in more serious trouble Shields would have mentioned it, but, it is known that Tom did depart from Tom Green county about that time, and went to live and work with his brother, Berry. He spent some time in the Devil's River country around Sonora for he was quite well known there later. He had returned to his home county often and did work on the Chisum ranch around Seven Rivers, later, as well as for the LFD outfit near Roswell, New Mexico.

Back home Sam Ketchum was working for Tankersly and other ranchers in the county, as were the Kilpatrick boys, Ed Bullion and a new comer, Will Carver, who had come up from Bandera county in the early 1890s. Carver worked on one ranch and another and came to know most of the local cowboys. He was considered

10

by folks of Bandera county, and later by the San Angelo ranchers, as a quiet unassuming young man who attended strictly to his own business. He came to know Sam Ketchum and often visited their ranch home west of Knickerbocker. The Kilpatrick boys, Ben and George, lived at The Hills, about half way between Paint Rock and Eden, in Concho county. It was in the little settlement of Knickerbocker that Ben met Laura Bullion, as did Carver. Both, later went about with Laura, Ben "taking care" of her after Carver's death. She and Ben were later arrested in St. Louis as a Mr. and Mrs. Rose, in connection with unsigned bank notes that had been taken in a robbery. Often the Kilpatricks, the Duncans, Ed Bullion, Carver and Sam Ketchum would take in the town of San Angelo, go on hunting and fishing excursions, scout the country for work, and the usual enterprises of young cowboys. Tom Ketchum had now drifted out into the Pecos country, working on ranches and often seen in Pecos City in west Texas.

Finally Sam left home and went west, worked for the LFD outfit with Tom. Sometimes he would return home and Will Carver was always happy to see his old friend. Tom returned home on one of these excursions and with an inheritance he had come into, some $1500, soon headed westward again, and alone. At Pecos City he renewed his old San Saba acquaintance with Jim Miller, bought himself a fine black suit, black hat, and sported a neatly trimmed mustache and settled down for a short go at being a gambler. There is a picture in the famous N. H. Rose Collection, showing a saloon scene in Pecos, with Jim Miller sitting at a gaming table, and in the background at another table, a handsome gentleman gambler figure that some say is a perfect likeness of Tom Ketchum. Soon tiring of Pecos he headed for northern New Mexico, to the new town of Clayton, and probably spent more of his money. Then he wandered on out through New Mexico, into Arizona and in a few weeks of playing the part of the loser, the high roller, his money pouring forth

11

like water, he had soon "thrown the helve after the hatchet" and was dead broke. His last days of the full-handed spending of his money, were spent in Phoenix and Yuma, Arizona.

Now broke, down and out in a strange town without friends, the heretofore elegant cowboy gambler, turned gentleman, was "on the town." He soon sobered up and took stock. He returned to the only life or work that he knew. Working awhile here, and there, he finally made his way back home to Tom Green county. He worked awhile on the ranch owned by Jonathan Miles, founder of the town of San Angelo, pioneer cattleman and railroad contractor. Jack Miles, son of Jonathan, worked on the ranch with Tom Ketchum. Finally he climbed his cow pony, strapped a blanket, slicker, coffee pot and skillet behind the saddle and headed east towards San Saba. In the small settlement of Lohn he Arbuckled at Morgan Stacy's store, headed south the few miles to Cow Creek and Cow Gap, astride the old cattle trail that Tom Ketchum knew so well. What he did during these several months it is not known, but he evidently did spend some time there at the old hideout beside the creek. He finally drifted down to the old home country around San Saba. At this point, it may have been that he was arrested for disturbing the peace as reported by Sheriff Shields, or for the killing of Powers, as reported elsewhere.

He may have included in his itinerary as a transit, the Sandies country, Gonzales county, Texas. As a young boy, I remember old timers around Nixon, talking about Tom Ketchum having worked around Nixon, in the very same area that Carver had worked later as a horse breaker. The point is of no significance except my early day informants had described a darkly dejected, deeply moody young man, tall, dark haired, of shaggy beard, who when in his cups vowed he was headed for hell anyway and anyone could easily hasten the end of the journey.

This was to be the start of his wandering, not the wandering of an itinerant worker, but the frenzied, horse killing change of scenery, almost daily, for the coming years was to so characterize his entire life from then on. He was to become the most active highwayman that the west has ever known or ever will know. Whether he was merely a good old cowboy, whether he broke horses or men's noses while in Gonzales county, is not known. He was little known by the towns people, but an old timer, or two, remembered the dark brooding eyes, the go-to-hell look, and the fatalistic attitude that was to mark him in the years to come. He soon disappeared, just like hundreds before him, and afterwards.

Back to Knickerbocker he picked up his brother Sam, their travelng gear, and they headed south. Freshened up a few days at brother Berry's place and moved on to the west, into the alkali flats of the Pecos River. It is said that as they paused on the high plateau overlooking the valley in which the Old Fort Lancaster ruins lay, there at the start of the steep Lancaster grade, Tom had vowed that this was his kind of country. Down the steep grade, they headed up river to the Horsehead crossing, then turned northwest, the hundred miles to Pecos City, "his kind of town."

It was in 1881 that Pecos Station had been established as a stop on the Texas and Pacific Railroad and for miles in every direction the railroad was to claim ownership of the land, the millions of acres of Texas land given to railroads for the building of these routes. There in that level to broken plains, the land of little rain, the town sat astride the railroad tracks, attracting land promoters, land hungry pilgrims, cattlemen and railroad camp followers. When the Ketchums rode into Pecos City, a railroad was building north from Pecos to Eddy, now Carlsbad. The Pecos Valley Railroad, nicknamed the "Pea Vine Railroad". W. L. Kingston, the grand old cattleman of the Davis mountains, had formed his bank a few years earlier. W. J. Mosely's hotel was headquarters for land prospectors, immigrants and cattlemen. Pecos was a town of about five hundred people

and in the near vicinity there was little opportunity
for straggling cowbys. The Ketchums are said to have
worked for the Halff brothers for awhile, then moved
on north to the new railhead town of Phoenix, a mile
south of Eddy. Here were the prostitutes, the card
sharks, outlaws, and camp followers, and some law
abiding citizens. It was here that Lon Bass, Martin
Morose, Jim Miller held sway. Later Phoenix was to see
John Wesley Hardin in his short rise, and rapid eclipse
in El Paso.

Tom convinced his brother that they should move
farther west, on to the Chisum range and there they
worked for awhile. In time they migrated to the cattle
country around the new town of Clayton, where they
were known, had worked before. There, near where the
states of Texas, Oklahoma and New Mexico join, they
worked again for the Prairie Land Company. It is not
known whether they worked on the Cross L spread at the
old Hall ranch, at the new headquarters ranch, on the
Cimarron, east of Folsom, but it is reasonable that they
first got work at the Beatty ranch holdings of the company, located southwest of Clayton, for Tom was seen in
that town often. Bob Haley was the wagon boss there,
Al Ferguson was the wagon cook. While there their camp
was near the head of Pinabetas Arroya, as well as near
the mouth of Leon Creek. It was there that only two years
before some fifteen thousand head of cattle had been
brought in by roundup by only twenty four cowboys. The
cattle were from the Colorado and Cimarron ranges and
were being moved back to the home ranch. Old timers
say that in this huge roundup and drive there were
brands seen belonging to PCC, W. L. & C. and the Mus-
catine company. When the Ketchums were employed by
the company, this time, Murdo McKenzie was the head
man for PCC.

Then, sometime later, Sam returned to Tom Green
county and Tom stayed on with PCC, spending his spare
time in the saloons of Clayton, telling all who would

listen of his experiences. This while drinking, when sober, he was quiet and moody. It may have been here that he gained the reputation of being a train robber, for it has been repeatedly said, in print and via the spoken word that he and Sam had robbed trains in west Texas, one for the unbelievable tune of $100,000. It is doubtful that his cowboy friends believed the rumors for Tom was living the life of a cowboy, spending the money of a cowhand, and drinking it up, like the rest.

Back at Knickerbocker, Sam found young Will Carver going around with Laura Bullion, spending a lot of time with the Kilpatrick boys over at The Hills It was then that Sam decided to open a gambling concession in a saloon in San Angelo. With the drifting away of the gambling fraternity after the closing of Old Fort Concho, he felt that there would be opportunity for those who stayed on. He felt that he would like to settle down, and he took Carver in as his partner in the undertaking.

They may have done well if trouble had not come hot-footing it into their place one fine day. District Court records did not indicate that Carver was charged wih a killing in the county during those days, but the most general theory of his leaving town was that he had been "abused by a local bully and had to kill him in self-defense." Knowing something about the nature of Carver, considering that he was just "a good old cowboy", real quiet like, tended to his own business and was not inoffensive generally, it could be that if he had been "abused" by "a local bully", that if need be he could have started a boring contest with a pair of single action Colts. So, may it be, if he did kill anyone then it could easily explain the closing of the Ketchum-Carver enterprise, and the reason for Carver hitting the owl-hoot trail.

Tom Ketchum, the roving cowboy was home, home from the Cimarron Seco, home from his travels, with a pocket full of money, and he had not received a new inheritance. When told about Carver's difficulty, if such

15

was the case, Tom rode down to The Hills and as an old timer in west Texas said: "He was persuaded by Ketchum that he did not have a chance at trial". A casual search of records did not bring to light any indictment against Carver for m u r d e r, but newspaper sources do agree that about this time Sam Ketchum and Will Carver joined with Tom Ketchum, for his return trip to New Mexico.

CHAPTER III

"Black Jack"

To attempt to list or record a good portion of the crimes committed during the 1890s through 1900, and laid to the hands of Tom Ketchum, and or his band, would be impossible. Quite a few of these incidents can be elaborated, for what it may be worth. Since all writers concerning themselves with the Ketchums, mainly relate the events attached to the robberies of the Colorado and Southern trains near Folsom, New Mexico, but some do mention bits of information about other robberies, robberies that "someone" was respnosible for. In all fairness, I must state that in the case of the Ketchums, never have I seen such a lack of recorded facts, indictments, charges, etc., that do characterize the cases of other prominent outlaws. Officially, the Ketchums, and their men, were actually officially charged with few crimes. Most were based on presumption, etc.

First, I must give some idea as to what the Ketchums were up against if they decided to start robbing railway trains. Outlawry and gunfighting had been in it's prime, those years before these boys had hit the trail.

When 1890 came into focus, an entirely new bunch of actors were to appear upon the stage, actually the last acts of the theme of gunfighting and outlawry, as we have come to know it, were then being assembled. In the mid-eighties it got so bad in New Mexico and Arizona the railroads brought their lobbies to bat and endeavored to strengthen the laws concerning the art of stopping railroad trains for financial gain, and illegal gain at that. The result was a new law, established by unanimous vote, that gave the law the strength it needed, the death penalty for anyone who would "assault any train, car, or locomotive with intent to commit robbery, murder, or any other felony upon any engineer, brakeman, conductor, mail or express agent, or passenger."

The knowledge of this new law in the territories may have forced Tom Ketchum to lay off the railroads in the beginning, and to work on isolated mining stores, post offices and the such. J. Marvin Hunter of Bandera, Texas says that it was in 1892 that Tom Ketchum turned outlaw and it was in 1893 that he received his inheritance and blew it all in. That it was in 1895 that Sam Carver joined Tom. We have seen some mention that Sam had joined Tom in his forays the year before, when he returned to open his saloon in San Angelo. In black print one report states that the two brothers were responsible for the death of a merchant in a post office holdup near Carrizo, and if true, we must surmize that this incident took place near the old town of Carrizo, New Mexico. Nowhere have I found any record of such an incident.

How Tom Kechum came to take, acquire or have bestowed upon him, the name of "Black Jack", is equally as muddled as are some of the reports of the crimes laid at his door. It may be that none of these reports are correct, but I will give them here for the what it's worth department. There comes into focus the name of a man known as William "Black Jack" Christian. It has been reported, from several sources, that Tom Ketchum decided he would usurp this man's nickname.

Will and Bob Christian were from Texas and had gone into the Indian Territory with their well respected parents and settled at Violet Springs, what is now Sacred Heart, Oklahoma. This account states that Bob hit the owl-hoot trail at age twenty and some months later Will joined him, and that young Will killed a U. S. Officer Turner at "Four Corners". It was said that Will got ten years and Bob fifteen years and that in their escape from jail in Oklahoma City, an officer was killed. There may be some inconsistency in this for the writer reported that it happened around 1900. Other reports indicate that there was a Will Christian who was well known in Indian Territory, who was a fast shooter and a hard rider, and escaped from the law and came to Arizona. When winter came, often cowboys were layed off their jobs and only skeleton crews retained to do the chores around the ranches. Sometimes cowboys holed up in dugouts, cabins, and sat out the winter. Sometimes they turned to other jobs, and this is what Christian had done. He was such a good wood chopper in the Black Jack oak hills of the Chiracahua mountains that he was given the name of "Black Jack". He was a fairly portly man, must have swung a mean axe. This report has him killed in the fall of 1897 by a posse headed by Ben Clark, later sheriff of Graham county, Arizona. The battle was said to have taken place sixteen miles south of Clifton, and this would have placed it somewhere near that terrific canyon near the New Mexico line, and which is known as Black Jack Canyon. I've driven through same from the Mogollon district, into the Clifton area and don't remember over one or two houses in the area at this late day. It is a pinon, ponderosa and cedar country, desolate as all get out. Whether this name was given the place as a connection with Christian or Ketchum, I do not know. One writer did say that Tom Ketchum and his men had holed up there. This is a reasonable point of view for there is no more direct route from the Alma section of New Mexico into the southern portion of Arizona where Ketchum had been so prominent in his activities.

It has been said that with the publicity of the chase and death of Black Jack Christian, Tom Ketchum had sidled up to a bar and simply stated that he was to be THE Black Jack, and all the world would sit up and take notice of him. Marvin Hunter said in 1951 that Black Jack Christian had a reward on him totaling $6,000, dead or alive. He further said that Ben Clark, Charlie Paxton, Bill Hard and one Shaw had decided to capture the outlaw and went to a cave he occupied and the next morning a fight took place. It was supposed that the outlaw and two men with him had escaped but later he was found badly wounded and in a dying condition.

Another account goes along with the Black Jack Christian story so far as to say that he was run out of Cochise county, and was killed in the White Mountains of New Mexico by Arizona Rangers. Marvin Hunter had worked in Clifton a few years later, and has stated that the scene of the death of Christian was on the Williams ranch, near Clifton. Somewhere along the line I picked up the report that he was killed "by a posse near Globe, Arizona."

Joe Chisholm, in his book, Brewery Gulch, says that Tom hied himself into a Bisbee saloon and bragged all around that he would be THE Black Jack, would take his name from Christian who had operated in the Chiracahuas. This writer also mentioned that a "lady named Black Jack" had helped open the new saloon in Bisbee some time before and the saloon had adopted the name.

Father Stanley, in his book on outlaws of New Mexico said that since Tom was of "swarthy complexion, and often wore a black broadcloth shirt or suit and the cowboys were fond of nicknames, and had named him Black Jack." Or as someone said, he could have picked up the nickname from his success at the game of oblongs, by the same name.

Some say he liked the name and often bragged that

19

he would live up to it, yet on page 28, volume three of Frontier Times Magazine, there is an account that mentiones the fact that when he was once called Black Jack, he drew himself up and announced that: "My name is Thomas E. Ketchum." He often claimed that he was not THE Black Jack, that everyone had so often heard of, but was just a cowboy trying to stay out of trouble.

At this late date folks are still all mixed up as to who was called "Black Jack", and who was not. A picture book published some time ago by a New York concern, goes so far as to identify Sam Ketchum as Black Jack and brother Tom just plain "Tom". In any event, at the time we are approaching, the start on the road to outlawry by the Ketchum boys, Black Jack, or Tom, was certainly a commanding figure. He could have acquired the name from his dark good looks. Joe Chisholm said that he was a "most spectacularly picturesque outlaw." Another early account said that he had eyes so penetrating that they could "Bore through a stone wall". Everyone agrees that he was fairly "large of stature", swarthy, in a dark and appealing manner, and a two gun man, who was equally adept at using his arms in either hand at will. He had black eyes and hair, a black mustache or beard as the case may have been. He was six feet tall and weighed at times 180 to 200 pounds. During and after the days at Clayton in the early 1890s, he was a character of bluff chivalry, often given to rough humor, sometimes boastful and at times nearly ridiculous but game to the backbone.

He and his brother were good cowhands as per the report of former Governor James Hinkle, of New Mexico, who said that although they had not worked for him around Clayton, they were often at his wagon for grub, Arbuckle, and for just plain talk. Clayton was but two years old in 1890 when Tom showed some of his brand of humor there one day. He had hid himself behind a pile of cross ties near the railroad station and as the engineer bent over to oil the drivers, Tom let him have it with a bean shooter. Rushing back into the saloon, he was exclaiming that he had "beat him to the draw!" The railman felt it was the better part of valor not to chase the cowboy.

CHAPTER IV

The Charge Of The Robber Brigade

It has been said that Black Jack and his band were responsible for over half of the holdups effected in New Mexico and Arizona during the years up to 1900. If this is true then this band will certainly find a place in history as the most active and notorious robbers and highwaymen ever to ride the American west. I do know that this man and his various associates did crisscross the states of Arizona, New Mexico, southern Colorado, and western Texas many, many times. You can hardly put your finger on the map and not touch one of those areas where there is either evidence, report, or rumor, showing that he, some of his band, or his associates had not operated around there. That Black Jack knew more about the back ways and the byways of these sections than any man before him, possibly afterwards, there can be little doubt.

In 1949 an old man died near Socorro, New Mexico, was said to have been an old time rustler, possibly the son of a wealthy ranch family of west Texas. It was reported that he had said on his death bed that Black Jack Ketchum was responsible for the deaths of Albert J. Fountain and his little son in the White Sands of New Mexico, in February of 1896, and which crime or disappearance has not been solved to this day.

A correct timetable of the forays of the band would

be utterly impossible to construct. Of the few writers who have attempted to sort his all out, in the articles and stories published over the years, in the most they deal mostly with the robberies of the Colorado and Southern Railroad in north eastern New Mexico in the late 1890s, as well as his ultimate execution at Clayton. Often these accounts have made some mention of certain events, but often the cart has been placed before the horse, with the wrong chronology, places and dates, if any.

One reports merely that Ketchum was in on the robbery of a store near Liberty, near the present Tucumcari, N.M., and responsible for the death of storekeeper Levi Herstein, who with others, had taken the trail after the robbers. No date or details is given. Another reports that Ketchum, whose identity was unknown at the time, had appeared on the Bell ranch near Liberty and that "the proprietor Levy Herstein, riding in pursuit was killed as he neared their camp." No one doubted that Black Jack was the man they sought, yet no one caught him, nor was he indicted for the crime, as far as I have learned. There were two men said to be in this robbery so it may have not happened before 1895 as is believed. Sam and Carver came west with Black Jack at that time. Another account gives more of a picture and names Ketchum as the killer, with the report that Herstein "reached for a gun, a foolish thing to do as the desperado had the bead on him. Exit Herstein."

Our next report in the supposed itinerary of the Ketchum band, was the robbery of a train near Grants, New Mexico. This is all I have heard on this matter. Another report has three men of the Ketchum's description who were seen ten miles north of St. Johns, New Mexico. Joe Pearce, Arizona Ranger, stationed at "Springerfield, Ariz.," said in later years that he met Black Jack and his gang there. Said there were four in the gang. "The next day they killed two young men who were trailing them—Frank LeSeur and Gus Gibbons." Perhaps he referred to Springerville. The Arizona Rangers were

22

organized some years later.

Next comes the report that the band robbed and killed two clerks at Camp Verde. Then the report of the robbery of the Resolute Mining Company office near "Ash Fork," July 30 or 31, 1896. This was reported in the San Angelo Standard of August 1899, in a story giving some sort of rundown on their activities. Then, the next day or so they showed up at the Hulaupi Mining Company near Kingman, and according to the same account several employees of the company store were confronted by four cowboys who asked to see some saddles. "One was bearded, a tall, dark complexioned fellow with deep set eyes, and mammoth tattooed stars on his hands, went about the store searching for money." They found $1400. "Jake A. Bishop, one of the storekeepers resisted and was stabbed to death." This article also told about the robbery at Ashfork, a day or so before.

If this was the same band, and the Ketchum band at that, they were really traveling fast, losing no time. If this was a factual account of their crime schedule then there is no doubt that they headed west from Clayton, knocking off anything that looked good, and easy. At Kingman the trail had turned south for the next account, in the Tucson Citizen of August 6, 1896, reported an attempted robbery of the International Bank at Nogales, which must have happened between the time they left Kingman on August 1st and before August 5th, the day before the paper came out. Fast travling, if you will check the distance between Kingman and Nogales.

The book Kill or Be Killed, by the writer, quoting L. D. Walters, it was said that Black Jack, Sam, Bill Carver and a man named "Spindel", and Cole Young, had ridden into Nogales and held up the bank. One report said that the robbers got away with sixteen thousand dollars while another stated that they got nothing but bullets for their trouble. One witness to the robbery was said to have recognized the above named men. The Tucson Citizen said "an unsuccessful attempt of five mounted Americans to rob the bank failed." Still another report said that. "President Dessort of the International Bank had mule headed notions of his own about how business was going to be run and he put up one whale of a fight right from the jump", and further that although wounded, the president stood the band off until help came, and the gang went on their way.

Actual evidence, as well as newspaper reports indicate that the five men escaped toward Calabasas to the north, then back tracked, turned southwest toward Lochiel and then crossed into Mexico. A Texas newspaper reported that during the robbery or attempted robbery of the bank, "over a hundred shots were fired in three minutes as the outlaws escaped up Los Animos canyon." This report concluded that Black Jack stole the Pima county sheriff's horse and on which the latter rode towards Mexico. It also reported that Cole Young was also known as Cole Estes.

The gang rode southeast to their hideout a few miles east of the mining town of Cananea. Here they had a fort which was constructed of logs and stones. It was located in the mountains surrounding the town, was well watered and offered a welcome retreat from the heat of the Arizona summer. Nothing was known of their activities while there but the record indicates that on August 27th, about three weeks after the Nogales fiasco, they were in Skeleton canyon, Cochise county, Arizona. This was near the same spot where Old Man Clanton, whose sons were central figures in the war between the cowboys and Kansas gunfighters around Tombstone some years earlier, was killed by smugglers. The Black Jack gang were camped there in Skeleton, taking it easy. On August 29th a posse out of Tombstone and Cochise county, were scouting the mountains and as Deputy Sheriff Burt Alvord of Cochise stuck his head up over a ridge, he was hailed from a distance by Black Jack, who taunted the sometimes officer, telling him he would "make daylight through that square head", if he would stand a little higher. Alvord declined to fight and smart decision it was although Burton was not famous for his quick thinking. Ketchum cursed him for a coward and Burton and former Slaughter cowboy Billy Hildreth, retired.

The gang then moved on to Mud Springs, then over the ridge up into the mountains. Sheriff Fly of Cochise county was told about the encounter by Alvord and Hildreth. Alvord was formerly a deputy under Slaughter, later worked under Sheriffs Fly and Wakefield. In 1899 he was implicated, while a deputy at Wilcox, in train robbery with Billy Stiles and Bill Downing, alias Jackson, who was said to have been the one who escaped the battle at Round Rock, Texas in 1878 when Sam Bass was killed.

Fly's posse trailed the band to their old camp at Mud Springs, then far into the mountains where a pitched battle was held. It was here that border rider Robson was killed in the flurry of gunfire. The outlaws escaped to the east, after Black Jack took Fly's horse and then had to mount another when it was shot out from under him. They headed up the west side of the Chiracahuas and were reported to have left some stolen horses "for the owners" near Dos Cabezos. September 17th they were seen near Wilcox, riding horses with the 96 brand, six men in their party, including Carver, Sam and Black Jack.

Now the gang was soon to split. Argument caused hot tempers to flame, as they neared the old hideout in the San Simon country, Rustlers Park. Here they were quiet for a while. Raids had been made in parts of the two states, so wide apart that one gang could not have been in both places at the same time, and these raids were attributed to the Ketchum gang. On October 8, 1896 part of the band, led by Cole Young, alias Estes, attempted to hold up the Atlantic and Pacific train about thirty miles southwest of Albuquerque, at Rio Puerco. Tom, Sam, Carver, and possibly others were holed up in the San Simon. Prematurely, the brakeman on the train had learned that the robbers were riding the coal tender and when found out Young was said to have taken a shot at the trainman. The conductor, hearing the shots, stopped the train and U. S. Marshal Loomis opened fire and killed Young as he was taking a shot at the brakeman. The reward for the dead man amounted to $3000. Evidently the rest of the Young group escaped from the scene.

While it is generally believed Black Jack and the rest of the gang were holed up in the San Simons, a robbery attributed to the gang ocurred October 28, 1896 when the stage was robbed between White Oaks and San Antonio, New Mexico, right down in the old Billy the Kid country. If Black Jack was in Arizona and some of his band robbed this stage, it could have been a portion of the group who had left under leadership of Young, and after Young was killed by Marshal Loomis at Rio Puerco. The stage robbery occurred as the stage approached Red Mountain station in the San Andres mountains. The old Jim Greathouse ranch, of Billy the Kid days was located some miles north of White Oaks.

Just about this time, the post office at Separ, New Mexico was robbed, just some twenty miles east of the old mining own of Shakespeare, former hideout of the old San Simon gang. Black Jack and his band were often referred to as the new San Simon gang, for their number two hideout during those days was at Rustlers Park, used for years by the owlhoot trailers. Number one hideout was near Cananea. Number three was in Black Jack canyon, near Clifton. A later hideout was on the ranch of respectable rancher Capt. Wm. French, at Alma, New Mexico, there in the edge of the Mogollons. Number four was the Robbers Roost in southeastern Utah, on the Green River, right there in the midst of our present day uranium activity. Number five, and I might add, their most desired hideout, was to be the cave faced with rock and logs, located high up in Turkey Canyon, off Cimarron Canyon, in Colfax county, between Ponil Park and Cimarron.

After the Separ robbery, if this group were guilty,

they holed up in the hills on the old Diamond A ranch, near present Hatchita. This brings to mind that if this was Black Jack's gang, then Broncho Bill Walters, alias Bill Anderson, the Texas cowboy, may have been along on this venture. He knew that country very well, had worked for the Santa Fe as a painter, then showed up in Cochise county. It was said that he participated in several train robberies. It was on the old Diamond A that he later met his death. Sheriff Shannon of Grant county, came down from Silver City and chased the band back into the San Simon. Black Jack again left stolen horses at a ranch, for the "owners", remarking that he was an "honest horse thief.".

If reports can be believed, the band returned to the San Simon country and then held up the post office at the town of the same name, on November 3, 1896. It is not clear whether this was station holdups or post office holdups, but San Simon was on the Southern Pacific, on their back tracking from Separ, on the same line. If the group stayed by the railroad on their return to Arizona they would pass through the towns of Lisbon, Lordsburg, Pyramid, Summit Siding and Steins Pass, the site of a train robbery the following year. They were pursued into or towards the Sulphur Springs Valley. They were known to be hiding there on November 11th. It was there that they had been joined by two more men, one Hays from McCulloch county, Texas and one Davis of San Saba county, Texas.

The next report indicated that two strangers, cowboys, rode up to the depot at Huachuca Siding, near the fort of the same name, quite a distance from where the band was supposedly holed up, and robbed the railroad agent. It makes one wonder, such a distance from where they were last seen. It was said that this robbery was done by Black Jack and one known as Jesse Williams, alias Jeff Davis, Jesse Johnson, whose real name was said to be George Musgrove, a twenty-two native of Texas. He was of light complexion, had a round, smooth face.

Anyway, shortly after the San Simon post office raid, a band which was supposedly Black Jack's men, rapidly hit the post offices at Bowie, fifteen miles west of San Simon, and then doubled back to rob the agent at Deming. Things may have been tougher around Deming for the gang immediately doubled back along the rails toward the west, and the San Simon. They were said to have been seen hiding out on Squaw Mountain when Steve Birchfield and his posse had a savage fight with them there. During the fight, one of the outlaws accidently killed one of his own group. Birchfield's family were old settlers of Turkey Creek, Uvalde county, Texas. The father had been wounded while serving the CSA in Arkansas. He was later an Indian fighter in Texas, armed with a Sharps rifle and a six shooter. Walter Birchfield, perhaps brother or kin of the aforementioned, later in 1900 was with George Scarborough when they had a battle with Will Carver and his group near the old Rustler's Park hideout and in which battle Scarborough was wounded and died of exposure. A Walter Birchfield, according to the Tombstone Daily Prospecter of January 14, 1889, and a group of cowboys of the Chiricahua Cattle Company, was in a fight with Mexican sheepherders of Don Pedro Montano on Bonita Creek in Graham county, near Solomonville. The paper stated that all but one of the herders were killed, Birchfield wounded, and that within six months all had either been acquitted, dismissed or not filed on.

But back to Black Jack and his band. On November 19, 1896 a band of men were known to have been holed up in the San Simon and according to cowboys in the vicinity, Will Carver was among them. On November 27th they were camped about sixty miles south of Separ on the Diamond A range. They were said to be Black Jack, Hays, Williams and Carver. Where Sam and Bronco Bill were, is not known. They were jumped by a posse and in the battle were chased to a place near Antelope Wells where they again dug in and entered into a pitched battle. Carver was conspicuous in this fight and was well remembered by the posse men. In this battle Hays was killed and Williams was wounded in the leg.

Black Jack's band and others, had kept things humming all over the two states area. After having made a complete swing across northern New Mexico, from Clayton through Liberty, Grants, St. Johns, Camp Verde, Ashfork and Knigman, they had turned south down through Arizona to Nogales and south into Mexico. Then back in Arizona, for two months had terrorized the southern portions of both states. Officers were in the field everywhere. They had been playing the game of strike, then run and hide, but now Federal troops had moved into action, being ordered from Forts Bayard and Grant.

Now Black Jack again advised that the group split up. Bronco Bill with several followers had gone his way. Jefferson Davis Milton, the Texas lawman, then a railroad detective, had been interested in the gang for some time. He was born in Marianna, Florida, November 7, 1861. Was the son of the later Governor of Florida. Milton made his first trip to Texas at sixteen years of age, in 1877. He worked first in Yarboroughs store in Navasota, then traveled on out to Fort Griffin to work for Billy Barry, nephew of old Buck Barry. In July 1880 he joined the Texas Rangers, spent a number of years in west Texas. Was in El Paso when the Hardin-Selman-Scarborough troubles were in full force. He was kin to Scarborough by marriage. Had once said, "I never killed a man that didn't need killing. I never shot an animal except for meat."

The fact that Jeff Milton was after the gang seemed to increase Bronco Bill Walter's temperature. After leaving Ketchum Bill sent word to Milton that he was holed up in the White Mountains and that he would appreciate it if he would bring him some blankets, horses and food, as he liked "to live in comfort." Taking up the bluff, Milton, with Eugene Thacker, George Scarborough and a man named Martin, went by special train to a point near Holbrook, Arizona, where it had been expected the gang

29

would attempt the robbery of a train. Nothing happened. Next Milton learned that the small band had robbed the patrons of a dance and had fled across the mountains to the vicinity of the Double Circle ranch in the White mountains. The posse trailed them and in a pitched battle, Bronco Bill was badly wounded by Milton and his men. He was found the next day in the bushes, was taken to Santa Fe where he finally recovered. Tried and found guilty of robbery, he was sentenced to life in the penitentiary. He served time at Santa Fe until 1917 when he was pardoned. He then went back to south-western New Mexico where he went to work on the Diamond A ranch near Hatchita. Some time later he was killed when he fell from a windmill which he was repairing. It was said that he lead a respectable and law abiding life as a cowboy.

CHAPTER V

Hideouts and Sanctuaries

As the band split there was left in the original band, Tom and Sam Ketchum and Will Carver, the three Tom Green county boys. Winter was coming on and Black Jack felt that they should again split into singles and hole up as cowboys if they could find jobs. He had always gone his lone way to a ranch near Kingston, New Mexico and it is believed that he again wished to go there, alone. Will professed an interest in returning to Texas for Christmas but Tom would not go home. The outcome was that probably Will returned to Texas and Sam stayed with his younger brother Tom and rode north with him, trying to beat the approaching snow storm. They skirted the western side of the Peloncillo mountains, turned east into the dark looming mouth of Black Jack's canyon. High in the pinons and pines they made camp for the night. It was cold in the mountains and during the night the first heavy fall of snow whitened their bed rolls. At Mule Creek they Arbuckled and tobaccoed-up and then pushed on east. They turned north at the San Francisco river, towards the Mogollon or Coney Mining District.

Captain William French, English born rancher on the San Francisco, a few miles north of the small mining town of Alma, Catron county, New Mexico, had just returned to his ranch from Silver City. He had just settled down to an evening with his pipe, with the early dark that comes on snowy evenings in the mountains, reading his mail and newspapers, when he heard a hallo from the gate. Investigation showed two bearded, travel weary gents, their worn-out horses shivering in the early darkness. They were invited in and after being warmed and fed, invited to spend the night in the bunkhouse. Next day French asked if they would like to rest up a few days, spend the winter on the WS working as cowboys. They accepted. Captain French said later that although Sam and Black Jack had received his hospitality, when they left without warning the next day they took with them his best saddle horse, and one of his buggy team. He said they rode into Wyoming with the horses. There is some indication that they did not get that far, however.

If they did get as far as Wyoming it would have been a long and hard ride in the middle of the mountain winter. Mid-December found them in southern Colorado and it is believed that they spent Christmas at the old Robbers Roost and it was there they spent the winter. This outlaw hangout is located near Green River of Utah, and was one of the most isolated places in the country. It was a barren sort of country, little tree growth but did have a fine creek of water for the camp and was just the sort of country they desired.

In that area south of the town of Green River and

northeast of Hanksville they made their hideout comfortable as possible under the winter circumstances. Now the midst of the great uranium activity, one can only wonder at the thoughts and activities of the two Texas cowboys as they wintered in the bleak and cold surroundings. A dismal Christmas it must have been. But as is always the case, spring was soon to come and they were probably making new plans for life again in the sunny days and cool nights of summer in Arizona and New Mexico.

Things were also happening among the other bands of the outlaw combine of the west. In April, 1897, George LeRoy Parker, alias Ingerfield, alias Butch Cassidy, and another, one Ellsworth Lay, or Elza Lay, alias Johnson, held up the mining camp at Castle Gate, Utah and supposedly got away with $8000. Cassidy was a Utah cowboy that had turned rustler, highwayman and robber. He was born in Circleville, Utah in 1865; was five feet nine inches in height, weighed 165 pounds. He had blue eyes, sandy hair, and mustache if any. In time he was to operate in Wyoming, Utah, Idaho, Colorado, Nevada, Montana, New Mexico and Texas, as well as South America. He had been pardoned and released on a grand larceny charge at Laramie, Wyoming in 1896. He was to become the leader of the Wild Bunch. Elza Lay, who was to be known as "the educated robber," was said to be the brains behind the most successful of the Cassidy gang forays. He was a native of Texas, was about 34 years of age in 1896. Was five feet and nine and one half inches tall, weighed 165 pounds, also. He was of erect build, of light complexion, and with hair of a blondish brown. His mustache was sandy, had light brown eyes. Somewhere along the line he got himself "a mouthful of gold teeth". He was a quiet spoken man, courteous, and said never to be given to violence if he could avoid it, but was dangerous when cornered.

After the robbery of the Castle Gate mining office, the two had retired to a hideout at Powder Springs in

Colorado. Whether they were holed up there during the previous winter or were with the Ketchums at Robbers Roost in Utah, is not known, probably not. At Powder Springs hideout the two planned the organization of the "Train Robbers Syndicate" and it was evidently a success for afterwards Cassidy recruited other gangs throughout the west and southwest. Among these were the Lee gang, the Curry or Logan gang, and there was a connection with the Black Jack gang. This gave the band a spread over an area from the Canadian border to the Mexican border. The northern headquarters was at Hole-in-the-Wall, middle headquarters at Browns Hole, and the southern base at Robbers Roost, with the alternate southern hideout at the WS ranch at Alma, New Mexico, this unknown by the ranch owner.

When the spring of 1897 came upon the land of southeastern Utah, the Ketchums must have left their Robbers Roost hideout. It is believed that they started to retrace their steps back down ino New Mexico and Arizona. It is known that they were seen heading south in April from southern Colorado. It is believed that they approached the Cimarron canyon country of Colfax county, on their way south, possibly for a reunion with others of the band, via the north fork of Los Animas river. Then a few miles above the mouth of middle fork, turned south down the mining road that lead to Stonewall Park, and the coal mines. At Stonewall store they may have re-vittaled, bought grain, received instructions for their journey into the Cimarron valley. The most logical path would have been down the Vermejos river, through Maxwell's beef pasture, past Clay Allison's old ranch house and across the rolling lands to Clayton, if that was their destination.

But, since there is some evidence to indicate that they continued south, directly through some of the most formidable mountains in western America, it may be that they intended to meet by prearranged agreement somewhere near the town of Cimarron. Mining paths lead through the valleys and there were a number of mines that had been operated in earlier days, some now were operating. Perhaps they felt that they could pick up extra money in some of the remote mining camps, or some work, which ever the case may have been. After leaving Stonewall Park, they took the trail through San Francisco Pass, crossing the Colorado-New Mexico border line, right square in the Maxwell Land Grant, at the 9354 foot elevation and where the Astronomical monument stood, just to the east side of the trail. Black Jack later described this spot.

They journeyed down through the small mining settlement of Vermejo, on the Rio San Ricardo, then took the southeast trail down by castle rock, and Castle Rock Park. At Van Bremmer Park they may have experienced the smell of pinon fire, Arbuckle boiling, the sight of aspens, junipers, ponderosa, and the brilliant dying sunset as the bright orb laid down beyond Costilla Peak, which rared itself up there in all it's glory, for some twelve thousand feet. Perhaps they spread their bedrolls, talked over future plans, or may have fussed as brothers often do. Again on their journey they would turn west at North Canon, and take the upper trail into Ponil Park, by the old stamp mill, past the old dykes thrown up to furnish water for the mill, and into the little mountain sawmill and farming settlement. That they had been in the area, has been established by personal interview with an old resident of the area.

What they did at Ponil, how long they stayed, is not known. It is felt that they merely stopped to get grain, food and directions. They could have gone directly to Elizabethtown, then east into Cimarron canyon to the town by that name, but they elected to take the middle Ponil trail to the southeast. If you are familiar with the Cimarron canyon country, you will know that the Ponil drains directly through the middle of the northern section of the huge Philmont Scout Ranch and it was into this section that the two riders traveled. Baldy Mountain with its old mines lay to their right, or south and ten or twelve miles out of Ponil they would enter the south Ponil canyon, which would carry them on down by the Chase ranch house. Then, as now, the only way to travel through these mountains, was down the canyons. Just above the Chase house is the mouth of Dean Canyon, running almost due west at its start. It may have been in error, but here the two horsemen turned up Dean, to the west, instead of continuing down the Ponil to the open lands leading to Cimarron town. Up Dean a few miles there is the slightest evidence that another narrow canyon takes off toward the south. This is Turkey Canyon, and the Ketchums entered there, traveling down the canyon. If they did this by direction, it was a mighty rough road to travel for there was no trail, just the creek bottom. Higher and higher they rode, into the juniper, pine and pinon country. Several times they had to blaze trail around huge boulders that had crashed down the mountains, many years before, to block the narrow confines of the canyon walls.

The gang had been on Turkey Creeks, Turkey Canyons before, down in Cochise country near Rustlers Park, up in Utah near Robbers Roost, and in Texas. It carried a sort of nostalgia, this Turkey Canyon. Finally, as they made trail around a lone boulder, they freshened themselves and their mounts in a cool, clear pool of water, made possible by countless years of freshets tumbling down the canyon over the huge rock, digging the water hole at the base of the rock. In April it is often cool, sometimes cold, high up there in the pinons of Turkey Canyon. If you were to camp out in Cimarron Canyon, beside Cimarron creek, you would need plenty of blankets, patches of snow cling in the shaded places. You will experience the pangs of well feeling, breathing the crisp mountain air, the pinons and junipers smelling up the place all around. Just above their drinking place, on the south wall of the canyon they saw the dark mouth of a natural cavern. Upon exploration they found that it receeded into the face of rock some ten or twelve feet. The walls and roof showed signs of habitations over the years, human and otherwise.

My description of this cave in Turkey Canyon, Colfax county, New Mexico, fifteen miles northwest of Cimarron can be more readily understood if I told how I came to find the place, and describe my travel up the canyon. I did not enter the canyon as did the Ketchums for I came up canyon from the Cimarron-Taos highway. As I replaced the chain, locked the gap that opened onto the highway, I could see no evidence of a trail leading into the mountains, much less the open mouth of a canyon. But, as we ventured farther, climbed, soon the mouth of the canyon came into sight. Following the dry creek bottom of Turkey, we went through an area of igneous rocks, a seemingly burnt out section, for six years of drought had left its mark. As we followed the trail through the rough, rock-strewn canyon floor, the flora slowly turned from cedar, to cedar and pinon. Here, we skirted the canyon walls, then back down into the dry bed.

As we climbed amid the tall pines the trail looped around a ridge and we were in a cool, green mountain park, the ruins of a sawmill location near the edge of the pines. The air was sharper, sweeter, as the pinon and ponderosa filtered in on the breeze. The trail turned abruptly up the face of the west side, climbing into the rock bluff, to bypass the narrow canyon base. Here in the trail bed were signs of bear, droppings indicating the presence of wild mountain plums in the vicinity. We had traveled some seven miles up the canyon with only a mile or two to go. Now the coolness of the dark canyon with the towering pines and juniper smacks you in the face, the air is sharp, fresh to one from the lowlands. We pause in the trail, to get our bearings; far down the canyon we can hear the jays fussing over the bread we had thrown to them. To the r i g h t we s e e t h e slight trace of a narrow trail leading through the sparse grass, amid the huge trees and giant boulders. We climb up the trail, peer into the darkness of the forest and see that the canyon had narrowed considerably, so narrow that a horseman could barely pass through the rock slit between the towering walls. Then we see the cave, on the south face of the canyon, some twenty feet from the very same cool pool of water that the Ketchums had found those many years before. It was April again, only fifty-seven years later. Black Jack's cave sat there yawning in the mountain sun, the dark cavity showing against the brown green of the wall. First we drank of the cool waters of the hole, then examined the walls of the canyon adjacent to the pool. Here were the pot holes cut into the rock by human hands to hold the ends of logs for the pole corral. The poles themselves lay in a tangled heap beside the pool. This was the corral wherein the gang kept their horses and pack animals. Beside the same pool that Elza Lay was to start for water that July morning in 1899, to be dropped by a shot from an officer's long gun, which started the live or die fight between the gang and a posse of officers.

As we climbed the few feet to the cave we passed trees and fallen logs that to this day bear marks of that battle. We scramble over a sort of fence of fallen logs, the tumble down walls of the cabin front that had enclosed the natural cavern. Here was the remains of the breastworks behind which the gang held off the posse. Here are signs of the slugs from the rifles and forty-fives of the officers, as they beseiged the band. We scramble over the remains of the barricade, into the flat, smooth floor of the cave, a floor worn smooth by booted feet of men outside the law, bare feet of the red men before them, as well as of the furry bodied animals of the mountains. It is cooler inside the cave, high enough to stand erect. Here is where they hid out. There is where Black Jack may have slept, here is where Sam lay, near the door, on the look-out, while his unimpressed younger brother probably snored on his bed roll. On the rock patio out front is where they probably built their fires to warm the cave on those cool summer days, those cold winter nights. Here they prepared and ate their simple meals. Here they ate canned horse with a Barlow, speared peaches, sucked on canned cherrys, drank Arbuckle, just like thousands of cowboys had, elsewhere in the great west.

In this stronghold they could stand off a small army if need be, but here they were safe for the place was almost unknown, so isolated and remote. They could hole up without fear, they felt, but Sam worried for he was the worrying member of the band. How long they stayed in this wilderness abode, is not known but I do know that if Will Carver had had his way, it would have been as long as possible. It took some time to build their hide-out, prepare it for habitation and security, for there is evidence there of a lot of hard work. But, sooner or later they were to drift down the canyon and head west up Cimarron canyon, to Ute Park, down through Moreno Valley, over Taos Pass, into the town of that name, and south to Steins Pass.

By Black Jack's own admission, while in prison awaiting the death sentence, the band robbed the Southern Pacific train at Steins Pass, near the Arizona-New Mexico border, and in the area wherein they had the year before been on the rampage. It has been said that Ed Bullion, the cowboy from Tom Green county, Texas was killed in this robbery which came off in August of 1897. This is the only mention I have found that Bullion was with the band at any time. One writer said that he was killed by a shot fired by a Wells Fargo messenger, Jennings, while another said it was a man named Adair who fired the shot. Three men were arrested and sentenced to ten years each, in prison, for this robbery attempt. Their names were Leonard Alverson, Edward Cullen and Dave Atkins. In 1899 Tom Ketchum wrote the President of the United States, while being held in prison, that "William Carver, Sam Ketchum, Broncho Bill and I did the job. I have given my attorney these names and a list of what was taken and where same can be found. I make this statement realizing that my end is fast approaching and I very soon must meet my Maker. T. E Ketchum." Evidently the three men were released from prison.

According to the Pinkertons in 1900, one Dave Atkins was "wanted for train robbery and murder". Said to be a native of Texas, a cowboy and farm hand, Atkins was born about 1875. He was five feet, ten inches in height, weighed a hundred and fifty pounds, was dark complexioned and had dark brown hair and mustache, with dark grey eyes. The Pinkertons indicated that he was "wanted at San Angelo, Tex. for murder. $300 reward." We note that in Black Jack's letter to the president he did not mention Ed Bullion, but did mention Bronco Bill, who must have joined the gang again for this foray. Or it is possible that he had not yet left the band, as had been reported.

CHAPTER VI

The First Folsom Robbery

The next report indicates that the band had ridden hard from the bottom of the state to the north and had returned to the hideout in Turkey Canyon. To Henry Lambert's bar next door to the St. James Hotel, in Cimarron, they did next go. At the old St. James there had strayed such figures as Kit Carson, Maxwell, Dick Wooten, Clay Allison, Dave Crockett, Doc Holliday, and all of the prominent, and notorious men who traveled the Santa Fe trail, Cimarron offered it's hospitality to all. Black Jack and Sam may have eaten from the same table from which a few years earlier Clay Allison had eaten his roast beef, his horse Still Toes, eating his oats from the same table top.

To the north of the hotel was Maxwells Mill, still in excellent repair. Behind the mill was Maxwell's horse barns and corrals. Across the street from Lambert's was the livery stable, where only short years before had been the famous Swink's Saloon, where Clay Allison dallied with his victims. It was there in Lambert's where a few years before Dave Crockett had killed a number of colored soldiers, from the door of the bar, now a window in the dining room of the Don Diego Hotel. After eating the Ketchums must have walked around town, down by the old jail still in excellent repair, over by Wilcox blacksmith shop, back north by the sheriff's home by the river, past Maxwell's corral, the court house and to the hotel. Some say that it was at Lambert's place or the St. James that Black Jack planned the first robbery of the Colorado and Southern train at Twin Mountain curve, near Folsom, and executed September 3, 1897. Some say he was never in Cimarron, but Sam and the rest of the band were there.

There is some doubt as to whether the band rode from Turkey Creek canyon directly to Folsom for the robbery of the train, or whether they were in the vicinity of Clayton, and then traveled up the Colorado and Southern tracks to the site of the robbery. It has been said also that the band were not in full force at Cimarron and met at Clayton. If this was the case they must have gone by Springer, on their hundred mile trip to the east. At Rock Ranch, after leaving Springer, they would have crossed the Red or Canadian river. At Chico Creek they would branch off on the old Buffalo Trail which led on east via Pecks ranch, crossing the Carrizo Arroyo at Martinz, then past Rolling Mesa, down Perico Creek, by the Lee and Foster holdings, into Clayton town.

The next heard from the gang was when Black Jack climbed over the coal tender about 9 P.M. on the night of September 3, 1897, of the Colorado and Southern south bound train to Fort Worth. The band had made their plans

40

well, having taken the road out of Clayton to the north-west, and which nearly parallels the rails all the way into Folsom, where the U. S Land Office had been located. The road crossed the tracks at Mount Dora first, then again at Grenville, then swinging wide of the tracks to the north by Black Spring, it skirted Des Moines and the road then ran flat across the double horse shoe bends at Double Mountain, some few miles out of Folsom. Ketchum had studied the schedule thoroughly; had had a lot of experience watching the trains during his early years around Clayton. The group had camped near the curves for two days, watching the trains, and completing their plans.

Black Jack had been left afoot in Folsom and when Conductor Frank E. Harrington's Fort Worth Express had pulled out of the station, Black Jack was on the coal tender, a trick evidently learned from the Cassidy bunch. He climbed over the coal and down into the cab and covered the engineer and fireman with two revolvers. He instructed them to follow his orders. Upon leaving the station at Folsom, southbound trains had to immediately begin a long climb up the heavy grade which stretched some several miles through the several curves which was necessary due to the grade. The first wide bend, a double horseshoe, was about three miles from the station. It was there that the robber commanded the crew to stop the train. This was done and the engineer and fireman got down to uncouple the Miller-Hook coupling device, and were ordered to pull the locomotive and the baggage and express car on up the grade, leaving the balance of the coaches at the curve.

This was done and the other three robbers came into view and while Black Jack and a confederate dynamited the express safe, the others stood guard outside the car. Black Jack had already knocked the express messenger to the floor when he refused to open the safe. Conductor Harrington, left on the abandoned cars behind, started up the tracks to see what had happened, when he was warned off with a shot out of the dark. Brakeman Dixon

41

had already started on the run up the tracks towards Folsom, to report the robbery. One writer says the take was around $3500. while another says that the passengers (evidently on the stalled cars) were frisked and the total loot amounted to around $5000. Another report has it that the total loot was "a bag containing 500 silver dollars."

In any event, the robbers disappeared into the darkness as the engineer backed the engine back down grade and hooked onto the stalled cars. Then the conductor either ordered the train pulled into the little sta tion of Grande ahead, or backed into Folsom, for there are two different versions of this. It was reported that the band had escaped to "the Taos hills", some forty miles west of Springer and that after a few weeks, their money gone, they headed into the southwest. "Then occurred murders and train holdups on the Southern Pacific." It is felt that in this report, happenings of the year before were confused with the dates and times. This author says Harrington ran the train back into Folsom and telegraphed the sheriff of Union county at Clayton. Also said that the conductor stormed at everyone and no one in particular and drew little crowds in Trinidad as he rehearsed the robbery.

Those in the robbery were Black Jack, who according to one writer wore a "black suit, black shirt", which would have hardly been proper for the road, his brother Sam and Will Carver. It was said that a fourth man was along. Some say this man was Harvey Logan, alias Kid Curry, who had at times worked with the Curry gang, Cassidy's Robbers syndicate, and later Ketchum's wild bunch. This must be in error for the records indicate that Logan was in the Deadwood jail; did not escape from that place with the Sundance Kid, until October 31, 1897, after the Twin Mountain robbery of the C & S. Others have ventured the opinion that number four man was Camillo Hanks, alias Deaf Charley, but again the records expells this for this Yorktown, Texas boy was doing time at Deer Lodge, Montana for his part in the Big Timber Pacific train robbery of the early 1890s. If a fourth man was there, possibly Bronco Bill was, for in August, 1897 he had been with the band at the robbery at Steins, although it was thought he had already left the band. It could have hardly been Bullion, for he was reported to have been killed at Steins Pass. A straw in the wind, possibly when Will Carver had gone home for Christmas, he may have brought a new man back with him. But, possibly there were only three men.

The band fled from Twin Mountain, into the darkness, down the Old Freight Road, which ran down through the Prairie Cattle Company holdings, and turned off then to the west from the road. They passed below Laughlin Peak, where in 1955 uranium ores were found. Only a few hours ride from the scene they had intended to camp near the base of Laughlin but were flushed from the area by the sound of horses on the road. They decided to continue their night flight and rode furiously into the mountain area west of Dorsey, on around Tenaja Mountain, where they holed up for the night. This night flight was unnecessary for Sheriff C. M. Forker and posse had not taken up the trail until early the following morning. The next day they traveled at an easy speed to the Canadian, crossed near Crow Creek, followed the Vermejo Ditch through the Maxwell farms and through Maxwell beef pasture, some five miles north of Maxwell City. Down the ditch they rode, to the Cimarron-Raton road and then southwest until they hit the Ponil, only a mile north of Cimarron. They turned up Ponil, down Turkey, and came to their cave hideout.

It is evident that they holed up there for several months, having arrived about September 5th. Although they were in the vicinity for quite some time, there was no suspicion of their residence. Perhaps they made partial purchases of supplies in Ponil Park, and other isolated mining camps to allay any suspicion. Perhaps they seldom ventured out of the canyon. First, they must have posted their lookout at the head of Turkey Canyon, where it joins the Cimarron, a few miles west of the town of that name. While roaming the hills and mountains of that area I found remarkable evidence that the foregoing was true. Sheriff Forker had lost their trail, Deputy Sheriff Loce of Clayton had studied the country and came to the conclusion that they had holed up somewhere above Taos, but did not find them. Black Jack had well laid plans for insurance against surprise attack and this was by having an all day lookout posted at the head of the canyon.

CHAPTER VII

The Stone Face

Just west of Cimarron a few miles is a low cedar and pinon studded mountain, located on the Philmont Scout Ranch Properties, which was formerly owned by Waite Phillips. It was to the east brow of this hill that I rode with my friend, John Stokes. Skirting the edge of the hill is an old water flume which carried water to the lowlands. It is at this point on the mountain where there starts the growth of scrub cedar, and pinon. We were looking for a huge boulder on the face of the hill, on which was the finely chisled face of a human being, and which had been there as long as some oldtimers remembered. It had been referred to as "the Christ face," but little attention had been given to it. I was told that the remains of an old tree and wire corral was there. From what I found, and the photographs shown elsewhere in this book, it is felt that this was the lookout for the Ketchum band.

Quartering across the face of the hill, we sectioned

off the area. Scrambling over and around the huge rocks we finally came to one that was more prominent than the others. There on the east face of the rock, facing the town of Cimarron and looking out over the entire flatlands of northeastern New Mexico, was "the stone face". The sun was near square-up and it left shadows on the eyes, showing finely chisled features of a mustached man, the bust only. The figure seemed to be intently peering out into the rich Cimarron valley. One can see for many miles in three directions from this point. The valley stretching from Maxwells farms, down south towards old Rayaldo Mesa, could easily be surveyed by one man. The activity in the small town could easily be viewed, with the aid of glasses, as could any pursuit from Springer, and from the north.

As I gazed at the face my attention was directed to the eyes and was shocked; here was the most perfect likeness of Thomas E. Ketchum one could hope to find anywhere! Located here in this mountain wilderness, peering out over the valley of the Cimarron, the figure was startling. The hair line was just right, the well defined eyelids, the shape of the nose, the sweeping mustache and the well defined chin spelled none other than Black Jack Ketchum! The eyes, most certainly the mustache and mouth, riveted my attention. Yes, viewed from any angle here was the likeness of Ketchum. In the picture section you may compare the "stone face" with those of Ketchum, taken at Clayton.

I was elated with this find for in my many years of investigating the lives of gunfighters of the old west, few times have I discovered such interesting and little known connections with the past. Upon examining the rear of the huge rock I found remains of barb wire imbedded in the trunks of trees, showing where a small corral had been located. Here someone had picketed their horse or horses. A perfect lookout for those on the owlhoot trail. Digging under the old rock I found portions of old whiskey bottles, a small rusty lock, which had been cut in years past by the sharp bite of the file or saw.

The "stone face" is there now, looking out across the valley in silence, the eyes forever wide awake, the jaw firm, poised for the sign of men or horses on the trail in the distance. If this is the likeness of Black Jack, then it can be said that he never sleeps, his vigilance is constant. Who created this fine work of art? I do not know. Mrs. Mary Lail, longtime resident of the area did not know either. She had heard of the tale but knew little about it. Could this have been the work of some little known native artist, an uneducated cowboy-outlaw who chipped at the rock in the long hours of watch? Who knows?

Back to Black Jack's cave and the work to be done there. They worked in the cool morning sun, cutting trees, hauling them to the cave with which to build the cabin front over the cave. They cut and notched the logs, hoisted them up the slight incline to be placed in position. A doorway was made, the roof laid on. Rocks and stones were rolled and lugged into place, to form the barricade around the front of the cabin. The holes in the logs were chinked with small stones and clay. After the place was policed, they were finished. They could then loll in the sunshine before the cold night descended, curry their horses and the usual camp chores. They led their animals to the grassy parks for feed to supplement the grain ration, hunted for fresh meat, and rested in their primitive hideaway. They spent some time there.

CHAPTER VIII

The Texas Expedition

Why they decided to venture out of their hideout is not known, possibly it was that they had gotten only a little loot in their C&S robbery, and went again to replenish their funds. But, there is some slight grain of evidence that the Ketchums, as well as others of the wild bunch in the West, came from their hiding places for a more patriotic reason. I like to think that there is some possibility that the Ketchum band came out, wanting to join with the United States in our fight against Spain.

The war was approaching and Assistant Secretary of the Navy, Theodore Roosevelt, was preaching intervention in Cuba. He was made a Lt. Colonel, proposed to make up several cavalry units from cowboys of the west, to serve against the Spaniards. It was here that the idea of the Rough Riders was born. Oklahoma, Indian Territory, New Mexico and Arizona territories were assigned a quota of 740 men, later this was raised to 1000. April 25th, Governor Miguel Otero was asked how many New Mexico could offer and he replied that 340 men could be produced. Thirty men were to come from Union County, mostly from the Texas cowboys who were around Clayton, some of them old buddies of Black Jack. Some had worked for the Halls, with PCC and other ranches in the area. They had gathered in the Favorite Saloon in Clayton, talked it over.

During this campaign Tom and Sam Ketchum may have wished to join their old friends at Clayton and at the time they were in Turkey Canyon. It is said that some back trail riders wished to join for they wanted to be where there was a fight, others felt they could escape through assumed names, through the United States Army, some few may have been mainly patriotically inclined. Albert Thompson, who had the job of enlisting the men in the Clayton country, said in 1946 in his book on New Mexico, that one night he was called from the Favorite by a messenger and instructed to go to a nearby bunkhouse at the livery stable. There he met two strangers, brothers on the dodge. "They had ridden 66 miles from the Neutral Strip, where in a deep canyon lined with cedars and scrub pine, they resided." The two men were originally from Texas and said they wanted to join the Rough Riders. According to Thompson, they were told they could join and go to Santa Fe, with the others, at a later date. It has never been said that these were the Ketchum brothers, and the author of this report did know Tom Ketchum, in later years as he awaited his death at Clayton. The Ketchum brothers were hiding in "a deep canyon lined with cedars and scrub pine." But, not too probable.

If the brothers Ketchum had really wanted to join up with Teddy Roosevelt, they must have had pangs of remorse when they learned that of those joining from around Clayton were Otto Menger, Bob Parish, John Roberts, Joe Duran, George Detamore, Jack Robinson and Bill Easley. All these men participated in the battle of San Juan Hill. Possibly the Ketchums knew them all. One point that had a lot to do with the winning of the west from the outlaw and badman, was that when the western cowboy-soldiers returned from Cuba, China and the Philippines, they brought with them the knowledge that the Krag-Jorgenson carbines were fine guns to handle, better to blast holes with.

It may have been a coincident but after leaving the hideout near Cimarron, the band rode down through the Clayton country, while the enlistment excitement was going on, finally wound up in west Texas. But, when they reached that area, they had been expecting to get to San Antonio, and possible enlistment with Teddy Roosevelt there, the boys from Clayton were already on their way home, the was in Cuba over. News traveled slow in the early west, especially if one was on the dodge.

About this time a band started robbing trains in west Texas, were referred to as "that gang recently seen in west Texas." The San Angelo (Texas) Standard said in 1899 that Black Jack had lead the robbery of the Texas and Pacific train at Stanton and also the Southern Pacific at Lozier, both in 1898.

As they approached west Texas, their flight across New Mexico brought them through the counties of San Miguel, Guadalupe, Chaves and Eddy. The officers had evidently been alerted to this fact for Dee Harkey, veteran officer who had known the gang in San Saba county during their early youth, said in 1948 that about this same time he and the Lincoln county Deputy Sheriff, John Leggs, were following Tom, Sam and Bill Carver. The band seemed to be just ahead of the officers all the way down from Carlsbad into Reeves county, Texas. The two officers finally located the men on Toyah Creek, eleven miles south of Pecos City, near the north fence line of a tract of land owned by myself. The two officers returned to Pecos and wired Roswell for Sheriff Charley Perry to come and help them. Perry was on the T&P train out of El Paso, coming to Roswell via Pecos City.

Harkey got on the westbound train at Pecos, met the eastbound at Toyah, eighteen miles out and Perry returned to Pecos with him. They borrowed two carriages in Pecos and headed south across Salt Draw, toward Toyah Creek. Deputy Sheriff Cal Carpenter of Carlsbad had joined them at Pecos, making four officers in the group. When they reached the Toyah, the outlaws had left and the trail led south, towards the Fort Stockton-Van Horn road, some ten miles east of Fort Stockton. Darkness overtook the officers at that point and they made camp. Harkey stated that when bedding down, he discovered a handful of gold pieces that fell out of one of the officer's pockets and said that the man replied that he had nine thousand dollars in his pockets. The next morning, according to Harkey, they followed the band down into old Mexico, where they "put them in jail." Certain papers were required and he and two of the officers left to deliver the horses and carriages back to Pecos and he was to meet the fourth officer in El Paso, where they were to get the proper papers and return to Mexico for the prisoners. Harkey said the man did not meet him in El Paso and that he had gone to South America for the money was said to be tax money belonging to a New Mexico county. If Black Jack and his men were in jail in Mexico, they evidently either were released or escaped jail. Harkey did not elaborate on the final outcome.

It may not have been while the New Mexico officers were on their trail through west Texas but the band did camp on Timber mountain, in the extreme north portion of the Davis Mountains, where now is located the old ghost town of Madera Springs. If they were looking for a Texas hideout to rival the Turkey Canyon place, they had come to the right country. As they progressed up beautiful but isolated Madera Canyon, crossing over into Nations Canyon, then into Little Wahoo, they may have paused, or camped at the old bear hunters cabin located on that beautiful little stream and investigated the huge Indian painting that covers the face of the towering rock shelf. I have been here, and marveled at the huge painting, located hundreds of Indian signs. Surely, for ages before the white men, the Indians too had sought sanctuary in this hidden place. Mortar holes pockmark the granite boulders all the way up and down the stream bed; here the Indians ground their grain, tanned their hides, fished and hunted the bear, the deer and the antelope and spent the long idle winters. Possibly the Ketchums stayed here a day or so. They did proceed up one of these canyons, it may have been Nations, until they came out on the old ranch road connecting the old town of Fort Davis, and Valentine. There in the shadows of Sawtooth Mountain, they camped in OH Canyon. This road is now the famous Loop highway which circles through the Davis Mountains, starting at Fort Davis and returning to the place of starting. Near the take-off road to Valentine from the Loop, is the old Barrel Sprigs ranch of former Ranger Jim Gillett, bought some nine years after the Ketchum's visit to the country. A fine camping place they had too; it was close to El Muerto Peak, where is was said that Sandy King, Curly Bill, Jim Hughes and another man, had buried the treasures stolen from the treasury of Mexico and the churches of Monterrey, some fourteen years before. Even as Black Jack and his men were in HO canyon, men were searching for the treasure at El Muerto, as they are today. To their east the gleaming shafts of old Sawtooth, and Mount Livermore reared into the 8500 foot levels of the azure sky, to rival El Capitan, miles to the north.

The boys came into the old Fort Davis for drinks, a turn at the oblings, for supplies. It may have been that Black Jack came in for a shave or a haircut for there is a story that the local barber was working on a stranger when a local resident stuck his head in the window to say that he had heard "old Black Jack and his men is up in HO Canyon." As the story goes, the barber, a respected citizen, ready for a joke, raised the hot towel from his patron's face and the local resident took to the hills.

If the band had been jailed in Mexico, as we have already reported, either before or after their Davis Mountain experiences, they did come back into Texas for the Southern Pacific train was robbed at "Lozier". You will not find "Lozier" on the map but there was a small station there where Lozier Creek crosses the tracks, to empty into the Rio Grande a few miles south. This is in Terrell county, about twenty miles east of Dryden, some fifty miles from where the SP train was to be held up at Sanderson Draw, west of Dryden, and was to end

51

in death for Ben Kilpatrick and his companion. This happened in 1912. Still, some say that Kilpatrick was with the Ketchums at Lozier Creek in 1898, had returned fourteen years later, after prison, to try again. The amount of the robbery, if successful, is not known. Whether it was robbed by Black Jack's band, I do not know. But newspaper accounts reported in 1899 that the Lozier job was done by this band.

One account indicated the train was forced to halt for rail ties had been stacked on the track. Black Jack entered the express car, placed a huge charge of dynamite on top of the big safe and held this down by a smaller safe as they felt this latter one held the money. The blast blew the small safe through the car top and the gang climbed the hill, opened the safe and left. Actually $90,000 was left untouched in the large safe it was said.

As to train robberies during the 1890s; the SP was robbed near Valentine. Also, another train, this time the T&P, was robbed near Kent, north of the HO canyon, some thirty miles. According to Judge Barry Scobee, about this time Bill Bell of Valentine rented a room to two strangers, a man and woman. A stranger in Marfa spent unsigned bank notes. It was thought that the gold or silver taken in the Kent robbery had been hidden for they were too heavy to carry in haste on horseback. After the robbery a man was arrested and convicted of robbery; said he had hidden the loot beside a small hill, had left a dagger with the ends cutoff driven into the ground over the spot. He told George Newton and Sheriff Dave Janes about this. The money was not found. When the man was released from prison he came to Valentine and took a rifle belonging to the Bell saloon and left town hurriedly. Thirty years later the rifle was found lying beside the dagger, the loot gone. The man's saddle and jacket was found in a cedar tree nearby, the saddle dried and cracked from the years of exposure.

Now comes the report that Black Jack and his band robbed the Texas and Pacific train near Stanton, in west

Texas. Stanton was named a f t e r Lincoln's Secretary of War. The drought of the late 1880s had cut into the population of Martin county, which was located some hundred and seventy-five miles north from Lozier and about ninty miles from Tom Green county. Stanton, in 1898 had about four hundred population, did not have a newspaper. It is not known just how successful this robbery actually was.

Either before, or after the Stanton robbery, the band had been seen in various parts of west Texas, as far south as south Texas. The San Angelo Standard had said that Black Jack had led the assault on the trains at Lozier and at Stanton. The paper also reported they had been seen in Tom Green county, also at Lockhart. Detectives had traced them getting on a train at that place, destination supposedly Llano, but they did not find them there. Pinkertons reported that after this the band went to the Hole-in-the-Wall country, then back to New Mexico, with the law on their tails. But they did visit old and familiar places in Texas.

Now, if we are correct in assuming that the Wild Bunch did actually make this wide swing down through New Mexico, through the Pecos Valley of west Texas into the Davis Mountains, then into Mexico, or to Lozier to rob the train, they were taking their time out to visit old friends or to hide out after jobs. Upon leaving Lozier, the Sonora, Sutton county area would have been directly on their course towards home and Tom Green county. They were well known around that section, as cowboys. It was in Sonora that Carver was to be killed later.

In 1898, near Sonora there lived the Taylor brothers, Bill and Jeff. They were known to the Ketchums. Berry Ketchum had ranched in the area. It may have been coincidence but on June 9, 1898, the Santa Fe train, running from Brownwood to San Angelo had been held up at Coleman, at night. It developed that the four were well known in the Sonora country. Noah H. Rose, the famous frontier photographer had his photo tent there at that time; his old friend Marvin Hunter, was working on the Devil River News. Hunter wrote in 1926 that the men were the two Taylor brothers of Sutton county, Pearce Keaton and Bud Newman, and that Newman was the leader of the band. He said that they had covered the engineer, James Stanton, with rifles and revolvers, forced the fireman, a man named Johnson, into the express car. Johnson was forced to tell the express messenger, L. L. White, to open the door. Before White got the door open, W. F. Buchanan, the traveling live stock man for the railroad, had fired several shots at the bandits. The fire was returned by the quartet and in this fight Johnson was wounded. Two of the bandits were wounded. Newman was shot in the left arm and Keaton through the right leg. They rushed to their horses and made their getaway to the Taylor ranch near Sonora. Fireman Johnson was brought to Santa Anna, and there died of his wounds.

Veteran Sheriff Shields of Tom Green county, ever on the lookout for the Wild Bunch, got on the trail of the four Coleman robbers, from the paper from dynamite sticks which had been left at the scene. He learned that they bore the name of a Sonora store keeper. Shield headed the posse, with Deputy U. S. Marshal Hodges, Sheriff Lige Briant, and several deputies. It was Sheriff Briant who later killed Bill Carver in Sonora. At the Taylor ranch Sheriff Shields fired one shot with a borrowed rifle with a defective sight. The men were arrested.

According to Marvin Hunter: "Newman turned state's evidence and gained immunity for himself, but the others were convicted, Keaton and Jeff Taylor receiving a term of 99 years each in the penitentiary for the killing of Fireman Johnson, and each got eight years for attempting to rob the express car." But Bill Taylor had escaped from Brown county jail where they had been tried. He was captured. Again he escaped and it was then that his trail was to lead close to the trail of the Ketchums.

After his second escape Bill Taylor, joined by Bud Newman, headed down into the Devil's Sinkhole country of Edwards county. There, it is felt, they devised the plan of robbing the Southern Pacific westbound train near the Pecos bridge. The place of robbery was to be as the train pulled onto the world's highest railroad bridge, "The High Bridge," over the Pecos, between Comstock and Langtry, in Val Verde county, where old Judge Roy Bean was holding forth. Hunter said that Taylor was captured by Newman "who inveigled him into the hands of the authorities at Comstock under the pretext of making an attempt to hold up a west bound Southern Pacific rain." The plan was that one was to climb the tender at Comstock station, the other to await he train at the High Bridge. The actual arrest was made by Val Verde officers.

This all happened in mid- 1898, when the Wild Bunch were rampaging from north to south, in west Texas and then south to north, to Stanton. The expected attempt on the SP westbound was to be made by Newman and Taylor, only about forty miles from the site of the assault on the same train at Lozier Creek, by the Ketchums. If this is other than coincidence, it is not known. The Wild Bunch may have been looking for a respite from their travels at the Taylor ranch, and learning of the trouble leading from the Coleman job, the arrest at Comstock, may have headed north and for the Stanton job. They then headed west and north into the alkali plains and pinon studded mountains of New Mexico.

But concerning the Newman band: Pierce Keaton was raised in Kimble county, was a well liked cowboy in Sutton county. When he was given the long sentence, it was regretted by many who knew him. He served some seventeen years at Huntsville prison and was pardoned and returned to Kimble county to ranch. He later died at Bisbee, Arizona in the early 1930s. Bud Newman was a dapper individual, cowboy and rancher, was raised in west Texas, lived near Sonora. After the arrest of Bill Taylor in Val Verde county, Taylor again escaped, the third time. He was reported to have made his way into the cedar hills northeast of Sonora, near the head of the north Llano river. Also, it was there that Bud Newman went to capture him, on the agreement that if successful "all charges against him" would be dropped. It was said that in the fight there, Newman was killed and Taylor escaped to Mexico, later to return to Texas to live a quiet and respectable life. Taylor is not to be confused with the Sutton-Taylor feud days in south Texas.

It is not known where the Wild Bunch spent the winter of 1898. It is not inconceivable that they holed up in one of their safe hideouts. No longer could they work for ranchers as cowboys. Their supposed exploits were now too well known. Cowboy jobs in those days were scarce, especially during the winter months. Only the old hands were kept on during the winter months. On such huge spreads as the Prairie Cattle Company, where Sam and Black Jack had earlier worked off and on for some years, there would be hundreds of men employed during the spring roundups and during the summer, but with the coming of winter, only a skeleton crew would be kept to keep up with the chores. So hundreds, yes thousands, of cowboys holed up in dugouts, cabins, etc., for a winter of doing nothing. Some went back home, to warmer climes, where they got work during the cold months. During those days, the winter layoff in northern New Mexico, Colorado, Wyoming, etc., was to be dreaded. The cowboys stocked up on Bull Durham, Arbuckle, beans, meal and sidemeat and settled down for the winter. Some worked as wood choppers, and at other such jobs. But, many batched it. So it was with the outlaws, bandits and night riders, too. Some few pulled the "certificates" from the bags of Bull Durham, sent them in for a batch of the some three hundred paper backed books, given as premiums, and spent days "follering the print." Others got their winter reading from studying the labels on tomato, baking powder and Arbuckle cans.

CHAPTER IX

The Ketchum-Cassidy Gang Merger

Some say the gang went up into Colorado, or Wyoming, to the Browns Hole, Hole-in-the-Wall country. Some bearing on this might emerge if we outlined here some information on Butch Cassidy's gang, and what they were doing in 1898.

When one starts explaining the Cassidy band, actually made up of the remaining lieutenants of the Curry, Lee and Cassidy gangs, one comes across some most interesting names, as well as some trouble correlating the information available. After working with the information a significant fact is soon grasped. Nearly all of these men "took" their outlaw names from someone for whom they cared a lot, from some random meeting, or even a locality. In the case of leader George Leroy Parker, if Harvey Logan actually was not their leader, he got his name from his old rustler friend, Mike Cassidy. William McGinnis, or Elsworth (Elza) Lay, alias Swede Johnson, probably took his name from the little town of Lay, near the Yampa river in northwestern Colorado, near one of their hideouts.

Of the Logans, there were Harvey, John and Lon, who with their cousin Bob Lee, first used the name of Lee, then went in with rustler George Curry, adopted his name and became the Curry boys. Harvey liked to use the name "Kid Curry". At times he used other aliases, such as that he used later when he was with Carver and the Kilpatricks, down in Concho county, Texas, when Oliver Thornton was killed. There, and at Sonora, he called himself Joe Walker, picked from his dead, old cowboy buddy, of the same name. The first Walker was killed in Wyoming. O. C. (Camillo) Hanks, the DeWitt county boy, who came back with the gang after his release from prison in 1901, did not feel his given name well fit, so he called himself "Charley". When the occasion arose, he used the name of Jones for his last handle.

Harry Longbaugh, the original "Sundance Kid," so named by his companions as he had spent his teens at Sundance, Wyoming, had served a short jail term for horse theft. Harry liked to use another alias, "Harry Alonzo," and the type he was too. He had Grecian features, a handsome guy, but on the prod. Will Carver, used the name "George Franks," and while he lay dying on the floor of a grain store in Sonora in 1901, when asked by Sheriff Briant what his name was, he replied that he was one of "the Off Boys," a joker to the last. Ben Kilpatrick had to have a handle and since he was evidently in little trouble, just a good old Texas cowboy until he got in with Cassidy, Carver and Logan, was a tall man, became known as "The Tall Texan." When he was arrested in St. Louis, late in the day for the Wild Bunch, he was known as "Ben Arnold," and registered in hotels there as B. J. Rose, with Laura Bullion, as Della Rose.

In 1898 this romantic bunch of fellows felt the blow torch flame of the law on their tails, in Colorado, Utah and Wyoming. Most of them decided to lite a shuck and they did. The governors of these states, including Idaho, decided to bind together and exterminate the outlaw bands. Some said they would ask the President to call out the troops, but as the gangs moved south, this did not come about.

Cassidy and the gang had decided to make one last raid, a large one, and proceeded to enter into the largest cattle rustle I ever heard of other than the one down in Texas in the 1870's when thirty cowboys drove off some nine thousand head. Their raid did not succeed, however. Then, a man known as "Johnson," who headed the Powder River hideout, was said to have killed a fourteen year old boy, Willie Strong or Strang. Whether this Johnson and Elza Lay, who had at times used that name, were the same, it is not known. Johnson was captured near the hideout near the Ladore River, and taken to Rock Springs, Wyoming. One by one many of the various gang members of the "Syndicate" were either killed, or arrested. Cassidy, Logan, Longbaugh, and Lay got away, but they had the law thinking.

One writer said that after the troubles in Colorado, Wyoming and Utah in 1898, Cassidy "was not heard from until September 10, 1900, when with a party of four he held up the First National Bank of Winnemucca, Nevada, and escaped with thirty-three thousand dollars in currency." Rewards were posted for these men and as an extra inducement, "twenty-five percent of all money recovered," added to this. Many oldtime gunfighters and the young ones as well, began the chase. The large rewards added as the inducement. The mainstays of the Cassidy gang were on their way south, to Robbers Roost in Utah. They then went down into New Mexico. One report says that the members of the Ketchum gang had gone up into the Hole-in-the-Wall country, then back into New Mexico "to escape the law up north."

If this was the case, they probably came down the road with the Cassidy bunch, with the law yapping at their dragging tails. Other reports say that they "had gone into Colorado on forays." But, it is sure they were back in southern New Mexico and the gang split again.

Things were really hot, they learned after they had returned from Texas that nearly every lawman in the two territories was out hunting them. They could not decide together what they were to do. Black Jack's leadership was waning. I have found hardly any indication that they were very active after their trip back from Texas. Sam was leaning to Carver's advice that they head north, to a safer country. One of these places was the ranch near Alma, Catron county, New Mexico, as well as Turkey Canyon. Black Jack did not like this in the least. He and another man struck out alone. Later Black Jack left his partner and went to his favorite hideout on a ranch near Kingston, New Mexico. This was an old mining town in Grant county, formerly Sierra county, 35 miles via stage from the A.T. & S.F. railroad via Lake Valley. In the Mimbres mountains nearby, mines were shipping silver ore which a few years b e f o r e had brought $8000 the ton, silver ore that one could squeeze in your hand like putty. Black Jack must have had a place picked out there, where he could retire, unknown, alone and possibly work as a respectable cowhand. He may have wanted the others to keep away from his "good thing." He was the little-boy-old-shoe type of man, now on the outs with his older brother, and the others and with a definite "I'll show 'em" attitude, as we shall later see.

With Sam Ketchum went Will Carver, and a man known only as "Spiedel." Others say this man was Red Meadows, others say he was Red Pipkin. They headed north. Sam and the other man went on north toward Cimarron and Carver up the San Francisco River, towards Alma. Sam had good reason for passing up Captain Wm. French's WS ranch for in his book, Some Recollections of a Western Ranchman, French said that sometime earlier, Sam and Black Jack were visiting on his ranch, had received his hospitality, and when they left, took one of his best saddle horses and one of his buggy team. This has already been elaborated elsewhere. When the brothers Ketchum were later put out of commission by the law, French was happy. But not so in the case of the other members of the band.

Alma, Catron county, earlier Socorro county, was located in the Mogollon Mining District, northwest of Silver City. It was connected by stage with Silver City. The Silver Hill Mining Company had placed the Silver Bell on a paying basis again, the Consolidated Mining Company was operating the Merrit Mine. In this narrow valley through which Carver rode towards Alma, there between the Mogollons and the San Francisco range on the west, were a number of small farms where alfalfa, wheat and oats were raised, as well as garden vegetables, some fruit. Resumption of work in the nearby mines had helped create the demand for these products. There were large ranches spreading out from the valley. In 1882 there was estimated to have been nine thousand head of cattle in the some five million acres of grazing land in the country. In 1886 there were about seventy-five thousand cattle and these numbers have risen sharply in the years since. Sheep raising had decreased sharply from the 1880's. The old town of Alma now has five or six families, located on the river about a mile off the Silver City road. The French ranch is located about five miles north of town, now known as the Thatcher place.

One day as Captain French was sitting on his porch, a stranger rode up to the ranchhouse. He said his name was Tucker, an experienced cowman. Said he had worked for a rancher named Golden and who was known to French. He came highly recommended and was given the job as foreman, as most of the hands had recently left his employ. The WS ranch had been bothered by rustlers and Tucker seemed to be the man who could handle such a job to the advantage of the owner. He whistled another man from the drinking trough, introduced him as Jim Lowe. A third man was introduced as Billy McGinnis. Impressed, French agreed to take on all three men. It was later decided that the first man was unknown, but the latter two were George Parker, alias Butch Cassidy, alias Jim Lowe, and Wm. H. McGinnis, alias Ellsworth (Elza) Lay, alias Johnson, who had been raised in Texas. The last named was about 33 years of age, five foot, nine inches tall, weighing about 165 lbs. He was of erect build, of light complexion, light hair and mustache, light brown eyes and had "a mouth full of gold teeth."

Cassidy and McGinnis had supposedly robbed the UP train at Wilcox, Wyoming, on June 2, 1899, a month before. Cassidy was a little older, more talkative, less educated and his features were hard to mistake when French later saw a photo. So Tucker was French's foreman, Lowe his new trail boss and McGinnis his wrangler. French was evidently happy with his new hands. Tucker ran his job with a close hand. Lowe was the best man on the trail French had ever had and was always ready for a joke, and on the long evenings, his conversation was witty and stimulating. McGinnis was a good man and French said he had no one better at breaking

61

horses. Things went along fine for awhile, French never suspecting that his new hands were none other than whom they had said they were. Soon the few older hands drifted on and Tucker hired new hands to replace them. They came to the ranch in ones and twos, none seeming to have known the others prior to their coming. The cattle losses dwindled, the men were held in check by Tucker and Lowe. When they went into town, which was seldom, their paydays were spent hanging around the saloon, the store, talking good naturedly with the townsfolk and visiting cowboys. Some drinking and card playing but there was none of the usual hurrahing the town or such cowboy fun at the local people's expense.

About this time Will Carver had headed up north from Silver City, after leaving Sam to head north to Turkey Canyon. Soon another man showed up at the ranch. French later referred to him as Tom Capehart, another of the Wild Bunch. From the description of this man, and from the views of others, there is little doubt that he was not Will Carver. Possibly French was mistaken in the surname for frequently ranchers hardly became acquainted with the last names of their hands, on such short acquaintance. Usually they knew them as Bill, Joe, Windy, etc. Carver immediately pitched into the work as Lowe's right hand man. He was well liked by all hands, including French. He was well behaved and preferred to camp in the open, out along the line. Often he went on the trail with Lowe and McGinnis. They seldom lost a head, brought the cattle money back to French, Other ranchers wished for such an able and efficient bunch. French marveled at the change in the work on the ranch. Possibly he had some reason to wonder about the men, but did not indicate same.

So, now the old Black Jack gang had spread out. Carver was at the WS ranch, Black Jack, when last heard from was heading for Kingston, and Sam was thought to have been holding out in Turkey Canyon, or working on a ranch near Springer. Of the Cassidy group at the ranch, there was Cassidy, McGinnis, Harvey Logan and possibly Harry Longbaugh. It had been said that Logan "could shoot three times before a poker chip hit the floor from his other hand." He had been a behind the scene leader in the Hole-in-the-Wall gang before coming with Cassidy; before that he had been with the Curry gang. His home town was Dodson, Missouri. He had three brothers, a cousin named Bob Lee. It was Lee's mother who had raised the four Logan boys. Lonny was killed in Dodson by Pinkertons as he resisted arrest. It was said the Logans had been born in Kentucky, orphaned as youngsters and taken to Dodson. All of the boys were said to have been dark complected, with black hair. Henry was the oldest, was a storekeeper, never a gunfighter or outlaw. Harvey used the alias, at times, of Tom Capehart, Harvey Roberts, as well as Kid Curry. Some say that Harvey later died "of lead poisoning" at a ranch near Thermopolis, Wyoming, while others say he was killed in a battle with officers near Glenwood Springs, Colorado. Some say he escaped to South America with Cassidy and Longbaugh.

Harry Longbaugh, the Sundance Kid, was born about 1870. As a youngster he worked around Sundance, Wyoming and when seventeen worked at the Suffolk ranch, on the Cheyenne River. He was arrested for horse theft and served a short sentence. At the time he said he was from Colorado. Like Cassidy, he was formerly a rancher, near Chadron, Nebraska. He was a pleasant, cool and friendly man. That Longbaugh and Cassidy later reached San Vicente, Bolivia, is for sure, for both were killed there in 1909 in a battle with soldiers. They evidently had operated as bandits there.

On June 2, 1899, Cassidy and his band were said to have robbed the Overland Flyer of the UP at Wilcox, Wyoming. Of those mentioned as being on the job were George Curry, Harvey Logan and Elza Lay.. If they had done the robbery, it was one of these men who placed the dynamite in the express car and blew the safe open. The loot was thirty thousand dollars in bonds and money. It was also reported that Sheriff Joe Hagen, or Hazen, was killed a few days later by Logan. The railroads, the UP and the SP put out a wanted circular, on June 10, for Lonny, Bob and Harvey "Curry," whose real names were actually Logan. The r e w a r d was three thousand dollars reward for the capture of each. But other reports lay this job to Cassidy, George Curry, Logan and McGinnis. If the report given out that Lonny Logan, alias Curry, was tripped up at his home town of Dodson, Missouri, because of a telegram being sent to the Pinkertons relating that notes from the Wilcox robbery had been spent there by him, that more were found in his home after he was killed on February 28, 1900, perhaps the railroad was correct in listing him as one of the three robbers.

So, in the summer of 1899 these four men were at the WS ranch, as was Carver. Where the other Logan brothers had gone is not known. A man named Weaver left at the same time. The last named man was either Red Weaver or Red Pipkin, or Harvey Logan. But if he had red hair, this may have eliminated Logan. Carver headed up through Albuquerque and on towards Santa Fe, while McGinnis and Weaver headed towards Las Vegas. In Springer Weaver was taken down by smallpox and his companion had to leave him. Evidently Carver and McGinnis joined Sam near Cimarron. This may have been around the middle of June, 1899. One author says that McGinnis came to Cimarron in the spring of that year, with some WS cattle and registered at the St. James Hotel. "He soon moved on out to the camp in Turkey Canyon. To this day he remains a mystery man. Miguel Antonio Otero, in My Nine Years as Governor, identified him as Ezra Lay. He was known as Will McGinnis, even to the courts. How he came by his refined ways n e v e r was explained." (Ferguson, Murder and Mystery in New Mexico).

CHAPTER X

The Second Folsom Robbery & Turkey Canyon Battle

The boys took up residence in Turkey Canyon, and one at a time went to the lookout where is located "the stone face." Some say the robbery that was next to unfold, the second holdup of the C&S train near Twin Mountain curve on July 11, 1899, had been planned, like the first one, in Lambert's bar, next to the St. James, in Cimarron. I think it was well planned, well ahead, on the WS ranch. One writer reports that there were no less than eight men who rode to Turkey, and who participated in the r o b b e r y. Of those named, the following can be eliminated: George Franks (listed separately from Carver), for this was an alias of Carver's; Red Pipkin (or Meadows) for it is k n o w n he got off at Springer with smallpox; Bob Hays, for he was either killed in the battle at Squaw Mountain, or had left the band with others; Bill Walters, for he had split with the gang a year or so before and got himself killed at Rio Puerco, Bronco Bill, which was an alias of Walters', and H a r v e y Logan either stayed with Cassidy, or was Pipkin or Meadows. Of those left, and who actually was on the excursion at Twin Mountain, there was Carver, Sam Ketchum and McGinnis, and possibly a fourth man.

By personal interviews with people who had lived in Colfax county during the time before and after the robbery, I learned something of their stay in Turkey Canyon. Mary Lail has lived in this county for many years. She lives in the old Maxwell house now, where the sheriff of the county formerly lived also. The once huge house now has only eight rooms, the other sections of the comfortable rambling multiple dwelling having been torn away over the years by storm and fire. She is loved by all, h a v i n g b e e n responsible in bringing into the world hundreds of babies in that area. When I visited her home, sat in the comfortable living room and talked, she had two of her "thirty babies" she has raised, at home then. She has many treasures, in her home there are fine antiques, those with definite historical ties with the early west. She has a beautiful round table that once was used in "the Maxwell house", and other fine items. She is the unofficial historian of Cimarron and writers usually wind up at "Mother Lails", as did I.

She had lived at Ponil Park, that idyllic retreat way up in the mountains, northwest of Cimarron. She told of her school days, of her beloved bicycle riding school teacher for whom she had written a beautiful bit of rhyme, many years later. She has written many more pieces that bring back mellow memories to the hearts of many who would like to "remember when." She looks to the day when she can again visit Ponil Park, stand among the tall trees and recall pleasant memories.

She "knew" some of the Ketchum band while they were in Turkey Canyon. On Sunday evenings the people of the little village would hold box supper dances and the frontier music would waft down the valley on the cool breath of the mountains. At one of these dances a young cowboy appeared at the door of the structure. As the music played, the dancers, young and old, tripped the light, the timid cowboy would peep around the door. Western hospitality, then what it is now, did not often wait on introductions. The timid young cowboy was invited in "and have some punch." He soon entered into the fun and would return to Ponil on other dance nights.

"These boys were just oldtime cowboys to us," Mrs. Lail said. "They would come to the door or windows of the house where we were holding our weekly dance and midnight suppers. They would look in, watch the dancers and timidly smile as we called to them We would invite them in and soon they would be having the time of their lives. We regarded them as good, polite cowboys and this they always were, in our presence I was sort of stuck on one of them, a tall slender dark haired boy. His name? Don't recall what he called himself."

But, he and the others came from Turkey to the dances at Ponil Park. Sometimes they came to shop, to buy grain for their toesack morrals. How long their pleasant life lasted at Turkey Canyon before they were to leave on their second foray against the C&S train at T w i n Mountain, is not known.

But, on the early morning of July 10, 1899, they rode up Turkey Canyon, made trail around the huge bolder blocking the canyon, and retraced their t r a i l across the Maxwell ranch country, through which they had fled back in September of 1897, after the first robbery of the C&S. Just as before, one member boarded the tender at Folsom, when under way covered the engineer and fireman and commanded them to stop the train at Twin Mountain curve, just one hundred yards from the place of the first robbery. They disconnected the first coach from the train, ordered it pulled down the tracks, where the rest of the band dynamited the safe in the express car, and escaped. Frank Harrington was again the conductor, as was he on the first robbery, and it was getting tiresome to him.

The newspapers reported that there were three men in the robbery, and there was a lot of excitement all over the state. When the hunt centered around Cimarron, law officers started to northern New Mexico from many points. When Harrington backed his train back into Folsom that night, the wires were soon humming with telegrams. That night Sheriff Edward Farr, Walsenburg, Huerfano county, Colorado, was roused from his bed and told about the robbery. He had worked with the railroads before and before morning he and his posse were heading south on the C & S, then changed trains for Springer, where they came to Cimarron on horseback and in public conveyances. With him were railroad special agents James Morgan and Captain Thacker. In Cimarron they were joined by special agent W. H. Reno. There they were aided by storekeeper Jim Hunt and organized a posse of seven men, four others including themselves. Among these were Deputy U.S. MarshalMemphis Elliott and Rains Thomas, long time citizens of Tom Green county, Texas, and who had known the Ketchums and Carver back in Texas. Also joining the posse was U.S Marshal Forsker, a young cowboy, Henry Love of Springer and F. H. Smith, a Chicago youth out to see the west. This was an experienced posse other than the last named two.

The alarm that had centered the hunt around Cimarron came when a teamster reported in Cimarron that he had seen three men on horseback coming up Cimarron Canyon and who turned up Turkey Canyon. He had been sleeping under his wagon. It seems that all outlaws made common mistakes and evidently the great mistake of Sam Ketchum and his band was in returning to their hideout by going "up canyon," from Cimarron. Had they gone in from the back way, as usual, perhaps they might not have been detected. And a more serious error was that evidently they had not posted an early morning sentry at the "stone face" lookout place, for they were surprised in their camp the next day.

On July 17, 1899, the San Angelo Standard, by wire from Las Vegas, had a bold head: "A Battle With Outlaws," further said that Sheriff Farr and his posse had run into the outlaws in Turkey Canyon and that "one of the outlaws was a dead shot. Sherriff Farr was killed and Henry Love and Smith, wounded. Love had been hit twice, one shot going through his thigh. The identity of the outlaws is not known but little doubt is entertained that they are the men who held up the train two weeks ago." It is believed the reference to a holdup "two weeks ago," was in error.

Before daylight that morning the posse had left Cimarron and when they had progressed some six miles up the canyon, Farr sent Memph Elliott on ahead to spy out the location. He soon hurried back to report that he had heard horses up the canyon. Farr assembled his forces and talked the situation over. He split up the forces, one to go up each side of the narrow canyon, leaving the horses behind.. Farr, Smith, Elliott and one of the railroad men crept along the west wall, while the other three, Love and the two other special agents went up the east wall. The cave was located on the east wall.

Soon they smelled smoke and as they paused to listen the billowy morning clouds were drifting over the canyon, the tall pines swaying in the morning swell. They soon saw the fire and the cave. Bill McGinnis had left the fire and had stepped down the rock steps the fifteen feet to the little pool of water, near the pole corral. He had a blackened agateware coffee pot in his hand. His hair was tousled from recent sleep, his suspenders down about his legs, shirt tails out. No one stirred from the cave, the only moving figure was that of McGinnis. As he reached to fill the pot, someone in the posse shot the young outlaw, who fell to the rocky ground. Erna Fergusson in her book said that Sheriff Farr fired the shot. Immediately Sam Ketchum ran out of the cave to help the wounded man and dropped behind the barricade in front of the place. As Sam started to fire toward the west wall, the sheriff's rifle got the outlaw in the right shoulder. "But somebody got Farr with a shot that penetrated a large tree where he had been sheltered, and pierced the man's heart."

F. Stanley, in his Desperadoes of New Mexico, says that Farr had announced their presence with: "We have you surrounded. Drop your guns and approach this way with your hands up," which started quite a lengthy conversation, entered into by both sides, as they took pot-shots at each other. He further reported that the gang decided to "ride straight towards where the sheriff was and shoot as they rode." It was in this fatal charge, he says, that McGinnis and Ketchum were wounded, but "not before he shot the sheriff." And, "the gang dispersed into so many different directions that the posse was at a loss as to which one to chase, . . . "

Of the fight, the August 5th issue of the San Angelo paper went into further detail with: "The Train Robbers: Vivid description of the fight between them and Sheriff's

Posse in New Mexico: Sam Ketchum's dying statement." The article went on to say that there were three men in the band, Ketchum, Carver, and McGinnis. The fight started when McGinnis went to the pool of water and "someone" in the posse opened fire, wounding him. Memphis Elliott who it was said, was quoted to say Carver fought "like a wildcat," was a crack shot and probably responsible for the killing of the sheriff and the wounding of several others. Elliott was the only man who escaped unharmed, according to the paper. He reported that Carver was in a good spot behind the barricade and lay there on his stomach, pumping shells into the brush. Twenty-three empty shells were found where he had lain. McGinnis was supposed to have been put out of commission when the fight started and in the first burst of shots Sam Ketchum was badly wounded, leaving Carver to fight off the seven or eight men in the posse. The paper further said that "it was supposed that he (Elliott) fired the shot which finally resulted in Sam Ketchum's death." Elliott further said that finally Carver drove the posse back, and both sides started their withdrawal; that the fighting had lasted **about forty-five minutes.** Elliott had killed two of the outlaws' saddle horses and one pack animal. He said that somehow Carver got the two wounded men on the remaining horse and got away but "finally Sam convinced them to leave him at a ranch of a friend and to look out for themselves but the friend went for the officers after getting Sam's gun."

Fergusson says that as the officers retired they saw a rider mount the rise, waving his hand, that it was McGinnis, who "shouted 'Adios!', and disappeared over the hill. Will Franks, well ambushed, had kept on firing until dusk when the posse all headed for Cimarron."

As to the length of time the battle went on, we have one writer who states that the battle went on all day, from early morning until six in the evening. Another says it started at noon and went on for several hours. Actually, the fight lasted about forty-five minutes, as reported by a participant. McGinnis had been dropped immediately as he was surprised and put out of commission during the first blast. He may have managed to throw a few shots during the fight, but he says he did not. Sam Ketchum had rushed from the cabin cave and was badly wounded "in the first burst of shots." This left Carver to fight off the posse. Memphis Elliott, who was there, made this report when it was fresh on his mind. Will Carver through presence of mind, stayed in the cabin, on the first firing from the posse. He had not a drop of fear in his veins, but was quick-thinking enough to hold back for a moment, and evidently succeeded in driving the posse off, as well as shooting them up badly. He knew the value of the hard hitting Krag carbine and he used his to best effect. Not considering who fired the shot that killed the sheriff, Carver must have wounded every man in the posse, excepting Elliott. He fired twenty-three shots, probably more. He was handicapped since the posse was on both walls, the east wall being to his back, up the slope from the cave. This offered him a protection, as well. Marks on trees years later showed the fury of the battle, as dished out by both sides, but the outlines of the barricade in front of the cave gives testimony that if Carver made that long fight alone with two wounded companions on his hands, he had a fine advantage. One writer, on writing about the Cassidy gang, condemned one of the possemen in this fight for cowardice.

The posse did withdraw and there is no doubt about this.

They had one man dead, and five wounded, one seriously and who died some days later. The outlaws withdrew also. One writer says that McGinnis had ridden over the rise waving an "Adios!", leaving Sam there and Carver "firing until dusk." Another reported that the gang "dispersed in so many different directions," that the posse did not know which to follow. Another reported Carver (Logan the writer said) left his two wounded companions and escaped.

Actually Elliott had killed two of their horses and one pack animal, and if none escaped from their corral, they probably had one horse and two pack animals left. It was reported by those in the fight, and by those who wrote the news story, that Carver got the two wounded men on their mounts and in some manner got them away from there. Is it true that "Sam convinced them to leave him at a ranch of a friend," or the statement that McGinnis rode over the hill, leaving his two companions? Elliott stated that C a r v e r helped the two wounded men get away. But we have the statement, said to have been made by McGinnis himself, that he had laid where he fell after he was shot by "someone," and that Ketchum was immediately wounded as he came out of the cabin, in the left arm and not in the right shoulder. He said that Carver was cursing the posse, taunting them to come down and get him and all the while laying down a terrific barrage of lead. McGinnis said that the posse finally left the scene, under Carver's fire. Charles Kelly, in his Outlaw Trail, a book about Cassidy, says that the report by McGinnis that Ketchum was unable to mount his horse and that he (McGinnis) and Carver left him there, probably is true. If this is the case then it is evident that Sam somehow got on a mount and went down the canyon, then west up Cimarron creek to what he thought was safe refuge at Ute Park, a beautiful grass carpeted park between Cimarron and Eagle Nest.

Ketchum had stopped at the McBride ranch house, there at 7500 foot elevation, where Ute and Cimarron meet. The posse's return to Cimarron had the people up in arms and a large posse returned to Turkey and removed Farr's body. One writer says that Sam was found "several miles out of Cimarron," and that he had suffered the wound when attacked by a "grizzly bear." A man who worked on the ranch put Sam to bed, and in some way got the wounded man's revolver from him and sent word to Cimarron. Special agent W. H. Reno and others went up to Ute Park and captured the unarmed and wounded man. He was brought into Cimarron in a wagon.

At Cimarron the posse paused at Jim Hunt's store and it was said that Sam admitted his identity. George Crocker, young brother of Frank Only Crocker, shouted the warning that alerted Reno, that Sam was edging toward the officer's gun, or as another report put it, "as Sam was in the act of lifting the rifle." Some say he was carried to Lambert's where his wound was dressed, others say he refused treatment of the arm wound and this led to blood poisoning which was to cause his death. He was asked about brother Tom, and was said to have remarked that Black Jack was "dead and buried where none will ever find him." Sam died in the Santa Fe Territorial Prison, July 24, 1899 and was buried in Odd Fellows Cemetery. Sheriff Gerome Shield of Tom Green county, Texas, and the elder brother, Berry Ketchum, came to Santa Fe to identify the body.

After the battle and escape from Turkey, one writer described McGinnis as being "up in the Cimarroncito hills," in agony, and alone, tearing off all of his clothes and that he was there captured. Actually Carver and McGinnis had ridden out via Ponil, down around Springer and down the Canadian where they again crossed at the old Rock ranch, then continued south. It was a long, hot and dusty ride of around three hundred miles. They were hardpressed to find the safety of a new hideout. McGinnis had advised against the Robbers Roost country of Utah and New Mexico was too hot. Southern Arizona had been off limits for them for some time, so they headed south, probably with the Davis Mountains, or Tom Green county, as their destination.

A month and five days after the Turkey Canyon battle, Carver and McGinnis were in camp on the Lusk ranch in Eddy county, New Mexico. Sheriff M. C. (Cis) Stewart, while out hunting a band of rustlers with his posse, came upon the camp. McGinnis was captured and Carver, who had viewed the arrest from a distance, had escaped. McGinnis was lodged in jail at Carlsbad and Jim Hunt of Cimarron was sent down as a deputy to return him. He went to trial for killing Sheriff Farr, was defended by an attorney said to have been hired by cowboys of northern New Mexico. The defense was that McGinnis had carried a rifle as he went down to the pool of water and that the sheriff's shot had knocked him out of the fight before he could bring the firearm into action. Prisoner number 1348, was tried as Elsworth (Elza) Lay and showed himself as a fairly educated witness. He was quiet and calm. Found guilty of second degree murder October 10, 1899, he was given life. Governor Otero felt he had not received a fair trial and commuted this sentence to ten years and he was released from Santa Fe January 10, 1906. That same month he rode to the WS ranch near Alma, to visit with his old friend Captain French. As a trusty in prison he had helped suppress prison breaks at the time that Black Jack was in the jail in Union county. He worked around Alma for a couple of years and in 1908 went up into Wyoming, opened a saloon, settled down as a respected and well thought of citizen. He was married, later ranched, and died in Los Angeles in 1933.

As to Sheriff Edward Farr, his body was returned to the coal mining town of Walsenburg, in Colorado, where he was buried. The name of Farr has been associated with the law for many years in Huerfano county. J. B. Farr was acting as sheriff in the years that followed the death of Edward Farr. In 1914, there was a lot of excitement in southern Colorado during the mining strikes and which resulted in numerous deaths and shootings, including the deaths of a number of immigrants and their families, which was referred to as "The Massacre at Ludlow." From a book presenting the viewpoint of labor, published in 1952 and entitled "From Out of The Depths," Sheriff Jeff Farr and the troubled situation was referred to and stated that Farr, "who contended he had won the 1914 election by a majority of 329 votes, was still sitting in the court house in June, 1916, when the Colorado Supreme Court gave the coal companies of Colorado their first major setback ... " He was referred to as "an employee of the coal companies." Further, on page 345 of the book, it was said: "Sheriff Farr and his henchmen had ruled over the Kingdom of Huerfano for twenty years." Also, "Jeff and his heavily armed lieutenants held on to the Walsenburg Court house for another week ..., and then Jeff Farr Abdicated." The Trinidad Free Press on July 20, 1916 quoted the former sheriff to have said when he got on the train, leaving his office to the newly elected sheriff: "When I die everyone will come to my funeral."

After the capture of Elza Lay near Carlsbad, Carver

changed his Texas plans and rode day and night across New Mexico to the WS ranch. There he found that Cassidy and his men were preparing to leave the state. Cassidy approched Mr. French and asked if he would make Lay's bail and was told that he would do so. Carver hung around awhile and when Cassidy and the others departed, he left and headed for Tom Green county. The San Angelo paper said on August 5, 1899: "The three remaining members of the Black Jack gang were seen in San Angelo, S u n d a y last. They rode through town two or three times, defying the authorities and Sheriff Shield has called in the Rangers." It further stated that the Wells Fargo Company and the Express Company shared all expenses of the rangers and other officers who converged on San Angelo. The men rode horses with a SMH brand, owned by a Sterling, Texas rancher. The third man may have been Ben Kilpatrick, recruited by Carver upon his return home. One may have been Logan, who was said to have returned north with Cassidy.

The number one actor in our drama, Black Jack has had no part in the foregoing, since he had retired to Kingston. It was said that he had been in New Mexico from October 1898 until August 16, 1899, when he attempted to rob the C&S train at Twin Mountain, for the third time, and his second attempt. This was within a month from the time that Sam and his companions had robbed he train, and had returned to Turkey Canyon and the great battle with officers. And on this robbery, Black Jack was alone!

CHAPTER XI

The Third Folsom Robbery
& Fatal Results

Conductor Frank E. Harrington, was working the Fort Worth Express when it was robbed by the Black Jack gang for the third time. He later lived at Houston, and Amarillo, Texas. He had said on the two earlier robberies that he "was unprepared to defend successfully against Black Jack and his gang and prevent the holdups." After the first two hold-ups he had told Mrs. Harrington that if Tom Ketchum ever held him up again, the attempt would not be successful, or he "would not come home." From then on he carried a dou-ble-barreled shotgun and a large supply of shells "loaded with buckshot," in his train box, which was located in the front portion of the combined mail and passenger coach. He was an employee of the Fort Worth and Denver Railroad, actually the crimes were committed on the section known as the C&S, out of Denver.

Just as before, Black Jack was on the coal tender when the number one train, the Fort Worth Express, pulled out of Folsom about 9 pm the night of August 16, 1899. Four miles out, Engineer Joe Kirchgrabber was intent on the curves and the long grade, when he felt the hard barrel of a gun in his back. There stood Black Jack Ketchum, and just as he had done before, he ordered the crew to take the train into the second bend of the double-horseshoe turn. When the train was brought to a stop, he ordered the fireman to get down and uncouple the Miller-Hook coupling device between the first car and the train.

Harrington, who knew w h e n t h e y stopped at Twin Mountain curve in the dead of night, trouble was afoot, had stepped onto the platform from the smoker section which was in the express compartment, turned out the lights, got his shotgun and assembled it and loaded both barrels. The shot that he had heard came from Ketchum's gun when Fred Bartlett, the mail clerk had stuck his head out of the express door and was shot in the jaw by the outlaw. Harrington crept through the dark car to the platform door which looked out on the uncoupling scene between the two cars. He had left brakeman R. B. (Bob) Harkins to care for the wounded mail clerk. He cautiously opened the door and through the slit he could see the engineer and fireman, Tom Scanlan, trying to open the stubborn coupling. As he opened the door farther, to enlarge the viewing area so as to get sight of the robber, the foreman inadvertantly raised his torch and Harrington was seen by Black Jack. The outlaw immediately backed some fifteen or twenty feet away from the train in order to survey the length of the train. Harrington warned the fireman to keep the torch down and stepped back into the doorway. He then eased the door open and blazed away with his shotgun. Black Jack had seen the conductor and had fired his rifle at the same time, the ball cutting through the conductor's forearm, slightly above the wrist. But, the buckshot from the conductor's gun had hit Tom Ketchum in the chest, tearing away his vest and shirt, and the main blast had torn away his right arm, between his elbow and shoulder, completely shattering it and rendering it useless.

The actual scene took only a few minutes and as Ketchum bolted away from the train, another shot rang out on the opposite side of the train. Since it was supposed that the bandit had been alone, it was never determined how this came about. He would have had to travel the length of the first car and locomotive to get to the other side of the tracks, or crawl under the car, but time between h i s d a s h and the sound of the shot from the opposite side would not have permitted this. Then, too, he was seen to bolt directly away from the car, into the darkness. Another strange part of the entire affair was that two "hoboes" were f o u n d o n the "blinders" and they had stayed there during the entire hold-up, and only left the train after it was all over. It was felt that they had had no part in the holdup, and that it was a one man job.

As to the capture of Ketchum, there are two writers who say that the next morning, a north-bound freight carried Sheriff Saturnino Pinard and a posse out from Clayton, as well as two special agents for the railroad. Near the robbery scene they saw a man's black hat being waved from a gun barrel. The train stopped and the sheriff ran to the wounded man, who surrendered. But, Conductor Harrington later told his brother that the crew of a freight train going north saw Ketchum, on the opposite side of the track from where he had been shot, sitting in the bushes and "holding his rifle with the barrel upward and a white handkerchief tied to it, indicating a flag of truce." The freight was stopped "and Ketchum, after surrenduring to the train crew was taken into the town of Folsom where he received surgical treatment." One writer wrote that after the sheriff had taken Ketchum the train took them into Trinidad "where it was found necessary to amputate the injured member at the shoulder." Another said that the sheriff was actually on the train when the outlaw was taken, and that he had his right arm tied in a black silk handkerchief, sobbed when taken aboard that he wished he had been shot through the head or the heart, and further said that he was placed on a cot in the baggage car and taken into Clayton.

Black Jack gave the name of George Stevens and told where he had hidden the dynamite and that he was on the job alone. Later the dynamite, his horse and pack saddle, bed roll, was found. In Clayton Doctor Slack gave him first aid and on his advice the sheriff was asked to take him to a hospital in Trinidad. There they removed "forty-two shots from that arm." Later Black Jack was put on the AT&SA and taken to the prison at Santa Fe, and there on September 9th, Dr. Des. Marias, the prison physician amputated his arm. It was said that he refused anything to ease the pain, just gritted his teeth and held on with his other hand.

He did not know of the tragedy at Turkey Canyon and the death of his brother Sam, a month before, or the robbery at Twin Mountain in July. The news of the attempted holdup on August 16th, had been telegraphed to papers all over the southwest. It was said that the robber had escaped, this was before the capture the next morning. The San Angelo paper said: "He lives in Old Mexico: Ketchum of all men. Lives in a Place as Magnificent as a King—He's Worth Millions; his name there is John Huiett."

After he was found the next day, badly wounded, claiming that he was George Stevens of the Panhandle of Texas, a wire was sent to San Angelo for someone to come to Santa Fe to identify the man. The paper there on September 9th said: "Sheriff G. W. Shield returned Monday from Santa Fe, N.M., where he went to complete the identification of Tom Ketchum, who was wounded by Conductor Harrington, while attempting one of the most daring feats known to the criminal history of this country—that of holding up—single handed, the Fort Worth and Denver train at Folsom, N.M. last month. Sheriff Shield was accompanied by Bige Duncan of Knickerbocker, a brother-in-law of the wounded outlaw. He (Ketchum) is a desperate and dangerous man, and his captors realize that fact."

In the meantime, when Sam died on July 24th, his older brother Berry Ketchum, had gone to Santa Fe, with Sheriff Shield to identify him. The well liked sheriff of Tom Green county, had gone to Santa Fe twice in less than a month to identify the two brothers, one dead and the other lying in his cell with an arm gone at the shoulder. Tom Ketchum was the first train robber to be indicted under the severe law which provided the death sentence for "assaulting a railway train."

Now, Will Carver was the last of the Black Jack gang. He had returned to San Angelo with Logan, t h e n disappeared. Said the San Angelo paper in September 1899: "The story of Will Carver's death as outlined in the extract from the Denver paper, which appeared in last week's Standard, Sheriff Sheild regards this as merely a blind. He thinks the man who was with McGinnis near Eddy, N.M. when the latter was captured by Sheriff Stevens and his posse was Carver and that he is still at large. The remaining member of Black Jack's gang. Carver, like all other members of this crew, is a cool, nervy fellow, and a dead shot and will likely make things pretty hot for the officers who attempt to deprive him of his liberty. A reward of $10,000 was offered for Ketchum, dead or alive, and the question as to its disputes will prove a most interesting one."

Then in another report a few days later: "Of the entire gang, G. W. Franks, Carver, the companion of McGinnis, who was captured at the Lusk ranch, is the only one still at large. Sam Ketchum, brother of Tom, was captured during the pursuit in July when Sheriff Farr of Huerfano county, Colorado, was killed." It had been said that the man got away at the Lusk ranch was Harvey Logan, not Carver, as well that Sheriff Cis Stewart was the arresting officer, while the Standard said that "Sheriff Stevens," captured McGinnis.

On the day that Ketchum's arm was amputated, the Southern Pacific westbound train was robbed by four men near Cochise, Arizona, at midnight. Newspapers reported that after dynamiting the safe the bandits got away with around ten thousand dollars. The papers further said that it was known that the old San Simon gang had robbed the train, and "not the men who had been running in Texas during the past month." This robbery was later charged to Burt Alvord, Billy Styles and Will Downing.

In the prison at Santa Fe, Elza Lay, prisoner number 1348, learned of the death of his old leader, Sam Ketchum, and of the capture and amputation of the arm of Black Jack, but was noncommittal.

Black Jack was to be tried u n d e r the sterner law at Clayton, N.M. On one of the trips to Clayton for a hearing (the trial was postponed), he and the officers were on Conductor Harrington's train and Ketchum had good naturedly talked with the conductor. While chained to his seat he told Harrington that with his help he c o u l d have robbed the Treasury in Washington. Harrington asked him why he had run away from the fight at Twin Mountain and was told he thought he was fighting a number of railroad guards. He said that if he had one of the guns laying on the seat in front of him, he could have gotten away. Harrington died in 1946.

Ketchum was finally brought to jail at Clayton and was placed in the steel cage just off the jail corridor. Rumors were afloat that he would be rescued by his friends but no attempt was made. Judge Wm. J. Mills held the trial, Jeremiah Leahy, the DA from Raton, was the prosecutor; William Bunker of Las Vegas was assigned by the court to defend him. When asked whether he was guilty or not, he rose and advanced to the bench, started to address the court, when he was stopped and returned to his seat. Evidence produced by the state was mainly on the testimony of the engineer, fireman and conductor of the struck train. Sheriff Salome Garcia had charge of the prisoner. Ketchum was pointed out in court as the man responsible for the robbery attempt, as well by Charles Drew, the express messenger. Testimony of Drew was that Black Jack had pounded on the door of his car and when he opened he was ordered to "fall out of there," which he did. Not on the stand, Black Jack agreed that this was true. Harrington testified that Ketchum was the man who had shot him.

Secundino Romero, court clerk, resumed his place at the recorder's table to start the minutes again, when the jury returned, handed the judge the verdict. They found that Ketchum was guilty of the charges and further found for the sentence of death. The date of hanging was set by Judge Mills for October 4, 1900. The defendant's attorney appealed the verdict, was denied and in the delay a stay was granted, with the sentence to be carried out April 26, 1901. Ketchum was returned to Santa Fe prison to await the final day.

During his stay at Santa Fe, his older brother came to visit him once. Governor Otero visited him often to talk and brought his son, who brought Black Jack peanuts and other items. While in prison awaiting death he dictated the now famous letter about the Steins robbery, stating that the three men in prison then, were innocent and that he and his gang committed the crime.

CHAPTER XII

Will Carver & The Wild Bunch

Early in 1900 the Black Jack gang has been practically wiped out, but for Will Carver. The various branches of the Cassidy gangs were broken up. On February 28, 1900, Bob Lee, cousin to the Logans, was arrested at Cripple Creek, Colorado. One day Lonny Logan, was killed in his hometown of Dodson, Missouri. The next report on the remnants of the Wild Bunch came in April, 1900, when it was reported: "Max Stein, Tom Capehart, George Franks, alias Bill Carver and Frank Laughlin, holdup men and all round crooks, departed from Tombstone in a hurry." This was from L. D. Walters' book. Max Stein was said to have been killed later in Utah in a train holdup attempt. "Tom Capehart," was evidently Harvey Logan, who had been referred to by that name while at the WS ranch. Cassidy and Longbaugh had supposedly returned to the north. The last named man, Laughlin, is not reported elsewhere in this story.

Another report said that the men had been up around Silver City and were trailed southwest by George Scarborough and Walter Birchfield, to the Steins area, where they had turned south into the lower San Simon valley, familiar grounds for Carver. The first report had them leaving Tombstone and traveling east by north to a point about thirty miles south of San Simon, which would have placed them near the old Rustlers Park hideout. Both accounts described them as Carver's gang. The Arizona papers reported that the band was from Silver City, N.M. and the New Mexico papers said they were rustlers from Arizona.

George A. Scarborough was born about 1858 in Louisiana. As a youth he came to McLennan county, Texas, later worked as a cowboy in McCulloch county. About 1883 he and his bride moved to Jones county, near Anson, where he ranched. He was deputy sheriff there, later sheriff, until 1888. In the early 1890's he lived in Jeff Davis county, worked on the very same ranches where Black Jack camped in 1898. He was considered a gunfighter then, on the side of the law. In 1894 he was named deputy U.S. Marshal, with headquarters in El Paso, where John Selman had been for nearly ten years an officer. Scarborough's friend Jeff Milton was chief of police there. Selman was constable. All three had different jobs, for the law. They all had to deal with John Wesley Hardin, whom Selman killed. Martin Morose, Bass Outlaw, and others were there then. Morose was killed there and officers Milton and Scarborough were said to have been the officers who attempted to arrest him. Selman was killed by Scarborough in El Paso April 5, 1896, who was acquitted. Dick Ware was U.S. Marshal and Scarborough's superior. He then went to Deming, N.M., to become a cattle detective and was instrumental in 1899 in the capture of three of the robbers of the SP at Cochise. He has been in posses that had chased Black Jack and his gang in 1898 and 1899. Now, he was working for the New Mexico Cattle Raisers Association and at times had five men working for him.

He and Birchfield were on the trail of a rustler band. They had trailed the group through the Burrow Mountains, and on through the Alkali Flats northwest of Lordsburg. Perhaps they got onto another trail in the San Simon, the trail of Carver and his gang. They found a freshly killed beef and trailed the men and when they came upon their camp they recognized the men and k n e w t h e y were up against rough characters. As the two officers went for cover, Scarborough was shot in the leg, all the time the outlaws were raining lead on their cover. Carver was seen standing, firing his rifle as fast as he could work the lever. Birchfield had pulled his friend to a place of protection, tried to stop the flow of blood. Finally the outlaws crept away and Birchfield cared for Scarborough, and although wounded himself, left for help to bring the wounded officer in. He made the thirty miles to the railroad and the next day brought back a wagon. Scarborough had been exposed many hours to rain and light snow. Put on the train at Steins, he was taken to Deming, and there he died of exposure and loss of blood. He was buried by the Odd Fellows, April 6, 1900, at Deming.

Walter Birchfield was a prominent ranchman and lived at Deming, having come from Texas some years earlier. From newspaper reports, it is evident that the gang split up and some of them, including Carver and Logan, went north into Wyoming.

Nearly five months later, August 29, 1900, train number three of the Union Pacific was stopped near Tipton, Wyoming and robbed by four men. It was reported that the four were Cassidy, Harvey Logan, Camillo Hanks, alias Deaf Charlie, and Bill Carver. Part of this is in error since Hanks was still in the penitentiary for the robbery of the UP train at Big Timber, Montana; sent to prison in 1894, he was not released until April 30, 1901. The fourth man may have been Longbaugh, alias The Sundance Kid. If this is true, Carver and Logan had met up with Cassidy and Longbaugh somewhere at one of the hideouts in Utah, Colorado, Wyoming, and had joined them in the raid at Tipton. After using three charges of dynamite, they blew the safe of the express car, got away with around five thousand dollars. The UP offered $1000 per man, and the Pacific Express Company, another $1000 per man. From then on out, the band stayed away from robbing trains, turned to banks.

Next the gang were heard from when the First National Bank at Winnemucca, Nevada, where they robbed it and got away with $32,600 in gold coin. It was said that the men on this job were Cassidy, Carver, Logan, Longbaugh and Ben Kilpatrick, the Tall Texan. It is possible that only four men were on this job. They escaped.

Next, they showed up in Fort Worth, for in November or December of 1900, they walked into John Swartz's photo gallery at 705 Main Street, had their picture taken. Swartz prepared a number of size 7 x 11 prints and this proved to be the best picture ever taken of an outlaw group. It shows all the men clean shaven. Carver and Logan standing, Longbaugh, Kilpatrick and Cassidy sitting. They had gone into local stores and purchased entire new outfits, down to spats and derbies. They headquartered in a rooming house, said to be a brothel, rode bicycles and spent their gold recklessly on the ladies of the evening. After the pictures were delivred, the photographer had placed his proud work in the window. Fred J. Dodge, a Wells Fargo detective, chanced to see it as he passed on the street, recognized Carver. It was he who sent out the alarm and soon the detective agencies and law officers were on the trail. A few months later Noah Rose, the famous frontier photographer, saw this same picture in the hands of a Texas sheriff. Col. Dodge gave Mr. Rose a copy of the picture. It was not until 1936 that all men in the photo were identified, and by Pink Simms, old time Jinglebob cowboy, who had worked the Texas trail, an ex-law officer, expert revolver shot, sent Mr. Rose the full identification of each of the men in the picture.

Alerted to trouble brewing, the band went to San Antonio, the detectives on their trail. There they made the rounds of the local parlors of favor, stayed at the best hotels, still on their spree. Tiring of this, Carver, Kilpatrick, and Logan went into Bandera county and stayed a few days at Carver's old home place. Cassidy and Longbaugh went elsewhere, probably back into Wyoming. Carver and his two friends went up into Concho county, to the Hills settlement, about seven miles from Eden, and camped on the Kilpatrick place. They hunted, rested, and generally laid low. It was there that a man named Oliver Thornton was killed by one of the group.

Said the San Angelo Standard: "One report is to the effect that some weeks prior to the shooting, Ben Kilpatrick and a man named Walker, who had several aliases, were camped at a spring on the Mollay Cattle Company pastures and had several good horses. John Dodson went to their camp one day looking around, thinking that the horses may have been stolen."

Oliver Thornton had worked for Ed Dozier, former sheriff of Concho county. He had been troubled with hogs said to belong to the Kilpatricks. A few days after Dodson was in their camp "Walker" and Ben Kilpatrick were playing croquet. Thornton went over to ask them to keep the hogs out of the Dozier pasture. Ed Kilpatrick later stated that Thornton had come up in the yard, where he, Ben and George and Walker were playing, and that Thornton was armed with a musket and had demanded that they keep the hogs out. He told Thornton that the hogs belonged to Boone Kilpatrick, and that they wanted no trouble. Ed said that "Walker" pulled his six-shooter, shot Thornton and when he ran, shot him again as he fell over a log and into the spring.

Mrs. Thornton, looking for her husband, found him lying in the spring with a wound in his forehead and and two in his body. Ed had gone into Eden to report that there was a dead man at his ranch. The paper further stated: "Another report to the effect that Thornton went to Kilpatricks unarmed and that he was a quiet, peaceful, unoffensive man. He was perfectly harmless." Evidently the boys then headed for the mesquite. Someone cut the telephone line in the Mollay pasture. A posse got on the trail, which headed toward Eldorado, found the wires cut to that town also. It was learned that strangers had been in Eldorado, posing as buyers of polo ponies, that they had bought one or two horses and were traveling in a rubber tired buggy.

The law agency put out a description of the wanted men and sent these throughout the southwest. Ben was described as about six foot tall, 180 pounds in weight, twenty-four years of age, of dark complexion, with about three-fourths of an inch of beard covering his face. He was riding a big bay horse, with no brand. Brother George was described as about six foot in height, about twenty-six years of age, light complexioned and riding a brown horse. "Walker" was a smaller man, 135 to 145 pounde in weight, dark complexioned with a heavy brown mustache, a bald head and between thirty-five and forty years of age. He was last seen riding a dun horse, branded on the left shoulder and left jaw. All were said to be wearing cowboy type garb and hats excepting "Walker" who had on suit pants with matching vest, and a narrow brimmed felt hat. No description was given of Carver, for it was thought that he was "Walker." Actually the last named man was Harvey Logan, alias Kid Curry. Concho county added their $100 to the reward for the apprehension of the men.

Nearly every writer that had mentioned the killing of Oliver Thornton had stated that he was killed by Will Carver. This one point has been a loose joint in western history and the brutal murder of Thornton did not fit the make-up of Carver. I have searched the archives and have never found one case where he was actually indicted for any crime, nor have I heard of any incident where he was brutal, or ruthless, as in this case. The law had felt that he was the guilty man for he had ridden into Sonora, a few days later, in company with one of the Kilpatricks. The newspapers seized on this and named Carver as the mysterious "Walker." George Kilpatrick, as he lay all shot up in Sonora, swore that the fourth man whom he knew only as "Walker," awaited them outside the town; that he was not Will Carver. The description of "Walker" does not fit the description and temperament of Carver, but does fit that of Kid Curry. Pink Simms said in 1936 that Logan was short, heavily built, not fat, and that he was very swarthy. He had black eyes and looked as he might have Indian blood. Also, he was slightly bald. Carver had a full head of hair. It was known that Logan, he alone of the Wild Bunch, often dressed in citified clothes, narrow brimed felt hat, sometimes turned up at the front, often looked like a railroad tramp, rather than a cowboy. Of course, one of his aliases was "Walker."

Back in Santa Fe prison Elza Lay was working with the brush gang and Black Jack was in the death cell. Over in Clayton authorities were constructing the gallows which was located behind the jail.

CHAPTER XIII

Death Of "Cowboy Bill"

But, back to Carver, his gang, and their troubles. On April 1st, 1901, they rode to the west of the town of Sonora, Texas, and camped on the T. Half Circle Ranch, near a water hole. Ben Kilpatrick was with the group, it is said. We know that George was there for he was to play a prominent part in the immediate future. Ben was a handsome young man, was from a respected family. It was said that his brother George was merely "with" the band, had no other connection with them.

Elijah S. Briant, was sheriff of the county. He was fairly slender, weighed about 160 pounds, had blue eyes perhaps and was sheriff, as well as the town's druggist. He was absolutely fearless in the face of danger. Called "Lige" by his friends, he had found no wide publicity as a peace officer. Carver and Kilpatrick were known in the county. Berry Ketchum had ranched on Devils River, and some of these boys had worked for him around there.

Noah Rose had his photographic tent in Sonora in 1898-1899, and Marvin Hunter worked on the Devils River News. Said Hunter: "Sonora was then a pretty wild western town, with several saloons and a gambling hall or two going full blast. It was in the heart of the greatest sheep and cattle country in Texas. Had a population of 500 and most of the ranch families lived in the town. Two big general merchandise stores, Hagerland Brothers and Co., and Mayer Brothers and Co. did a big business. Mrs. McDonald and Mrs. Traweek conducted the two hotels there The first still is operated by Mrs. McDonald . . ."

On the evening of April 2, 1901, Will Carver and George Kilpatrick went into the Mexican settlement, on the west side of Sonora to buy feed for their horses. It is felt that these two went into town, for some reason their descriptions had not been broadcast, as had those of the two others. Finding no feed there they went up town, to the Red Front Livery Stable. Then on down the street to the local bakery, located just to the rear of the bank, and across the street from where the Devils River News is now located. The City Variety Store is now on this present site.

Said the San Angelo Standard of April 6, 1901:

"Will Carver, alias Franks, McDonald, Walker, who was killed this week by Sheriff Briant of Sutton county, was not a Robin Hood character. He was a plain, unassuming, quiet sort of desperado, of a very retiring disposition, and rather shunned than courted notoriety. He was adverse to society, and preferred to dwell in the solitudes of the great southwestern plains, with a few choice spirits."

"Will Carver, who was wanted for the killing of Oliver Thornton last week was the son-in-law of a well known citizen of Knickerbocker. He was well known in this section and at different times worked for Berry Ketchum, the Half Circle Six ranch, Ed Jackson, Lee Aldwell and others. Of medium size, 140 lbs., a fine roper and horseman and a crack shot with six shooters, in either hand."

"A few years ago, he and Sam Ketchum ran a gambling house in San Angelo. He disappeared from Angelo and was next heard of after the robbery of a train at Folsom, N. Mexico and was in a fight at Cimarron, N. Mexico, between Black Jack gang and the officers."

The paper went on to tell that although he had a cut in his thigh, his two companions wounded in the fight near

Cimarron, his unerring marksmanship brought death to officer Love, who lost his life in the bloody encounter, "in which Memphis Elliott, formerly of San Angelo, took part. A year ago last July, a month after the Cimarron f i g h t, Rains Thomas was in the party that went after the gang after the Folsom robbery. They got McGinnis after a fight when he was badly wounded in the arm and shoulder. McGinnis is now serving life for the killing of Officer Farr during the Cimarron fight. Here Franks (Carver) waived an affectionate adios to the officers and disappeared over a hill, leaving McGinnis wounded. Four weeks ago four men were seen in Knickerbocker, Carver and Kilpatrick b o u g h t f e e d at Tweedy's store."

And here is the newspaper account of the actual battle:

"Before He Could Cock His Pistol"—"Last of Black Jack Gang Killed. Reward $5000."

"Sheriff Briant, The Hero of The Hour: Sheriff E. S. Briant received last week a description of the men who killed Thornton in Concho county. The description of the parties caused Sheriff Briant to suspect two men, who were in Sonora two weeks ago buying horses."

"Tuesday nite at 8 p.m. two men bought some baking powder at a store in the Mexican part of Sonora and wanted some grain. The Mexican storekeeper did not have grain for sale. The two men rode up to Becketts livery stable, opposite the First National Bank and inquired for grain, but again being disappointed, rode to Jack Owen's Bakery and were buying their supplies when Bossie Sharp recognized the smallest man as one of the 'rubber tire' buggy men for whom the officers were on the lookout. He informed his brother who was a deputy under Sheriff Briant, who in turn told Briant. Briant, deputies Davis and Sharp, Constable W. H. Thompson, went to arrest them. Briant knew one was Carver and one Kilpatrick."

"He told his men to get ready and the four officers stepped into the store. Sheriff Briant covered the men and required that they hold up their hands. The tall man, Kilpatrick who was nearest the door, made a surprised or fumbling motion with his hands, but the other went for his gun at once. Sheriff Briant saw the movement and shot instantly, and the man fell to the floor before he could cock his pistol. The next shot was fired by Thomason and almost simultaneously with that of Sheriff Briant, brought down Kilpatrick. And the four officers shooting as quickly as possible filled the prostrate bodies full of lead. Sheriff Briant then fell on Kilpatrick and disarmed him."

Bill Carver was game, even though the sheriff and posse were advancing with drawn pistols, he went for his gun a mite too slow. He was then one of the fastest on the draw in the country at the time. His pistol hand was shattered by he first charge and he attempted the border switch, throwing he revolver into the other hand, but fell to the floor, riddled before he could cock his pistol. Later when Marvin Hunter came to Sonora for his second time, this time to establish his own newspaper in the very same building, the holes were still visible in the floor. It may be of interest to mention that three of the gang had their hands or arms blasted, Sam, Tom and Will Carver. The Black Jack gang was now fully out of commission, only Black Jack remained, he soon to die.

The two wounded men were carried to the court house. Given a narcotic, Carver raved: "Keep shooting them boys. Will you stay with me? Will you sweat it out? Die game boys!" Finally he admitted that he was Will Carver, known as Cowboy Bill around Sutton county. He had been asked if he was "Walker" and he had replied that his name was Franks. "Don't you know me, Bill?" an old cowboy had whispered in his ear. The Sheriff asked him his name and he had replied, "I am one of the Off boys." And this he was. But, in the end so many of his old cowboy friends, former employers, had come see him, he admitted he was Will Carver. Then "Cowboy Bill" died, there on the court house floor.

Upon close examination it was found that he had been shot through the right lung, right arm, in the right leg, twice in the left arm, in the hand and had a wound near his left temple. It took seven wounds, and more shots, to finish Bill Carver. His right arm and left leg was broken, each in two places.

George Kilpatrick was badly wounded, but he said that Carver was not the man known as McDonald or Walker, who had killed Thornton. He said he had known Carver for years, the other man only two or three weeks. It is surmised that with all the shooting in town, Ben Kilpatrick and Logan took off for the brush.

Sheriff Howze of Concho county came and identified George and Carver, said they were two of the men he wanted. Said that the fourth man was merely a myth and indicated that Ben Kilpatrick was the only one left of the group.

At the time of his death Will Carver carried three short arms. One was a 45 Colts, with ivory handles, silver mounting, Number 20916. Another was a 38 hammerless S&W. Under his armpit was a derringer. In addition to his arms he had "one gold Elgin watch, a silver compass case, a handsome diamond ring and a thin gold band ring." Each of the men had twenty-five dollars cash in their pockets. Carver was riding a horse fifteen hands high and unbranded. George was riding a saddle made by Mose Harris of San Angelo. The horses were sold to pay for Carver's funeral.

George Kilpatrick was more shot up than had been Carver, receiving fourteen wounds, yet he lived. He was placed in the jail, later recovered and was never connected with any of the crimes of the gang and was released.

CHAPTER XIV

Death Of "Black Jack"

Black Jack Ketchum was to be hung April 26, 1901. He was taken from Santa Fe prison on April 23, 1901 on the order of Judge W. J. Mills and brought to Clayton on the AT&SF and C&S railroads. The officers, as insurance against an attempted rescue attempt, changed trains three times before they got on the C & S, first at Lamy, then at Glorietta and for the last portion of the trip at Las Vegas. He was in good humor. He had been outfitted in Santa Fe with a new suit of black clothes, a new black derby which he wore tilted at a sporting angle. His black mustache had been trimmed and his hair cut. Crowds thronged the stations through which the train passed and on one stop when photographers poked their cameras toward the window, he pulled his coat over his head. The trip to Clayton was uneventful and upon arrival there he was placed in the steel cage off the jail corridor and there he remained for three days as the finishing touches were put on the gallows. The drop was designed to take a fall of eight and one half feet for Tom had gained weight during his prison inactivity and regular meals.

The day before the execution a priest came to the jail and talked with the condemned man but Ketchum refused consolation. It is said that he slept fairly well that night. The sheriffs of Trinidad, Colorado, and Las Vegas were sent to help Sheriff Garcia with the execution. Reporters from many southwestern papers were on hand to cover the story for their editors, as were several photographers. Conductor Harrington and Charles Drew were present also. On the morning of the execution a message was received, supposedly having come from the governor, which was proved bogus. Several moments before 1:15 PM on the afternoon of April 26th, the rear door to the brick jail opened and Black Jack strode down the steps, flanked by guards. He climbed the thirteen steps to the gallows without a falter. He was bareheaded and once he attempted to raise his left hand, chained to his side, to stroke his temple. The right sleeve was neatly held by his coat lapel. At 1:15 PM the sheriff asked Black Jack if he was prepared and was told that he was. He surveyed the crowd, shrugged his shoulders under the black shiny coat. The natty bow tie was removed, the soft collar unbuttoned from his neck. He stepped onto the four foot trap door, moved to the center of same, stood motionless. There were six other men on the platform. The rope was adjusted around his neck, the hood placed over his head.

Black Jack Ketchum had always been obsessed with the idea that he was born only for hell. He showed his fatalistic attitude to the very end. He was reported to have made a remark about hurrying up the process. Some say it was something like this: "Hurry up, I'm late for dinner in hell now." The sheriff held the hatchet poised. The brick walls of the jail was a backdrop. The hatchet fell, the trap sprung and the tall man's body shot through to the length of the rope. The head was severed from his body, so sharp the drop, so heavy the man. Photographers had shot the scene; with head bare, standing straight, another as the rope was adjusted, another with the hood on his head, the third photo showed the body laying before the gallows, the head in the foreground. At the undertaking parlor the head was neatly sewed back to the body. An hour or two after the execution the coffin was hauled in a wagon down Clayton's main street, to the new cemetary north of town. Then the coffin was opened before interment. With no ceremony the body of the notorious outlaw was delivered to the sod in an unmarked grave.

September 10, 1935, the public was invited to witness the removal of Ketchum's remains to a new cemetary a short dsitance away from the old one and over one thousand people attended. The coffin was opened for the curious to see that the once black mustache was now a dull red, the elements had been good to the remains, during those 34 years.

Black Jack was hung for the crime of "assaulting a railway train—". He had been officially charged with nothing more, as far as I could find in the archives, during his long career. Will Carver was the lucky one, for he was never caught, never forced to stand trial for any indictment, if any ever existed. As to Sam Ketchum, the same. Elza Lay, charged with second degree murder in the death of Sheriff Farr, was indicted for this crime, found guilty and imprisoned. Of the gang, he was the only one to remain alive, died a natural death years later.

CHAPTER XV

The High-Five Gang

This story would in no means be complete if we left it at this point. Since the Wild Bunch were closely associated with the Cassidy Gang, the Carver gang, etc., since at the time of Ketchum's hanging, some remained unaccounted for, it is necessary that the story continue.

On May 30, 1901 Camillo (O. C.) Hanks, alias Deaf Charley was released from the Deer Lodge, Montana pen, after serving nearly eight years for his part in the Big Timber robbery, having been arrested in Teton county,

Montana in 1894. Cassidy and Longbaugh had returned from San Antonio where they left Carver, Logan and Kilpatrick. They returned north to Wyoming and Montana shortly after the first of 1901. Kilpatrick and Logan must have hotfooted it from Sonora in April when Carver was killed, and joined the rest of the bunch in one of their old hideouts. Sometime between the early part of June and 1st of July Hanks had joined them, probably in their Montana hideout. They next planned the strike at the Great Northern train number three near Wagner, Monana.

Those said to have been in on this robbery were Cassidy, Longbaugh, Logan, Kilpatrick and Hanks. It was said that Laura Bullion had taken up with Kilpatrick and was waiting for the band in their hideout. Shortly after noon of July 3, 1901, Harvey Logan was in "the blinders" of the express car as the train pulled out of Malta, Montana. Harry Longbaugh was in the coaches. The other three were along the tracks between Malta and Wagner. At a prearranged point, Kid Curry climbed into the locomotive and commanded that the engineer halt the train. The Sundance Kid, usually of even and quiet demeanor acted, the robber part. As he commanded the passengers to remain calm, he ran up and down the isles intimidating them with his two sixshooters. As the engine crossed a bridge near Wagner, Montana, it was stopped and Hanks and Cassidy got into the act. From either side of the train, with high powered r i f l e s, t h e y kept the passengers in the coaches. Logan marched the engineer and fireman to the Express car and the safe was dynamited. As Logan left the car with the loot, Longbaugh swung down from the coaches and the two others ran with them to their horses and were away. The loot was forty thousand dollars, in tens and twenties, being shipped from the U. S. Treasury in Washington to the National Bank of Montana in Helena. Rewards were posted for this robbery and for convictions totaling $10,000. We are well acquainted with the members of the band, excepting Hanks. He was a native of DeWitt county, Texas, born 1863. At the time of the robbery he was about 5 feet 10 inches in height, 156 lbs. weight, sandy complexion, blue eyes, of stocky build, auburn hair, and a sandy mustache, if any. He was a cowboy in DeWitt and Gonzales counties before going to Las Vegas, New Mexico, in the late 1880s.

The band split up after the Wagner robbery, their last. Ben Kilpatrick and Laura Bullion went their way, Cassidy and Longbaugh theirs. Hanks went it alone, as did Logan.

The United States Secret Service was on the job and when some of the unsigned bank notes from the Wagner job, with forged signatures, showed up in a St. Louis bank, the alarm was sent out by John Murphy, agent at St. Louis. At a jewelry store on Pine Street in St. Louis a man had given some of the notes for jewelry. Detective John Shevlin, in charge of the case for the city of St. Louis, said in 1927, that it was from this store that the trail was picked up. He was aided by Detectives Guion, Burke, McGrath and Grady. The saloons were canvassed in the "district". In a saloon at Twenty-first and Chestnut, they found a porter who came in with a twenty dollar bill to buy beer. It proved to be one of the stolen notes. The porter led the police to a place on Chestnut and one of the detcetives under the guise of drunkeness, went into the room where the suspect was sitting, surrounded by several women. The detectives soon had the man's arms pinned back. Shelvin said that two revolvers were taken from the prisoner. His pockets were full of cartridges. A group of authors have reported that a bank teller intercepted some of the bills in St. Louis and identified the man and woman who gave the bills as Kilpatrick and Laura, and that they posed as a cattleman and wife from Texas named Arnold. Detective Shevlin in his 1927 report stated that he and his men located them by the finding of the porter in the saloon wth the forged bill and also stated that "We

97

did not know until a few days later, but our prisoner was Ben Kilpatrick, one of the most dangerous members of the 'Hole-in-the-Wall' gang who, despite his gory record, was now undergoing the humiliation of his first arrest." From a key found in Ben's pockets, the detectives captured Laura as she was leaving the hotel the next morning. They had been registered as J. D. Rose and wife. It was said she had seven thousand dollars of the unsigned notes in her bag.

That the officers did not know who they had nabbed is known for a newspaper printed pictures of Kilpatrick and Laura, accompanying an article headed, "Harry Longbaugh Identified As 'The Lone Texan'." The picture identified Kilpatrick as "Harry Longbaugh", and this was some several days after the arrest. It was Sheriff House of Eden, Concho county, Texas, who identified the pictures sent him as that of Kilpatrick and Laura. Some have confused the police St. Louis picture, wherein they identify a frontal pose as Kilpatrick and a side pose as "John Arnold", his St. Louis alias.

During the grilling of the prisoner one of the detectives kicked him in the shins, and Ben threatened revenge. He finally admitted his identity and was tried for the robbery of the Wagner train and given 15 years in the Federal pen at Atlanta, and was released from prison in 1912. In September 1913, as reported by ex-Detective Shevlin, while living in South Dakota, a man named Henry Gibbel was killed near the town of Winner. It developed that Gibbel and Shevlin's auto had one distinguishing mark; both cars had a cream stream-line near the top of each door and they looked very much alike. Both men wore the same type of driving cap. Shevlin came to the conclusion, those many years later, that Harvey Logan or some other surviving gang member had tried to kill him and had killed the farmer under mistaken identity.

About December 15th, 1901, a few days after Kilpatrick had stood up for his sentencing in Federal Court, Harvey Logan wound up in Knoxville, Tenn., after "papering" the southwest as far south as Fort Worth. During an argument over a game of pool, he pistol whipped another player and the law descended on the scene. Two cops were wounded in the gun battle and he escaped wounded, only to be captured some thirty miles west of town. His appearance had not changed any for the better. He still looked like a railroad tramp, nothing of the west lived with him. Only his use of a revolver and the cunning that had showed him so much success as a badman and bandit, marked him as a man of the west.

In February 1902 Cassidy and Longbaugh were in New York, again dressed to kill. They had their pictures taken there. They booked passage to South America and were killed in the Argentine some years later, after embarking on a career of outlawry there.

In November of 1902, Kid Curry was convicted of the last train robbery. An appeal was filed but it was denied. He was taken to prison at Columbus, Ohio, supposedly escape proof, where he seemed to be a fairly model prisoner.

Now there remained only Orlando Camillo Hanks. After the Wagner robbery he had gone to the home of his brother near Abilene, Texas. There he visited with his mother, buried part of his loot and had started back north when for some unknown reason he turned again toward Texas and the southwest.

The Pinks had a wanted bulletin out for Hanks, number fifteen, which gave his description. Said he was wanted in DeWitt county, Texas and in New Mexico on various charges.

On April 16, 1902, a year after Carver had been killed at Sonora, the San Antonio Light carried a head to a story which read: "A Stranger Killed." It seemed that an unidentified man had been killed in the rear room of a saloon at the corner of South Laredo and West Nueva streets. He was first identified as Tom Tumlinson of Pleasenton, then as Hermann Brodt of Seguin, finally as Wyatt Hanks. But in a few days the officers were to learn that he was Camillo, who had his brother's name sewed in his coat. His mother contacted, wired: "Hold body of so called Hanks until identified." She came, viewed the body, and said that he was her son, Camillo. Burial was in City Cemetery number three at 10 a.m., September 24, 1902.

Camillo had came into Texas via Longview, to Beaumont, Flatonia, and then San Antonio via train. He had gone to Flo Williams place, sat in the rear room drinking. Had said that he had recently been released from prison. Witnesses later said that he had shown two pistols, had become unruly. At 1:50 A.M. Flo blew her police whistle and summoned the police. Mounted Officer Pink Taylor entered and Hank pulled out a revolver and fired once, just as two officers grappled with him. A double-action self-cocking revolver saved a number of lives that day. As Camillo struggled in the officers grasp, he kept pressing the trigger harded and harder. He had forgotten to release the trigger on this double action revolver. He gritted his teeth, as he struggled his first and only shot had hit officer Harvey in the mid-section. Officer Taylor fired three shots, all fatal. Hanks had used a 38 pistol and in his hip pocket was a 45 Colts and a full belt of 50 calibre cartridges. This is one of the enigmas of Deaf Charlie Hanks. The paper mentioned that he had been a Sutton follower in the Taylor-Sutton feud in DeWitt county. Officer Taylor was not one of the DeWitt county Taylors.

Detectives rushed into San Antonio and identified Hanks as one of the men who had robbed the train at Wagner. "He was perfectly fearless and reckless," one detective said, "and would rather fight than eat. He was the toughest one of the gang." And the last one to be "taken" for all the others were "out of commission," for the time being! Another officer stated: "This was one of the most desperate gangs in the country and for a long time the detectives of the country were on the lookout for them."

But the terrible "Kid Curry", Harvey Logan, was not to be dealt with lightly. The Pinks had warned officers that he was the one criminal "who does not have one single good point", and that he would escape if given the slightest opportunity. He seemed to be a model prisoner and it appeared that the warning from Pinkertons was wrong. He was locked in the Knoxville jail. Then on June 26, 1903, he slipped a wire over the head of an unsuspecting turnkey and jerked him to the bars, tied the guards hands to the bars. With improvised "fishing gear" he got his hands on a box which contained two revolvers, of the same calibre as those on Hanks when killed. He then took the keys from the guard's belt, let himself out of his cell. He used the outside turnkey as a shield, mounted a horse and was away. This happened late the afternoon of Friday, June 26th. His conviction had not been completed and he was to be resentenced July 10, 1903. Wanted circulars were put out all over the United States, but somehow Logan seemed to dodge the officers.

It is thought that he tried to join Longbaugh and Cassidy but without success. Somehow he got word to Kilpatrick, possibly Ben had gotten word to him. Ben knew he was trying to find Cassidy. As to what happened to Kid Curry I cannot say for sure. Reports had it that ten days after his escape at Knoxville, he had already organized a new gang and from their hideout near Parachute, Colorado, July 7, 1903, attempted to rob a train, blew the safe and ran away. When cornered one of the men killed himself, and that the Federal case against him was closed. They say this was Harvey Logan. Folks around Glenwood, Colorado, where he was buried said that he was "Tap Duncan" a Texas cowboy. The body was exhumed and an operator, who had known Logan during his trial at Knoxville, came to Glenwood and identified the body as that of Logan.

But the writers who say that Logan tried to rob a train near Parachute on July 7, 1903, and killed himself two days later "near Glenwood Springs" also report that on June 7, 1904, he held up the Denver and Rio Grande train at Parachute, Colorado and that the next day, June 8, 1904, he "killed himself near Glenwood Springs". Possibly this is merely a mistake in reporting, possibly a mistaken identity. Some say he went to South America and there died with Cassidy and Longbaugh. But, those eastern writers who claim that the man buried at Glenwood Springs was Kid Curry, would certainly be surprised to learn that Tap Duncan did exist. He was a Texas cowboy from Richland Springs, San Saba county, cousin of Black Jack Ketchum, and brother of Dick and Bige Duncan. He had testified for Dick at his trial in Eagle Pass, where Dick received the death sentence for murder and was hung in 1891

So, with Logan disposed of, we have left, of the Black Jack-Wild Bunch-Carver Gang, two members, both in prison. Elza Lay, soon released and lived out his life as a law abiding citizen, cowboy and ranchman, to die in 1933. Then we have Ben Kilpatrick and Laura Bullion. Laura served a portion of her sentence and disappeared.

CHAPTER XVI

Death Of "The Tall Texan"

Ben Kilpatirck, The Tall Texas, had served nearly ten years of his sentence at Atlanta Federal Prison when released early in 1912. He returned to Texas to Concho county, then drifted on out to Sonora, Ozona and Sheffield, near the Pecos river. He was visiting with relatives, old acquaintances, etc. He had changed a lot. From the dapper handsome gentleman pictured in the photograph in

Fort Worth in 1900, he now weighed more; he wore the clothes he had gotten on release. In 1912 Marvin Hunter was publishing a weekly newspaper and Ben came into the shop several times, told Hunter that he had been "dead wrong" in the past, had fully reformed while in prison. He had hoped to find some land around Sheffield where he could run a small herd of sheep. But, only a few days later, Ben was killed while attempting a train holdup, between Dryden and Sanderson, only forty or fifty miles from where the Black Jack gang had held up the SP at Lozier Creek.

It was on the night of March 13, 1912 that Train Number Nine of the SP was stopped at Sanderson Draw. The procedure was the same, as if a stamp of authenticity had been given by Black Jack Ketchum and Butch Cassidy. At Dryden, The Tall Texan, had climbed onto the tender and when the train reached the wide curve at Sanderson Draw he threw down on the engineer and fireman.

Since Dave A. Trousdale, the Express messenger, was the true hero of the holdup, this part of the story will be told as given in an interview two days after the holdup.

A moment after the train stopped, Trousdale, in the express car, was summoned to the door by the porter who told him that robbers had stopped the train and for him to come down from the car. As he opened the door he "looked down the barrel of a gun one of the robbers was holding on me and I got out of the car." None of the crew were armed and along with the others Trousdale was made to get onto the engine as the engineer took the first car down the tracks a safe distance. It was there that the engineer was instructed to blow the whistle four times and with this the confederate, said to be one Ed Welsh, then identified as Ole Beck, who had been in prison with Ben, came to the side of the engine. Ben had been successful so far in his one man holdup of the train. Ben climbed into the mail car while Beck held the crew, and found five pouches. One of these was cut open and some registered letters were selected and the others were returned to the pouch, with the idea of taking them be fore they left.

"There were only two express packages removed", Trousdale said. "One of these was valued at $2. and the other at $35., so you can see that there was not a great deal obtained by the robber who was doing the work. But you know, this fellow was making me madder all the time. If I was not holding my hands high enough he seemed to take delight in jabbing me in the side with his gun. However, I kept on jollying him along and when he got into that section of the car where the express packages were stacked he broke open a few of these. It was while he was doing this that I wondered how to kill him. I was mad for I was determined I would have it out with him for jabbing me in the side and bruising me up. I would have fought him with my fists had it come to that."

Trousdale remembered that there was a huge ice maul lying on top of an oyster barrel in the car and he felt that if he could get the maul and maneuver the bandit into the right position he could hit him with it. "You know", he said later, "you can hit an awful blow with such a maul. Why, I've broken up a box of ice at one blow."

Finally, Ben became more friendly with the express messenger, "and I got his confidence and could lay my hands on him, helping him along the car. I showed him packages I said I had never seen before. He was looking over these packages in a stooped sort of position and as quietly as I could I lifted the maul from the top of the oyster barrel and he did not detect me. While he was stooping over I struck him at the base of the skull. The first blow broke the man's neck. I struck him a second and a third time. On the third blow the maul crashed through his skull and the man's brains spattered over the side of the car."

"After I saw he was done for, I took two Colts pistols

from his body and his Winchester. About the first thing I did after that was to find the gas key and turn out the lights in the car. Then I waited for some time. Nothing developed so I decided to fire a shot through the roof of the car to attract attention. Then I took up my position about midway of the car, there being one door still open, and that was the one where the porter first called me. The light of the combination car was shining through the end doors of the car and had the other robber entered through the other car I could have seen him and had he come in at the door of my car I could also have gotten a bead on him."

"After firing the shot I did not have long to wait for I soon heard the other robber on the outside of the car talking low and pretty soon he was calling for 'Frank'. Pretty soon I saw a head poked out from back of some baggage, I could not get a bead on him at once so I waited for a little while. It was not long and I saw his head again and I cut down on him. The bullet struck him about an inch above the left eye. It passed through his skull and then passed out through the ear. There were just these two shots fired, the first to attract attention, and the other was used with deadly effect on the second robber who was the smaller of the two. It was with the first robber's gun that I killed the second man. This rifle is of 1910 model."

"From the two men I got four pistols and two rifles. One of the pistols I brought back with me and the officials at Sanderson told me I would be given the rifle with which I killed the second man. I gave the other two pistols to the mail clerk and my express helper. At Sanderson I appeared before the grand jury in the morning and yesterday afternoon I attended the coroner's inquest."

"The first man I killed was six feet one inch in height, weighed 201 lbs., and the other man, who was always addressed as 'partner', was baldheaded, of medium stature and I should say, weighed about 160 or 165 pounds.

'Partner' seemed to be the man who directed the operations. It was the big fellow who looked to be green at the game."

"At the time I killed the first man the mail clerk was in the combination car and my helper was about ten or twelve feet from me in my car. At the time none of us had any guns on us. My shotgun and pistol were on my desk and then when I laid for the second man I decided I would use the first robber's rifle because I could work that faster than the shotgun I had in the car."

"After (the shots) the fireman came back to the car and asked me to open the door. I told him I had killed two men, and told him to go back and get the conductor and some passengers. When he first called I believed there might be some more robbers on the outside with him who were making him talk. After awhile he and the conductor and probably fifteen passengers came back to the car."

M. E. Banks was the mail clerk. When questioned about the incident he said that he was alone in the mail car when the train stopped. He had looked out and the fireman had tried to signal and tell him what was happening and he did not understand and sat down to read, then came a call from the engineer, "There is a man out here with a gun who wants you to come out and hold up your hands." He came down and was marched to the express car and there the porter was commanded to call express messenger Trousdale and his helper from his car. The porter then was instructed to uncouple, they were herded onto the engine and the two cars were run a mile up the track.

"Then one of the desperadoes remained aboard the engine guarding the engineer and fireman while the rest of us were told to go back to the cars and assist the other bandit in securing the valuable packages supposed to be in the mail and express car."

Banks continued: "The masked man looked through the mail car and asked me to unlock the registered pouches. I assured him I did not carry the keys to the pouches and showed him a few registered packages which had been tied out for transfer to the agent who would relieve me at Sanderson, the end of the division. He cut a long slit in one of the pouches, shoved in the loose registered packages, and then had me dump all the pouches out the door and on the ground. He then went to the express car with the messengers. I remained in the mail car for a while and then opened the door into the express car just after Trousdale had felled his entertainer with a blow from the ice mallet. He dealt him a second blow to make sure he wouldn't bother us any more. Trousdale grabbed up the highwayman's rifle which fell to the floor, and I reached underneath the dying man's coat and removed his six shooter. Trousdale turned out the lights in the car and after Reagan had armed himself with a revolver the three of us went to the far end of the car and waited in the darkness for the appearance of the other robber. Reagan climbed upon some trunks piled in the end of the car and Trousdale and I remained standing on the floor. It was understood between us that Trousdale should fire upon the robber first and if he failed to get him, we would then open up. I do not know how long we waited but it appeared to be an age. After a time, an hour or so, we heard the other robber call 'Frank' to his pal, who was then dead. We did not answer and he opened the door and clambered inside. Trousdale's aim was perfect, and as he shot we saw the bandit lurch forward and fall to the floor without a groan. We were afraid he was stalling and not dead and remained in the dark end of the car. After a long time the train crew and passengers came up to investigate and find out whether the bandits had killed us or we had silenced them."

"I shudder when I think of what might have happened had Trousdale's shot hit the dynamite and nitro the other robber was carrying. That was my first experience of that kind and I hope it will be the last. Too much cannot be said of Trousdale's bravery. He was not at all excited, and while we were marched to the engine he had told me that the bandits were "green" and if we watched our chances (we) 'would get them sure'."

So, the bodies of Ben Kilpatrick and Ole Beck were taken off the train at Sanderson and the two dead bandits were held up by the crew and local people and a photographer took their picture. They were then buried and now lie in unmarked graves in the Sanderson cemetery.

Here was ended a reign of outlawry and highwaying that started in the early 1890s, by the bands of Black Jack Ketchum, the bands of Butch Cassidy, and the Carver gang with the all embracing title of The Wild Bunch and that kept the southwest and west on fire for over ten years. These bands had roamed from central Texas to the very borders of California west, from the interior of Mexico to the very Canadian border. The deeds laid to these bands would number into the hundreds. They robbed trains, stage coaches, banks, army pay masters, mining camps and any place that seemed profitable. Now, in 1912, all were gone excepting Elza Lay, the one lone member of those associated directly with this story, and he was spared violent death and permitted to live a law abiding life.

But, considering how the others had died, had they been alive to read the papers, the manner in which the once "Tall Texan" had died, would have been a crashing and resounding defeat to their morale. The Tall Texan, the last of the Wild Bunch, the last of the early western train robbers, had been downed by the crushing blows of an ice mallet, wielded by an unarmed and mild mannered express clerk, who had thought of the famous outlaw, "a green hand".

BLACK JACK KETCHUM, while in prison and prior to his execution.

BILL CARVER AND BEN KILPATRICK, as they
appeared in Fort Worth in 1900

GEORGE PARKER, alias Butch Cassidy, as he appeared in 1894.

HARVEY LOGAN, alias "Kid Curry", as he appeared in Fort Worth in 1900

WILLIAM WALTERS, alias "Bronco Bill", as he appeared in 1899.

GEORGE SCARBOROUGH, veteran Southwestern peace officer.

BLACK JACK'S CAVE, in Turkey Canyon, near Cimarron, New Mexico

THE STONE FACE, said to be the likeness of Black Jack, located in the mountains near Cimarron, New Mexico.

BLACK JACK KETCHUM, on the gallows at Clayton, New Mexico.

BLACK JACK'S decapitated body beneath the gallows.

Deputies with equipment captured from Black Jack gang.

The Arizona posse who fought Black Jack gang:
1. Steve Birchfield, 2. Baylor Shannon, 3. Charles Bollard,
4. J. L. Dow, 5. Fred Higgins, 6. C. S. Fly.